AF837384

Talent Management in the Developing World

Dedicated to my lovely wife (Felicia), and two children (Etana) and (Omokeshi) for sharing my vision, and inspiring my life with purpose and meaning.

Talent Management in the Developing World

Adopting a Global Perspective

JOEL ALEMIBOLA ELEGBE

Routledge
Taylor & Francis Group
LONDON AND NEW YORK

First published 2010 by Gower Publishing

2 Park Square, Milton Park, Abingdon, Oxfordshire OX14 4RN
711 Third Avenue, New York, NY 10017

Routledge is an imprint of the Taylor & Francis Group, an informa business

First issued in paperback 2018

Copyright © Joel Alemibola Elegbe 2010

Joel Alemibola Elegbe has asserted his moral right under the Copyright, Designs and Patents Act, 1988, to be identified as the author of this work.

All rights reserved. No part of this book may be reprinted or reproduced or utilised in any form or by any electronic, mechanical, or other means, now known or hereafter invented, including photocopying and recording, or in any information storage or retrieval system, without permission in writing from the publishers.

Notice:
Product or corporate names may be trademarks or registered trademarks, and are used only for identification and explanation without intent to infringe.

Gower Applied Business Research
Our programme provides leaders, practitioners, scholars and researchers with thought provoking, cutting edge books that combine conceptual insights, interdisciplinary rigour and practical relevance in key areas of business and management.

British Library Cataloguing in Publication Data
Elegbe, Joel Alemibola.
Talent management in the developing world : adopting a
global perspective.
1. Employee selection--Developing countries.
2. Employees--Training of--Developing countries.
3. Creative ability in business--Developing countries.
4. Delta Steel Company--Personnel management.
I. Title
658.3'0091724-dc22

Library of Congress Cataloging-in-Publication Data
Elegbe, Joel Alemibola.
Talent management in the developing world : adopting a global perspective / Joel Alemibola Elegbe.
p. cm.
Includes bibliographical references and index.
ISBN 978-1-4094-1813-9 (hbk.) -- ISBN 978-1-4094-1814-6 (ebook) 1. Manpower planning--Developing countries. 2. Human capital--Developing countries--Management. 3. Personnel management--Developing countries. I. Title.
HF5549.5.M3E39 2010
658.3009172'4--dc22

2010024947

ISBN 13: 978-1-4094-1813-9 (hbk)
ISBN 13: 978-1-138-37971-8 (pbk)

Contents

List of Figures

List of Tables

Acknowledgements

In writing this book a number of professional colleagues and friends have contributed in no small measure to the final product, even though I am fully accountable for any shortcomings that may be found in it. Dr Austen Isamah was the first person to read the zero draft of the first few chapters of the manuscript and was the laboratory where I tested my ideas. His words of encouragement and incisive critique inspired me to continue, and he was a bastion of support and inspiration throughout the writing of the remaining chapters. I am immensely indebted to him. Professor Francis Odemerho's critical review and suggestions, particularly with regard to the target audience, were invaluable and provided me with a broader perspective. I am profoundly grateful to him. I am also deeply grateful to Professor Ben Elugbe who found time, despite his hectic schedule, to review the manuscript for intelligibility, sequence and logic. I also thank Mrs Yomi Afolabi for her professional comments on the initial chapters. Many thanks also to Dr Abdul Karim Bakri and his team at the African Development Bank's Knowledge and Virtual Resource Centre (KVRC) for their unflinching assistance in searching for and providing me with relevant materials within and outside the KVRC.

Finally, I thank my wife and children for their immense love, support, understanding and unceasing prayers. Many a time I almost ruined our carefully planned vacations because I spent most of my time in libraries and book stores. They bore my bad behaviour with good humour.

Reviews for Talent Management in the Developing World

'Tapping from his rich experience as a Human Resource Practitioner in both national and international settings, Dr Elegbe has come out with a brilliant, well-researched and well-written book, in simple prose, devoid of technical jargons. The book will no doubt fill a vacuum in the available knowledge resources on International Human Capital Management and it is therefore a 'must read' for scholars, practitioners and training institutions in the field, in both developing and developed worlds.'

Dr. Olatunji Kolapo, formerly Divisional Chief of Human Resources, Nigeria (Coca Cola) Bottling Company. Ambassador Kolapo is Policy Study Group Director at National Institute for Policy and Strategic Studies, Nigeria

'The author's experience in the field has been brought to bear in this book and that makes it easy to read and understand. It is a powerful and invaluable contribution to the discourse on manpower development in all kinds of organizations around the world. Both scholars and management professionals will find it a useful companion.'

Matt Mogekwu, Ph.D., Chair , Journalism Department, Ithaca College, NY

'This book is an irresistible call on us all to share new creative ideas on Talent Management. As the discipline (of TM) is fast becoming an essential component of HR strategy, I find the book most useful in examining associated limitations of the established best practices in talent management while it heralds fresh vistas for more progressive strategy appreciation and development.'

Jude Iyitor, HR Director, Whassan Eurest Nigeria Ltd

'This book's central proposition is that there is a right mindset and approach that enterprise leaders should adopt in managing their organizations' talent in order to achieve a sustainable competitive advantage in the marketplace. The author's lucidity makes the well researched content compelling for Human Capital Management practitioners as well as business leaders who want to leverage an appropriate talent management strategy for competitive advantage. The context in which the content is situated makes its reading a contemporary imperative, given the forays that enterprises from the developing world and emerging markets are making and will continue to make at the world stage.'

Emmanuel Imafidon, Director Business Services, Chevron Nigeria Limited

Preface

Globalization is a universal phenomenon which has benefited many countries all over the world. Four decades ago, it was not certain that countries like China, Brazil, Russia, Korea, India and South Africa would be recognized as strong economies with the capacity to make a global impact. Today, they have produced organizations that are competing successfully with multinational giants of the developed countries. As a result of globalization and the various economic and political reforms implemented by the developing world, particularly in Africa, there is emergence of an impressive array of manufacturing, telecommunications, banking, financial, and oil and gas companies. Many of them have performed so well within their national borders that they have now ventured into the international arena: they are becoming multinational corporations. However, the transformation is not generally accompanied by a change in the way these organizations manage talent. A major challenge which globalization therefore poses to these organizations is how to manage human resources effectively within the international setting.

It is axiomatic to say that great organizations are the creation of great talent and great leadership. In his best-selling book, *Good to Great*, Jim Collins wrote: 'if you have the wrong people, it doesn't matter how great your strategy may be, you still won't have a great company' (2001: 42). Pfeffer (1998) noted that talent and the way in which it is managed is what gives companies competitive advantage. According to him, process and product technology, protected or regulated markets, access to financial resources, and economies of scale may provide competitive leverage but to a lesser extent than in the past and by far less than people will provide if properly managed. In other words, traditional sources of competitive advantage are no longer as effective, reliable and sustainable as talent management. Unfortunately, many managers are still fixated with the traditional sources of competitive advantage while ignoring this brutal truth. Although they probably appreciate the fact that people are the bastion of success for any organization, the challenge they face is how to fundamentally alter their paradigm about how to attract, hire, engage, develop and retain the talent which they so much need for their success.

Human resource management policies, systems and practices that were successful within national boundaries are still being deployed with the same vigour and frenzy to serve a completely different and diverse group of people working in different countries, cultures and socio-economic environments. It can safely be predicted that not only will the HR policies, systems and practices be inadequate to meet the value propositions of the diverse employees, but that they may also in fact be dysfunctional to talent management. In reality there is a disconnect between globalization and talent management even though we know that no multinational corporation can be effective or sustain its success for long without a strong, strategic and dynamic approach to the management of talent.

Aligning talent management with globalization must begin with a change in the paradigm of organizational leaders. First, they have to accept talent management and retention as their responsibility. For too long many organizations have abdicated this responsibility to the HR department. The role of the HR department is to develop policies and systems and guide managers, but the actual management of talent falls squarely on the shoulders of line managers. Second, managers need to change their hedonistic philosophy about employees. Developing countries may be poor (in Africa about 300 million people live on less than a dollar a day), yet not every employee is necessarily an 'economic man'. People are motivated by factors other than pecuniary reward, and those factors should inform the way managers manage the abilities, potential, aspirations, needs, wants and concerns of their talented people.

Third, global executives have to perceive themselves differently – not just as managers but rather as *entrepreneurial leaders* who have a stake in the business. Yet, it is not enough to be leaders – they must be global leaders and have an entrepreneur's mindset that enables them to see how critical talent is to the success of their firms, and also be able to manage talent with a passion and integrity amidst socio-cultural pressures to adopt a nationalistic or parochial approach which invariably vitiates diversity and creates a glass ceiling for certain categories of talent. Fourth, the approach to attracting and hiring talent has changed from being a mere transaction to being a marketing enterprise. Managers must flow with the tide. Recruitment brand has become a pre-eminent feature, and information technology an incredibly useful instrument in the war or competition for talent. Hiring talent should be not only for the job, but also for a global career – not only for today, but also for tomorrow.

Fifth, recruiting talent is brutally hard but getting the best out of talent could even be harder. Managing the performance of talented people of different generations with conflicting value propositions in diverse cultures and countries is a huge challenge to multinational corporations (MNCs). It is not about merely setting objectives, providing resources and evaluating performance at the end of the year. Rather, it is about how managers support and guide employees, proactively remove blockages to performance and reward performance equitably without any form of racial, ethnic or gender bias. It is also about how to identify, design and deploy appropriate employee engagement drivers taking cognizance of the fact that because of the diverse demographic, national and cultural differences and backgrounds of employees there can be no one-size-fits-all engagement drivers. For instance, for some employees, gone are the days of the 'organization man'; work–life balance has become a cherished value. For others, empowerment, a socially amiable environment and work teams in which interaction is devoid of excessive formality and paraphernalia of status are what drive their engagement. Yet for others, growth, development, rapid advancement and career resilience are the *sine qua non* for their engagement and retention. Lifetime tenure has become history to such employees. Talented people are a high-risk and volatile asset.

The high turnover rate of global executives certainly leads to the inescapable conclusion that failing to plan for succession, or basing it mainly on seniority, translates into failing to plan for the future leadership of a corporation. The high turnover of global executives underscores the imperative need to prepare high-potential managers for strategic and critical leadership positions in the future. Successful leaders in national enterprises may not necessarily be successful as global leaders. Hence previous national track record alone is not a sufficient determinant for succession to global executive positions. Potential is critical.

The approach to preparing future leaders and successors deserves a review in many corporations. Many years of executive training aimed at producing leaders have not yielded the desired results because development is not aligned to the context and strategy of the business. Instead, it tends to focus primarily on today's business with little or no regard for the leadership of tomorrow's business. Besides, executive training in high-profile business institutions is not synonymous with leadership development. It is only one instrument in leadership development; other tools which are critical to leadership development but are often ignored are job rotation, international assignment, action learning and mentoring. When selectively used, they are mutually reinforcing and create synergy. Multinational corporations should move towards building learning organizations.

Finally, the HR department should be allowed to play a more strategic role in multinational corporations. The HR function has to be represented on the board so that it can have a voice in planning and executing the business strategy. HR specialists need to slough off the garb of 'personnel management' and transform the function into international strategic human resource management. It is only in this mode that it can provide global executives with the kind of professional advice and support they direly need to manage their most important asset. The change must begin with a change in the paradigm of line and HR managers about talent management. This change cannot take place unless they can both see its urgency and criticality. That is the enterprise of this book.

Joel Alemibola Elegbe

1

The Challenge of Talent Management

Talent Scarcity – The Global Scenario

No subject in the past 15 years has received as much attention in the human resource management literature as 'talent management'. There is a cavalcade of literature produced by eminent scholars and experts like Ulrich (1989, 1996, 2005), Pfeffer (1998), Woodruffe (1999), Barner (2000), Michaels, Handfield-Jones and Axelrod (2001), Pucik (1996, 2005,) Sullivan (2004a), Meisinger (2009), Berger and Berger (2004), Rothwell (2005), Lawler III (2008) and Cappelli (2008) on what organizations should do to attract, hire and retain talent. Based on his wealth of experience, Welch in his book, *Winning* (2005), has also written about the practical approach to hiring, developing and retaining great people. All the literature recognizes that talent provides companies with a competitive advantage, and it shares a common concern not only that talent is scarce, but also that most companies are not doing enough to manage and retain what they have. As the greatest source of competitive advantage for any organization, (Pfeffer, 1998), human resources deserve the attention and time of managers more than any other organizational resource or asset. This chapter attempts to define the scope of the war for talent, explains what talent and talent management actually mean and identifies the cause of the talent scarcity, particularly in Africa despite its high rate of unemployment. Finally, it provides a synopsis of the subsequent chapters in the book.

The concern about the scarcity of talent is almost universal. In 2005 the Aberdeen Group and Human Capital Institute carried out a research survey which covered '170 human capital management professionals and executives' who are members of the Aberdeen Group and Human Capital Institute's global online communities (2005: 11), as well as executives in human capital management in North America. According to the survey's findings, 57 per cent of companies cited the inability to both get the talent needed and address talent requirements over the next five years as their top overall challenge. In addition, 79 per cent of the companies stated that their chief concern was continuity in executive leadership for the future, while 61 per cent were concerned about the potential cost of disruptive succession from one leader to another. The study also revealed that 71 per cent and 65 per cent of organizations had formal retention plans for executive and mid-level management staff respectively, but 60 per cent of respondents viewed their retention programme as 'haphazard at best, and heavily reliant on paper files and manual efforts' (Aberdeen Group and Human Capital Institute, 2005: 5–7). Another survey conducted in 2005 of human resources executives from 40 countries around the world revealed that virtually all the executives indicated that they had 'an insufficient pipeline of high potential employees to fill strategic management roles' (Ready and Conger, 2005: 69).

Barner (2000: 337) cited a study conducted by Elizabeth Chambers and Associates, which found that only 10 per cent of the 6,000 respondents reported an ability to retain the large majority of their high performers. Clearly, the number one people-related issue is the retention of high performers. Dychtwald, Erickson and Morison (2006) noted that there were too few young workforce entrants to replace the labour, skills and talent of baby-boomer retirees. The loss of skills and experience threatens the performance of many corporations.

Workspan, a magazine of WorldatWork, corroborated this view by stating that finding talent during the years ahead would continue to be difficult particularly in highly specialized areas such as finance and accounting. It noted that a worldwide survey conducted by Deloitte with the Economic Intelligence Unit revealed that 67 per cent of respondents from the Asia-Pacific region claimed that the current supply of finance talent was either limited or inadequate. This view was supported in the same survey by 54 per cent of CFOs from Eastern Europe, 53 per cent from Asia-Pacific, 52 per cent from Western Europe and 47 per cent from North America (News Notes, 2007: 11). The challenge is global and has been compounded by the fact that companies are currently facing the departure of the baby boomers from the workforce. High rates of turnover attest to the challenge in retaining talent in various occupations.

According to Axelrod, Handfield-Jones and Welsh (2001: 1) of McKinsey, a study of 4,500 senior managers and corporate officers revealed that 89 per cent of those surveyed thought it was more difficult now than in the past to attract talented people, and 90 per cent thought it was more difficult to retain those hired. A survey conducted by Howard, Scott and Bruce (2007: 1) revealed that competition for talent had increased since 2005, and that 79 per cent of the survey respondents expected it to heat up even more in 2007. It said the war for talent was hot and getting hotter. The same report showed that the toughest competition was for executives followed by mid-level managers and professionals. The Newsline of WorldatWork (2008a) noted that 86 per cent of British organizations were finding it difficult to fill their vacancies despite the economic slowdown.

The demographics, especially in the United States, reveal a compelling reason why organizations must strive to retain their good people. According to Lebovits (2005), the US Bureau of Labor Statistics estimated that, by 2010, the United States would have a shortage of 10,033,000 workers. Cadrain (2008: 23) noted that the Bureau of Labor Statistics had indicated that, in 2005, one in four US workers was over 50 years old, but, by 2012, it would be nearly one in three. The situation might be further complicated by the fact that with the growing economies in Asia – India and China in particular – large numbers of immigrants may be returning to their homelands where salaries are becoming very competitive and the cost of living is comparatively lower than in the United States. The attraction to their countries is further reinforced by the natural desire to return to their cultural roots and contribute to the development of their homelands.

Unlike other writers and commentators on the war for talent, who are concerned about shortages of local talent within a particular country or region, Sullivan (2004b) is concerned about a truly global talent war. He calls it 'World-wide War II' for talent. Sullivan believes that instead of fighting for talent primarily within the home country, firms will in future fight to attract and retain the very best in every region around the globe. Global competition is increasing because firms are becoming larger due to mergers and acquisitions. As firms expand their operations into foreign countries they naturally seek and hire experienced people working in other firms. Telberg (2007) also notes that all businesses which operate on a global scale face a talent shortage and that a survey of 32,000 employees across 26 countries, conducted by Manpower, found that the shortage in professional talent was undermining opportunities for growth worldwide.

Certain conclusions may be drawn from this literature review on talent scarcity. First, there is a high demand for, but a low supply of, talent in the labour market. In the information age there is an exponential demand for knowledge workers. Second, all organizations are seeking the same kind of talent very aggressively, and are employing a variety of strategies to attract and hire, or even poach, great people from competitors. Organizations must therefore develop counterstrategies for dealing not only with external 'pull factors' which attract organizations' talent, but also with internal 'push factors' that tend to make talent leave for other organizations.

Third, the war for talent is becoming global and is no longer localized in individual countries. Managing talent is a challenge to all organizations in the context of globalization irrespective of the country. As will be demonstrated later, many poor African countries have lost some of their highly skilled professionals to the United States, Canada, France, the United Kingdom, Australia and the Gulf States. Fourth, it is fatal to assume that the recruitment drivers that enable an organization to attract and hire talent will also enable it to engage and retain the talent. Recruitment drivers are very different from the drivers that keep employees motivated, committed and highly engaged in an organization. Finally, talent management is a business imperative. It is a process and not a product; a journey and not a destination. It is strategic, dynamic and must be driven by top management but owned by all levels of management. It must be holistic and inclusive in the sense of encompassing all functions and levels of the organizational hierarchy.

What Constitutes Talent?

In 1960 an unknown athlete by name Abebe Bikila, a corporal in the Ethiopian army, lined up barefooted for the marathon at the Olympic Games in Rome. His co-contestants must have giggled at the African athlete and apparently regarded him as a jester to think he could compete in the race barefooted. Abebe Bikila amazingly won the race in 2 hours 15 minutes 16 seconds, breaking the world record at that time. The secret of his success was that he had a talent in athletics. Four years later, Bikila won gold again at the Olympic marathon in Tokyo.

Talent has been defined in different ways. It generally refers to mental power, a natural endowment, an aptitude, ability, a natural capacity or a special gift. What is common to all these definitions is that talent is not acquired but inborn, and a person either has it or does not. Someone who has a talent – for example, in music, dancing, acting or sport – stands above the rest of the population in the sphere of his talent. The possession of a talent alone does not make the possessor great; it is the development and utilization of the talent that makes them achieve extraordinary results. It is thus argued that those who have talents are under a moral obligation to develop and use their special gifts for their own benefit and that of their society.

A problem with these definitions is that there is an assumption that people who have talent will perform exceptionally in all situations. But this is not true of any human being. Talent cannot be meaningfully understood without reference to its relationship with the environment or context of the individual. Talent is specific to situations. That implies that no matter how talented an individual may be, he or she may never be successful or effective if the environment is not conducive or appropriate for the utilization of the talent. Talent has to be socially defined because it can only be understood to exist through behaviour. Barab and Plucker (2002) noted that the existence of a talent is manifested through behaviours that are consistent with ways that are socio-culturally defined and endorsed.

Every talent is relevant to a given situation or role. While a musical talent will be most appropriate to an orchestra, it may not be suitable for an IT function. An artistic talent may be most useful in architecture or sculpture but completely irrelevant to an accounting function. Every role has a corresponding talent. The incumbent of a role who has the pertinent talent makes a great employee or leader while those who do not have it make, at best, average leaders. Nurses who have empathy make better nurses than those who do not possess that talent. No individual can be a great soldier or firefighter without the talent of courage. Talent is therefore of no value if it is not matched with an appropriate role. The challenge which executives face in selecting candidates for positions or preparing their successors for future leadership roles is to determine the talents that are appropriate to the roles.

There is no universal definition of talent that is applicable in all organizations. In general, those who are regarded as 'talent' provide a firm with a competitive advantage. It is their abilities, skills and commitment that determine the long-term success of their organizations. However, organizations recognize the fact that every employee cannot be a talent. Talent is sometimes used as if it is synonymous with hot or scarce skills. In other instances, it refers to leadership capability and yet in others it connotes knowledge workers. Despite the variety of definitions, a common denominator is that individuals who have talent have technical capability and leadership 'potential' to contribute significantly to the effectiveness of their organizations.

The Towers Perrin survey (2006) considered the following groups to be 'talent':

- senior leadership
- mid-level employees with leadership potential
- key contributors or technical experts
- entry-level employees with leadership potential.

These groups are estimated to constitute about 15 per cent of the total workforce. We operationally define talent to mean individuals who have skills, competencies and abilities to make an impact on organizational effectiveness now and in the future through their contribution, performance and high level of potential. Talent is not required for its own sake. It is a business imperative; hence classical economists refer to human resources (labour) as a factor of production.

Talent Management

Talent management means different things to different organizations. To some, it refers to the process an organization adopts for managing those with scarce or hot skills or recognized as having exceptional technical or managerial abilities. Yet others define it in terms of how they manage all their human resources irrespective of the worth, status and capabilities of each individual employee. Following a survey of 518 people and subsequent review by a panel of experts, the American Society for Training and Development in collaboration with the Institute for Corporate Productivity adopted the following definition:

> *... a holistic approach to optimizing human capital which enables an organization to drive short and long-term results by building culture, engagement, capability, and capacity through integrated talent acquisition, development, and deployment processes that are aligned to business goals. (Cited in Paradise, 2009: 68)*

Talent management is therefore not merely a process of managing physical human bodies or disparate human resource management processes and systems, but rather an integrated and comprehensive approach to managing the abilities, competencies, skills, needs, concerns, careers, fears and expectations of the people that an organization values and needs to make it great and highly effective. Successful talent management is driven by a 'talent mindset' in which every manager in a firm regards talent management as their business and not the sole responsibility of the HR department. Whatever the conception of talent management by the various organizations, in general it is a process by which an organization hires, engages and develops its most valuable resource. It consists of various interrelated components that are shown diagrammatically in Figure 1.1 as an integrated system.

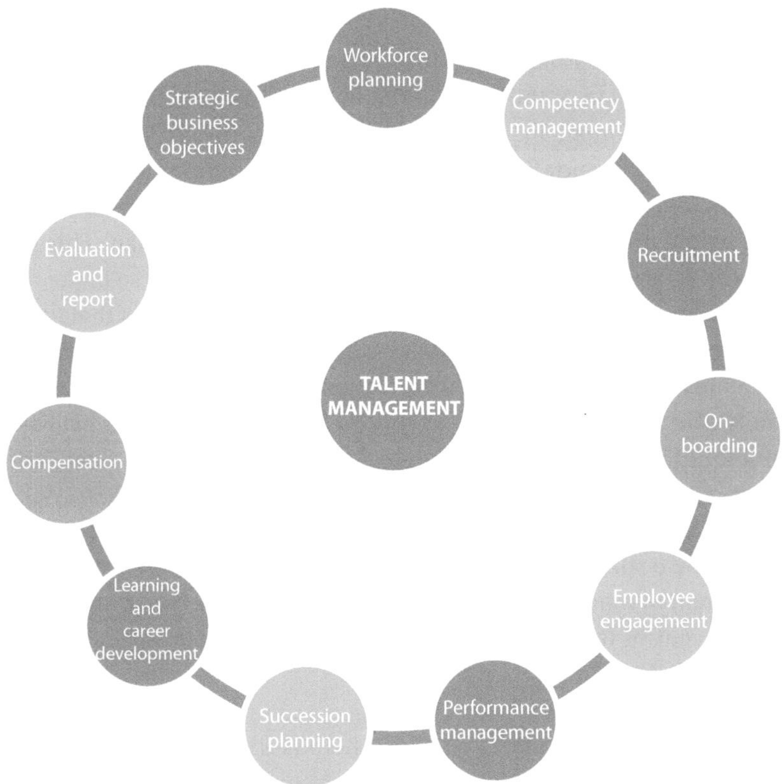

Figure 1.1 Talent management system

The Etiology of the Talent War

While companies all over the world may express concern about the war for talent, it is important to note that the causes of talent scarcity in the developed and industrialized countries are not the same as those in the developing countries of Africa. According to Dychtwald, Erickson and Morison (2006: 4) three major factors are responsible for the growing shortage of talent in the United States, Europe and Australia. First, the baby boomers, born between 1946 and 1964, are reaching the traditional retirement age, and this is culminating in a 'massive exodus of skills, experience, customer relations, and knowledge'. A second factor is what the authors refer to as 'longevity boom'. Life expectancy is higher now than it was in 1900 when, at birth, life expectancy in the United States was 47 years. With good healthcare and quality of life practices, this has increased significantly to almost 80 years. Nevertheless, despite their longevity, there is a point at which people are no longer as productive as organizations may require.

A third factor in the 'age wave' is the 'birth dearth' – an unprecedented shift in the age distribution of the population. In the mid-1950s the average number of children per woman in the United States was 3.7. It has since declined significantly. Dychtwald, Erickson and Morison also noted that countries like Italy, Germany and Japan with fertility rates of 1.2, 1.3 and 1.4 respectively are now below the replacement rate of 2.1 children per woman. This situation portends an enormous implication for the size of the workforce in the future. Is this factor also applicable to African countries in view of the fact that the fertility rates in the continent are significantly different from those of Germany, the United States and Japan? For instance, the fertility rates in 2008 in the following randomly selected countries were as follows: Uganda, 6.77; Burkina Faso, 6.28; Mozambique, 5.18; Kenya, 4.56; Ghana, 3.68; Egypt, 3.05; and Botswana, 2.60. These rates are higher than the world's overall fertility rate of 2.56 (Wikipedia, 2010a). While the developed countries have an ageing population because of extremely low fertility rates as noted above, Africa has a high fertility rate with the result that, in many African countries, young people constitute between 35 and 45 per cent of the population. By implication, a youthful population is a potential pool of talent.

A fundamental question is whether there is a scarcity of talent in Africa. This question is relevant for the following reasons. The unemployment rate in African countries is in double digits and can be as high as 30 per cent or more in some countries. Africa has a huge population, particularly of young people. Furthermore since the 1980s there has been a remarkable growth of tertiary institutions and in the number of graduates who are churned out annually in most African countries. For example, Nigeria's first university was established in 1948 with a total student enrolment of 104 students. By 1963 there were five universities with a population of 3,646. Ten years later the country had six universities with a student population of 20,889 and by 1999 there were

39 universities with a student enrolment of 236,261 (Oni, 1999). According to Jibril and Obaje (2008: 1) the Nigerian higher education system had, as at 2008, a student enrolment of 1.4 million, and consisted of '92 universities, 57 polytechnics, 90 specialized colleges and monotechnics, and 72 colleges of education'. The first university in South Africa, the University of Cape Town, was established in 1892 followed by two others in 1904 and 1916 respectively. As at 2010, there are 23 universities and about 25 degree-granting institutions (Wikipedia, 2010b). Uganda has 27 universities and two degree-awarding institutions. The famous Makerere University was established in 1922, and no other university was established until the 1990s (Wikipedia, 2010c). The exponential growth of tertiary institutions is repeated throughout African countries over the last 20 years. In theory, many African countries, including Nigeria, Ghana and Kenya, should not suffer from a scarcity of talent; in reality, it is a veritable challenge in Africa.

It is the paradox in Africa that although the unemployment rate is high, organizations are complaining of shortage of talent. The African Association for Public Administration and Management (AAPAM) rightly observes that the continent has not been able to recruit and retain needed well-trained and skilled personnel due to several challenges which include, among others, poor compensation, and an uncompetitive working environment (AAPAM, 2008: 2). These factors translate into low institutional productivity and the migration of human resources. The Association concludes that institutional and human resource capacity limitations are among the most evident frailties of most African countries.

According to Gara (2007), there is a huge demand in Egypt for skilled professionals of all stripes, particularly those with technical or quantitative skills such as telecommunications engineers, information technologists, financial planners and investment bankers. Gara (2007) further observed that since the oil boom began in the Gulf region, the temptation for Egypt's best and brightest professionals to take up more lucrative positions abroad has been strong. The exodus of highly skilled professionals to Europe and the United States is a daily occurrence in many African countries such as Nigeria, Ghana, Kenya and Ethiopia, and is largely responsible for talent scarcity.

Anekwe (2003: 1) noted that the Presidential Committee on Brain Drain in Nigeria estimated that between 1986 and 1990 Nigeria lost about 10,694 academics from tertiary institutions. In fact the total number of professionals who left public, industrial and private organizations was estimated at 30,000. According to Mberu and Ponguou (2010), the World Bank Development Prospects Group reported in 2007 an estimated emigration rate of 36 per cent for Nigerians with tertiary education. For physicians and nurses, the rates were about 13.6 per cent and 11.7 per cent respectively. The impact of the brain drain or human resources haemorrhage is evident in many tertiary institutions. According to the former National President of the Academic Staff Union of Universities (ASUU), Abdullahi Sule-Kano (2008), Nigerian universities, as at 2008, required no less than 60,000 lecturers to be effective – that is, within the university system alone. The shortage of talent so greatly affected tertiary institutions in Nigeria that most of the new and private universities began to recruit holders of Masters degrees as lecturers. In response, and to safeguard the quality of university education, the National University Commission – the regulatory body for tertiary education – immediately imposed a ban in 2006 on the recruitment of academics who did not possess doctoral degrees (Vandu, 2010).

Olita (2007: 17) noted that, in 2000, one in five Ugandans who finished tertiary education left the country for 'greener pastures'. He also noted that in 2000 Gambia lost 64.7 per cent of its 'tertiary educated people'; Somalia 58.6 per cent; Eritrea 45.8 per cent; Mozambique 42 per cent; and Sierra Leone 41 per cent. Notably, with the exception of Gambia, all these countries were involved in conflicts at one time or another. Other countries such as Tanzania, Kenya and Ghana also lost people but not to the same degree. The story is the same all over Africa. The average number of African–born scientists and engineers per million people in Africa is less than 200 as compared to 3,000 per million people in developed countries (Hassan, 2008). The underlying factors include poor-quality education and brain drain.

The health sector is most hit by the African brain drain phenomenon. According to the former Nigerian Health Minister, Dr Ihechukwu Madubuike, as at 1995, 21,000 Nigerian doctors were practising in the United States alone. It is estimated that about 10,000 Nigerian doctors were also practising in Europe, Australia, Canada, the Gulf States and African countries (Anekwe, 2003: 2). The numbers might have doubled by now. Stilwell *et al.* (2004: 1) estimated that between April 2001 and March 2002, 432 Nigerian nurses emigrated from Nigeria to Britain. In 2002 there were 175 Ugandan doctors practising in the United States and only 722 doctors practising in the whole of Uganda (Olita, 2007: 1). Professor Edward Ofori-Sarpong (2003: 1) also estimated that Ghana lost about 60 per cent of its doctors in the 1980s and an average of 20,000 professionals annually between 1985 and 1990.

In Lesotho there were fewer than 100 doctors in 2007, and most of them were foreigners. According to Médecins Sans Frontières, one nurse looked after 100 sick patients in a ward. The same organization also revealed that in Mozambique there were only 2.6 doctors, 20 nurses and 34 healthcare providers per 100,000 people. It warned that a shortage of healthcare workers was paralysing the healthcare system in Lesotho, Malawi, Mozambique and South Africa and threatened the lives of millions particularly in the rural areas (Nduru, 2007: 1). According to the International Council for Science (ICSU 2007: 22) of the 57 countries that are critically short of health workers, 36 (63 per cent) were in Africa. Sub-Saharan Africa has a mere 4 per cent of the world's health workers even though it has to deal with 25 per cent of the global burden of disease. In comparison, the Americas have 37 per cent of the health workers, but only 10 per cent of the global disease burden.

The exodus of Africans from the continent is due essentially to political and socio-economic factors. At independence the few Africans in diaspora returned home to work for their countries. Those who were abroad for higher education scurried home as soon as they completed their education in order to use their knowledge and skills for the development of their countries. As the political and economic situation in many African countries deteriorated due to military rule or civil wars, many of these educated Africans sought refuge abroad while those already abroad postponed any plans for returning home. For instance, many professionals left Ethiopia, Somalia, Rwanda, Liberia and Sierra Leone during the conflicts in those countries, for the United States, Canada, Germany, France and other European countries. Some of these Africans are highly educated, highly skilled and renowned in their respective professions.

Another reason for the exodus of African professionals is that countries like the United Kingdom, United States and Canada operate programmes aimed at attracting highly skilled labour to become permanent residents or citizens of these countries. The programmes provide Africans with an opportunity not only to escape from the harsh conditions of war, poverty and political violence in their home countries, but also to use their skills and creativity to earn a decent living. The opportunity to acquire British, American or Canadian citizenship is highly valued and a great attraction. Furthermore, in the past, most of these countries stipulated that as soon as foreign students graduated from universities they must return to their own countries. This regulation was subsequently reviewed. Students could remain in the United States and Canada, for about a year or two after graduation during which period they were expected to be doing internship which, until the current financial crisis and the consequent high unemployment rates, usually culminated in the intern's employment.

This practice is a subtle way of identifying, attracting and hiring highly skilled foreigners to fill the void being created by the large number of managers and professionals (so-called baby boomers) who are retiring or will be retiring from active labour force in those countries. Like a zero-sum game, what these countries gain in terms of highly skilled talent is a loss to African countries. Emeagwali (2003: 4), a well-known Nigerian computer guru in the United States, puts it even more pungently: the contradiction in brain drain is that 'Africans who immigrate to the United States contribute 40 times more wealth to the American than to the African economy'. African countries spend millions of dollars annually to recruit and pay a few expatriates to work in Africa, but fail to spend even a third of that amount to attract and recruit the African professionals now working outside Africa.

The causes of shortage of talent can be attributed not only to the brain drain, but also to the educational system. The shortage of talent in Africa is also traceable to the declining quality of the products of the educational system. Since the 1980s the continent has witnessed a proliferation of universities in an attempt to meet the demand for higher education but with the unsavoury consequence that the available funds are spread thinly among these institutions and quality is compromised. Poor funding has resulted in the lack of essential facilities, equipment, tools and high-quality academic staff.

The quality of education, especially at the tertiary level, is low when compared to the quality that existed prior to the 1980s. The Nigerian former head of state, Shehu Shagari said that it was sad that tertiary institutions in Nigeria that once had international reputation have been allowed to deteriorate abysmally (Idoko, 2010). In explaining the cause of the decline in the quality of education in the country, Tijani Momodu Yesufu, an erudite economics scholar, lamented the situation in a lucid description of the state of affairs: 'The student-teacher ratios are worsening in virtually all disciplines. Laboratories are either non-existent or completely denuded of essential equipment and experimental consumables. Libraries cry out for updating with current books, periodicals and research findings' (Yesufu, 1996: 207). Unfortunately, 14 years later, the situation has not improved and it is the same in most African countries.

Furthermore, not only do lecturers lack the tools and resources for research and teaching, but they are also poorly paid. Yesufu (1996) notes that teachers are grossly underpaid and that many have had to resort to emigrating to other countries both to seek higher pay and further their intellectual development. Many others have abandoned academics for employment in private industry, banks and consultancies. Those who have remained are tempted to compromise their commitment to academia by engaging in non-academic pursuits to earn more money through part-time jobs and moonlighting with the result that they no longer devote enough time to research and teaching. It is therefore not surprising that the quality of education is declining and that there is no African university among the world's best 100 universities. Yet some argue that the low rating of African universities is political!

The curriculum of most of the educational institutions does not equip students with the skills required in industry and in the information age. There are inadequate linkages between educational output and the labour-market requirements in Africa. Quite often, employers have to retrain new graduates to equip them with relevant basic skills which they should have acquired in their colleges. Education programmes in virtually all disciplines are designed and delivered from narrowly defined and theoretical perspectives that fail to produce graduates with the knowledge, skills and business orientation needed to meet the industrial, technological and developmental needs of their countries.

The African economy is increasingly becoming knowledge-based. The structure of the economies of middle-income African countries like Egypt, Morocco, South Africa, Botswana and Tunisia is shifting from primary sectors to service sectors with the consequence that there is less demand for unskilled labour and greater demand for knowledge workers. The rapidly growing economies of Africa have created the need for more talent. The average annual growth rate of most African economies was 6 per cent in 2007 and 5.75 per cent in 2008, although it was estimated in 2009 that, as a result of the current recession, the growth rate might decline to 2.9 per cent (Kasekende, Ndikumana and Rajhi, 2009). The private sector in Africa is increasingly becoming an engine of growth and development. The financial and telecommunications sectors have been developing at an exponential rate in Nigeria, Tunisia, Morocco, South Africa, Kenya and Egypt amongst others, naturally stimulating the demand for knowledge workers and high managerial capabilities in these countries. In addition, many companies in these countries are 'going global', expanding their businesses within and outside the African continent.

University graduates who do not have the relevant skills in disciplines or professions such as engineering, finance, accounting, information technology, telecommunications, biotechnology, and so on are becoming less relevant to the industrial and commercial needs of African businesses. Unfortunately, Africans who have gone abroad to acquire quality education and expertise in the desired disciplines and professions are reluctant to return home. The shortage is affecting not only private-sector organizations, but also governments' capacity to implement development programmes.

Shortage of talent is more acute in the post-conflict countries of Africa. These are countries that have suffered not only from the violence and destruction of physical infrastructure, but also from the decimation of human capital as a result of internecine wars. While some skilled people fled the war-torn countries, many others could not escape and became victims of bullets, diseases and other calamities of war. The acute shortage is exacerbated by the fact that human capital takes many years to develop.

Scarcity of talent in many African countries is also caused by the problem of spatial immobility of labour. Many African countries would rather hire expatriates from Europe, Asia, China or the United States than from an African country, even though they may have to pay five times the salary they would pay an African who has the same or even better capability for the job. This problem exists even within national boundaries. For instance, in the colonial era, labour moved easily between the three regions of Nigeria. With the creation of states (of which there are now 36), the labour market has been compartmentalized into states or zones in which only the 'indigenes' of a state are eligible for employment into a state's civil service or corporations. As a result, while some states appear to have a surplus of skilled human resources, others are experiencing severe shortages. The imbalance is artificial and politically induced. The tragedy is that expatriates are recruited at a high cost to make up for the shortage. This is also true of many other African countries.

All these multiple factors have cumulatively created a high demand for talent in African countries. The situation points to a need for organizations to comprehend the various exogenous factors that determine the availability of talent. Otherwise, they may live in the self-delusion that the required talent can easily be obtained in Africa because of its large population of unemployed college graduates. However, the challenge is not the number of graduates, but the quality and relevance of the skills of the teeming, unemployed population to the leadership and technical needs of African organizations and institutions.

The Global Economic Crisis and its Impact on Talent Management

Economic crisis always creates the pain of downsizing, but it is comforting to know that it usually terminates in a recovery, and smart organizations think beyond the crisis in planning for and utilizing talent. The global financial and economic crisis which began in 2008 was the aftermath of the dramatic failures of gigantic and apparently impregnable institutions such as Lehman Brothers, Merrill Lynch, American International Group (AIG), Fannie Mae amongst others. The crisis has impacted on global economies, including the fragile economies of Africa, but to different degrees. As a result of the crisis the forecast is that the average annual economic growth in African countries in 2009 would decline from 5.75 per cent in 2008 to about 2.9 per cent (Kasekende, Ndikumana and Rajhi, 2009). The sharp decline is due to: decline in trade flows and remittances from Africans in the diaspora; a faster decline in exports than in imports, thus creating a negative balance of trade where there are no substantial foreign reserves; and shrinkage of liquidity in international financial markets which are a source of investment capital for the private sector. The impact of the crisis varies from country to country in Africa.

A predictable consequence of the current situation is the increase in unemployment. A contraction of the economy and decline in revenues affect the profitability and expansion of businesses. Without profits and expansion there will be limited employment. A second possible consequence, which is related to the first, is that private-sector organizations may resort to downsizing in order to reduce staff costs. Unlike in the United States and Europe, the statistics on job losses resulting from the economic crisis in Africa are not known, but what is known is that organizations have either frozen recruitment or laid off some of their employees. Where such drastic cost-cutting actions have not been taken, employers are not increasing salaries, paying bonuses, promoting employees or providing training for development. Salaries and benefits constitute one of the largest 'costs' for any organization. Finally, employees may be required to make great sacrifices in terms of taking on additional responsibilities of those who have been laid off or working extra time without commensurate compensation.

It is important at this point to state a principle which has proved historically true and incontrovertible – namely that countries and businesses always recover from a financial crisis if they do the right things and manage their talent effectively. They rise from the ashes of recession and thrive better than they did before the crisis. The Mexican financial crisis of 1994 spread to neighbouring countries like Brazil and resulted in a depreciation of the exchange rate, a fall in stock prices and capital flight. The countries recovered. The East Asian financial crisis began in Thailand in 1997 and later spread to Indonesia, Malaysia, Philippines and Korea. The exchange rate and stock prices collapsed. The countries recovered and prospered. Finally, in the 1998 Russian financial crisis the ruble depreciated by 34 per cent, stocks fell and there was a huge capital flight. Russia has since recovered and become financially and economically strong.

The recovery from the financial and economic crisis began at the end of 2009. Hopes for recovery were particularly noticeable in commodity sectors with the increase in prices of raw materials and energy which are particularly sensitive to shifts in global production. Organizations must therefore look beyond the crisis in managing their most valuable asset at this time. Well-managed, futuristic and people-centred organizations recognize the fact that this difficult time will not last for eternity. While the tough time imposes on organizations the need to reduce cost, be lean and healthy, it is an error of judgement to sacrifice talent management at the altar of cost control. The economic environment has changed dramatically, but the need to invest in talent has become even more important. O'Neil (2009) puts it succinctly: 'a skilled, educated workforce is essential for our recovery and future financial security. This was true before the current downturn, it's true today, and it will be even more so when economic health is restored.' Jones and Schweyer (2009: 1) have similarly noted that every recession of the past has been followed by a recovery. They opine that 'It is not a matter of if, but when'. Indeed, Reich wrote a year later that profits that 'plummeted in recession have bounced back. Big businesses have recovered almost 90 per cent of what they lost' (Reich, 2010: 6). Leaders must therefore take the right decisions at this time about talent and manage it in a way that not only supports their organizations to survive the recession, but also repositions them for greater performance in the post-recession era.

About This Book

This chapter began with an overview of the war for talent in Europe, the United States and Africa. It demonstrated that talent scarcity is a reality and a universal phenomenon. Sullivan (2004b) refers to it as 'World-wide War II'. The chapter also demonstrated the paradox in Africa that, despite the high rate of unemployment, there is talent scarcity! Chapter 2 shows that organizations that maintain the same approach to talent management even though they have gone global may lose competitive advantage in the international market. It invites managers to make a significant shift in the way they perceive and manage talent by shedding obsolescent managerial philosophies and behaving not as managers but as entrepreneurial leaders of their organizations.

Chapter 3 outlines the strategies for hiring talent and emphasizes the need to link hiring to business strategy; recruit not just for today and the job but for the future and the globe; mainstream diversity into hiring, development and succession planning; and leverage information technology in the process. Chapter 4 states that talent cannot be effectively attracted and hired if the process is not based on the following three principles:

- a recruitment brand for attracting quality candidates; recruitment involves marketing or relationship management;
- a competency-driven selection process to ensure candidate-organization-job fit; and
- integrity, which is critical for fair and honest decisions by those who are involved in the selection processes. There are ethical issues in hiring in every country and organization.

The chapter emphasizes that successful hiring of talent is not fortuitous but is a result of commitment, integrity and professionalism. It outlines the pitfalls to avoid when selecting candidates. Chapter 5 seeks to answer the question of how organizations can generate and sustain high employee engagement. It identifies three categories of critical employee engagement drivers: instrumental, normative and professional. The pith of Chapter 6 is that having successfully recruited talent, how can an organization obtain the best from such talented people through the management of their performance? It also outlines causes of ineffective performance management and what could be done to restore effectiveness.

Chapter 7 underscores the fact that performance appraisal is, by definition, a differentiation of the workforce according to performance and potential and that the investment in talent through development, advancement and retention must be based on the outcome of the differentiation. Reward must also be based on differentiation. Chapter 8 makes a clear distinction between succession planning and replacement planning. It provides a succession planning framework which should guide organizations in undertaking succession planning and emphasizes the need for top management commitment and ownership. It also provides the principles that should guide top management in implementing a succession plan. It concludes on the note that having a succession plan is not enough; implementation is the main challenge.

Chapter 9 focuses on growing and developing leaders for tomorrow's businesses, and states that hiring talent is not enough. It identifies tools for executive development. Finally, the chapter highlights the value, challenges and pitfalls of external assignment, and outlines an approach for its effective management. Chapter 10 examines the reasons why executive development programmes are often ineffective – failure to link development to business strategy, slow pace of response to development needs of future leaders, confusing executive training programmes with development, failure to have a holistic approach to development and so on. Chapter 11 is concerned that human resource management in most organizations, especially in African countries, is lagging behind globalization and technological development with the result that HR functions are not adequately providing their organizations with the kind of services they sorely need in their globalization efforts. The chapter defines the competencies of global executives, describes the state of HR management in African organizations and outlines what the strategic role of the HR function must be in companies that are going global.

Chapter 12 is the final chapter of the book and is a case study based on Nigeria's first integrated steel plant with over 4,500 employees. Its mission of 'Reinforcing Nigeria with Steel' was incredibly inspiring in hiring talent. About seven years after the establishment of the company, things began to fall apart and the centre could not hold. The prospects of establishing the second phase of the steel plant became a mirage: individual and corporate visions dissolved into thin air and opportunities for advancement shrank by the day. Internecine conflict in top management erupted; the work environment became toxic; and teamwork and bonding went up in flames, thus engendering distrust and suspicion. Staff turnover followed, and then a decline in production and a loss of revenue, and finally, the shut-down of the plant. In 2005 another company bought it over.

2

The Need for a Paradigm Shift

The previous chapter sought to establish the fact that talent scarcity is universal and that African countries, despite their high unemployment rate, also experience an acute dearth of talent. Unfortunately, few managers recognize that reality. This chapter presents a business case for a paradigm shift in talent management and specifically identifies the areas where a shift is imperative so that organizations, particularly those of African countries, can compete effectively in the global market. The message that pervades all the subsequent chapters is that the level of talent management does not resonate with the demands of globalization. Furthermore, organizations are not doing enough to equip managers with what it takes to operate in a global setting. A change is therefore imperative for the effective management of talent.

The Imperative of Paradigm Shift in a Changing Context

Progress in human society is a product of continual generation of innovations and adaptation to change. Without change the human society would decay or at best become static and remain what it was prior to the Industrial Revolution. History tells us that the fall of great empires and kingdoms, whether in Europe or in Africa, was largely due to rulers' fixation with current dominance. Because of their dominant position, emperors and kings often believed that they were invincible and that change could not take place except at their behest. Decline inevitably occurred, though gradually and imperceptibly, due to a festering pathology of complacency.

The same malady afflicts organizations. In general, employees are blinded by current success and achievements. They are in a state of complacency and revel in the belief of their invincibility in the market. Their market share may be gradually etched away or eroded by other emerging innovative and dynamic firms, and there would still be denial of any loss. They only see and hear what they want to see and hear. Their blindness and deafness deaden their sense of urgency. Therefore in introducing change, the greatest challenge is to reverse the sense of complacency (Kotter, 1996).

However, there are organizations that inexorably pursue innovation, challenge the status quo, traditional views and hallowed practices, and seek to respond effectively to economic, technological, scientific and environmental changes. In an age characterized by rapid global changes, an organization's capacity to innovate, create and sustain interventions that endow it with competitive advantage is critical to survival, competitiveness and progress. Indeed, change is absolutely vital for the survival and future progress of any organization. No firm can survive for long in the increasingly competitive global environment if it continues to deliver the same products and services in the same way. The principles that provided competitive advantage in the 1980s may be necessary but are certainly no longer sufficient for the information age. Rank Xerox was the first firm in the world to develop personal computers in Palo Alto Research Center (Xerox PARC) in 1973, long before Apple and IBM. Today, it is hardly associated with computers.

The economic, technological, scientific and social environment impacts on all organizations, yet organizations react differently to the same impact or environmental conditions. Some proactively seek to change and control the environment through innovations, others merely react to it and yet others are completely incapable of either and soon suffer fatal atrophy. These varying reactions are a reflection of the varying organizational paradigms (Barker, 1992). The Swiss once ruled the world in watch-making. A research institute in Neuchâtel, Switzerland invented the electronic quartz and presented this revolutionary idea to Swiss manufacturers at a fair. The major Swiss watch-makers saw it and dismissed it as unmarketable because they thought the prevailing analogue technology was supreme and invincible. The researchers were allowed to showcase their 'useless invention' at the World Watch Congress in 1967. Seiko of Japan was impressed with the invention and, ten years later, it flooded the world market with digital watches, and the Swiss dramatically lost a substantial proportion of the market as well as their dominant position in the industry. The rest is history. What the business leaders of the Swiss industry suffered from is what Barker called 'paradigm paralysis', a terminal disease of certainty, a situation in which the individual's paradigm becomes *the* paradigm (Barker, 1992).

A paradigm is a mindset, a mental map or the way we perceive the world. We all have paradigms in every aspect of our lives. The paradigms in an organization could vary with departments and divisions. For instance, while the HR department perceives people as an investment, the production department perceives them as a production resource and the accounts department perceives them as a cost. The problem with paradigms is that they can sometimes distort new reality by either exaggerating negative aspects or undermining what is positive. They impair the ability to acquire new learning or accept new ideas because they vitiate the capacity to see the need for change. As Barker noted, paradigms that are too strongly held because they have proved successful in the past make it difficult for the holder to see the need for change. This is the point at which mental maps paralyse the ability to respond proactively to change. Here lies the dysfunctionality and danger of paradigms. A paradigm shift means making a change, rejecting the status quo, embracing and accepting ideas and practices that contradict existing beliefs and practices. It means being proactive.

The irony of the Swiss tragedy is that it was the Swiss themselves who invented the electronic quartz that sounded the death knell of their watch industry. Many organizations may be making the same kind of mistakes in Africa and elsewhere either by sticking to an obsolete approach to managing talent or by refusing to anticipate and accept change necessitated by globalization. Michaels, Handfield-Jones and Axelrod rightly note that it is not better HR processes that make the difference in talent management. Rather, it is the mindset of leaders throughout an organization that makes the difference. They conclude that 'without this mindset, recruiting becomes an activity, development happens by serendipity. Average managers are tolerated in key spots. Attrition increases. Performance suffers' (2001: *x*). Evidence exists that there is some disconnect between globalization and the way in which talent is being managed in African multinational enterprises (MNEs).

The State of Talent Management Practices

Human resource management occupies a strategic position in the globalization of an organization. Yet, as noted later on, in Chapter 11, most organizations do not appear to recognize this strategic role in the formulation of corporate strategies and business plans. The human resource function is generally relegated to the background as evidenced by the fact that the head of the function may not be on the company's board and the position may be filled by an individual whose background is in no way related to the HR function. Stern (2008) in fact noted that less than 10 per cent of FTSE 100 companies have an HR director on the board. In addition, HR may not be involved in strategic business decisions. Part of the explanation has to do with the current state of HRM practices in African organizations.

How can the HR function help its organization play a strategic role in its globalization – for instance, in attracting, recruiting, developing and retaining executives with the kind of disabilities described above? The challenge facing many HR functions is that they are still operating in the mode of 'personnel management' of yesteryear – lacking in vision and strategic orientation to partner with the business. Budhwar and Debrah (2001) note that, despite the pressures for change facing HR managers in developing countries as a result of globalization and international competitiveness, most HR departments are not involved in the formulation of business strategies, and there seems to be no movement from personnel management to human resources management. African organizations are not developing HR strategic responses to globalization and do not have an integrated and focused approach to HRM.

HR policies, practices and systems are still oriented to a single-country operation and are not oriented towards globalization or aligned to a strategic business goal. Many HR executives have little knowledge of HR practices within and outside African countries or of the impact of globalization on HR management. Many HR processes are still procedure-driven rather than business-driven. There is scarcely an integrated approach to HR management – policies and systems are generally compartmentalized and introduced piecemeal. The rate of change from HRM to strategic international human resource management (SIHRM) is painfully slow.

Organizations whose HR practices have undergone transformation into SIHRM are generally foreign multinational corporations operating in African countries. Their main distinguishing characteristic is that their HR policies and practices are closely aligned to the business of the organization. Although their headquarters are in Europe or the United States, their HR practices seek to meet global challenges and at the same time satisfy the local needs of the operations in individual African countries. Their HR policies and practices may not be ideal, but they sufficiently demonstrate flexibility and orientation towards ensuring the effectiveness of not only individual national operations, but also the global business.

Managers' Paradigms

The challenge of talent management in African organizations does not inhere only in obsolete HR systems, policies and practices; it also has its roots in the paradigms of managers. Managers' paradigms affect the way in which they manage or fail to manage talent. One of the paradigms is that talent management is the responsibility of HR specialists. The second is that they perceive themselves primarily as managers who should drive efficiency and the third is that they conceive workers as 'rational-economic men'. Each of these paradigms is examined in detail below.

TALENT MANAGEMENT IS THE RESPONSIBILITY OF THE HR DEPARTMENT

In most organizations, line managers typically believe that they should not take on what they consider as 'additional' responsibility for the management of human resources in their domain. They believe that there is a division of labour and that they are only responsible for production, procurement and inventory control, marketing and sales, or financial control, but not human resource management. Michaels, Handfield-Jones and Axelrod (2001) note that talent management is not about HR processes but about managers' acceptance of their role as leaders who strengthen the talent in their respective functional domains. What managers often ignore is the need to build what Ready and Conger (2007) called 'talent factories' – that is, the ability to marry a rigorous talent process that supports strategic and cultural objectives with an emotional commitment on the part of management that is reflected in daily actions. A talent factory allows managers to develop and retain key employees and fill positions quickly to meet the organization's evolving needs.

The reluctance of line managers to take on the responsibility for talent management can be attributed to a number of factors. First, many organizations fail to define clearly the roles of the HR department vis-à-vis the responsibilities of line managers. Most job descriptions and performance evaluation systems are completely silent on the role of managers in hiring, developing and retaining talent. In the absence of an explicit allocation of responsibility, managers have leeway to think that managing talent must be the responsibility of the HR department. Second, the implementation of HR policies and systems is highly centralized and unduly deprives managers of decision-making authority. HR specialists become oracles that must be consulted on every issue before a decision can be taken by line managers. Finally, there is so much emphasis on results and non-human aspects of their jobs that managers do not sufficiently understand that the greatest asset entrusted to them as leaders is not the production line, equipment, maintenance tools, raw materials or even a huge financial account; rather, it is people. Their responsibility is in fact to manage both people and performance.

The paradigm shift required is for line managers to accept their responsibility for people management and refrain from holding the HR department accountable for talent management. Managers have annual budgets; they monitor how the budget is being used and are accountable for the way it has been used or misused. The same managers are hardly held accountable in the same way for the manner in which they manage or fail to manage their people; yet people are more critical for their success than the budget. The role of the HR department is to provide the regulatory framework (policies, procedures and systems), training and guidance to managers on how to manage their people.

When top management accepts responsibility for talent management, middle managers easily adopt a talent management mindset. To make a paradigm shift, it is important for top management to understand the profound effect their behaviour can have on managers. The latter spontaneously come to understand, almost as an epiphany, that they will be held accountable for failure to identify, develop and retain talent for the enterprise, and that such a failure could impact negatively on their own individual career advancement. Ready and Conger (2007) noted that, in HSBC, each organizational unit has a talent implementation strategy. Each unit's growth objective is linked to its people development. Leaders make talent acquisition, development and retention a priority at every level of the organization. They support recruitment strategies, are deeply involved in the development of talent, have a holistic view of the employee, and not only demonstrate commitment to identifying super-performers, but also invest appropriate resources in them in order to ensure their retention. Procter and Gamble is reputed for growing leaders. Its former CEO, A.G. Lafley staunchly believes that the greatest impact he could have on the long-term success of the firm is to ensure the development of its leadership. The focus of the company is not merely on attracting and hiring the best people but, more importantly, on developing them as future leaders.

Attitudes and behaviours cannot change overnight. To facilitate the change in the mindset, top management must empower managers and also involve them fully in the talent management process, including hiring, talent pool creation, talent development, succession planning and career advancement.

Systematic and consistent communication of the desired change by top management is imperative. Human resource policies, procedures and systems need to be reviewed with a view to empowering line managers to take decisions. Thereafter they can be held accountable.

RESPONSIBILITY FOR MANAGING, NOT FOR LEADING

A second major paradigm of managers is that their responsibility is to plan, organize, control and ensure efficiency and productivity. They hardly see themselves as business leaders. They do not understand that being a manager entails leadership and that a transition in terms of thinking and behaviour is imperative. Being a manager does not automatically transform the individual into a leader. Yet, ironically, no manager can succeed for long if he or she does not provide effective leadership. Unfortunately, the world-view of managers is limited to their immediate tasks, targets and results here and now. Managers are unduly preoccupied with daily planning, monitoring, controlling and evaluation of results with the consequence that they largely lose sight of strategic issues that impact on the business from the environment. The 'manager mentality' is myopic and not strategic. It is reflected in the fact that many managers do not see the big picture of the enterprise and how talent management fits into that picture.

For instance, many managers conceive of the products, markets and technologies only within the context of their national frontiers. They do not comprehend the organization's business within the global framework. They rarely pursue innovations or do things differently. When hiring, they think of filling a vacancy with a competent person but not of hiring for a career or hiring a global executive; in training, their orientation is merely to equip the employee with relevant skills to perform a particular task but not to develop his or her capacity to innovate or grow. They perceive performance appraisal as a means and an opportunity to increase the pay of good performers and punish poor performers and 'uncooperative employees' but not as a tool for employee development. They regard promotion as a means to reward loyal employees or high performers but not as recognition of potential and commitment to grow future leaders. International assignment is an opportunity to set up 'difficult' employees for failure or get rid of them but is certainly not considered as part of an integrated succession plan.

A paradigm shift is necessary, and it is a transformation from being efficient managers to being effective leaders and global executives. There is a wide gap between managing and leading people. As noted earlier, managers are preoccupied with efficiency and doing things right whereas leaders focus on effectiveness and doing the right things at the right time. Leaders develop a vision, communicate it, create teams and energize them to achieve the vision. They create an appropriate ambience for performance. What African organizations need in their effort to globalize is entrepreneurial leadership which should take the form of the following behaviours:

- a long-term vision of the enterprise within the global environment, and ability to build and inspire teams to innovate and actualize the vision
- a deep understanding of the international business environment and its impact on the organization's competitiveness and effectiveness
- An ability to think strategically and link talent management to departmental and divisional business objectives and success
- a passion for, and commitment to, the development, motivation and management of talent pools
- integrity characterized by a commitment to strategic organizational goals that override personal and parochial considerations.

THE WORKFORCE IS ESSENTIALLY DRIVEN BY MONETARY REWARDS

A third paradigm of managers has to do with their philosophy of the workforce. The way in which managers conceive of their workforce influences the way in which they manage them. Many managers in Africa still operate in the mode of the classical manager who insists on control or micro-management. In the face of the ravaging poverty in Africa where about 300 million people subsist on less than one dollar a day, managers tend to conceive of every employee as a 'rational-economic man'. The philosophy of the rational-economic man was derived originally from hedonism and it states that human behaviours are aimed at maximizing self-interest. The philosophy essentially implies the existence of a psychological contract involving the exchange of extrinsic rewards for performance and commitment, and it has had the effect of devolving the responsibility for individual and organizational performance entirely on to management. Hence, the strategy that naturally emerged is epitomized in the characteristic managerial functions of planning, organizing, motivating and controlling. The philosophy also institutionalized a culture that produces managers, but not leaders, and a workforce that is totally disempowered to use their talent and potentials. To effectively manage talent, managers have to make a shift in the paradigm.

Research and experience have shown that although workers need money, there are other needs that dominate their lives. First, people are basically motivated by social needs and are more responsive to their peer group and self-fulfilment than to economic incentives and controls of management. Second, employees are capable of improving organizational effectiveness (quality and productivity); they have a reservoir of relevant knowledge and competencies which can be tapped through their involvement and empowerment. Third, organizational performance is the responsibility of all employees. While extrinsic rewards may be important to the workforce, the basis for motivation and high performance must be a combination of extrinsic and intrinsic rewards. Managerial philosophy must give accent to individual autonomy, to the need to challenge workers with responsibilities, and to the need to develop their capabilities and draw out each individual's infinite potentials. This kind of philosophy will resonate with the philosophy of talent management. In addition to the fact that the philosophy of rational-economic man is questionable, it is misleading for African managers to see the global workforce through the African prism.

Spheres for a Paradigm Shift in Talent Management

Talent management is an integrated process which comprises workforce planning, recruitment and selection, development, performance management, compensation, employee engagement and career development, among other functions. Managers have mental maps as to how each activity in the sequence of managing talent should be performed. Many of these are, incidentally, not in synchronization with globalization. Therefore, multinational corporations, which by definition are global organizations, may not be optimally effective until there is a transformation in their paradigms about talent management. Table 2.1 summarizes the areas where a paradigm shift is necessary. It would be pretentious to assert that the list is exhaustive. Some people may not even accept some of the paradigms. They are an analytic tool on which research can build. The table shows current paradigms and practices and also the kind of practices that resonate with globalization.

Table 2.1 A framework for paradigm shift

Managers' paradigms	Global thinking and practices
There is no scarcity of talent, particularly in Africa, because the rate of unemployment is high.	The war for talent is global, including in Africa. The continent suffers from perpetual talent haemorrhage as a result of brain drain.
Talent management is the responsibility of the HRM department.	Managing talent is the most important responsibility of all managers. It is their duty to build a 'talent factory' for their organizations. They must have a talent mindset.
Workforce planning is about negotiating and competing for more people by organizational units. The larger the number of employees the more important the organizational unit is.	Workforce planning consists of strategic decisions on the allocation, development and utilization of talent where they are most needed for the achievement of strategic business goals.
Hiring is a transaction – it is essentially the purchase of the services of a competent individual for the performance of a job for an organization.	Hiring is marketing in which employers must demonstrate their brands in the competition for talent or why they are 'an employer of choice'. It is about managing relationships with potential employees. The focus of the recruitment process should be on the company's recruitment brand.
The most important instrument for hiring is the job description accompanied by a person specification.	A competency model for each job is imperative because what it takes to succeed in one job is not what is required to succeed in another job. Competency models are also the basis for development and career advancement.
Hiring aims at selecting the people who have just the skills required to do a particular job for the organization today; tomorrow will take care of their career. In hiring for vacant positions emphasis must be on educational qualifications and years of work experience in similar positions because they are strong predictive indicators of performance and success on the job.	Hiring must be for a career and not merely for one particular job so that people can grow and develop in the organization. Hiring has to be for tomorrow and with global mobility in mind. While not discounting years of experience, candidates' diversity of experience and potential are more critical to, and predictive of, success than paper qualifications and the number of years of work experience.
Growth and mobility mean promotion or vertical progression up the career ladder. Employees are expected to remain with the organization until retirement.	Orientation is towards global mobility within and outside their organization. The purpose of growth is career resilience, and there is no plan for tenure in one organization.
Pursuing individual passions that are not job-related is not compatible with an employee's commitment to an organization. Spending many hours at work, even at the cost of time with the family, is a clear testimony of commitment.	Employee engagement is enhanced when organizations provide employees with the opportunity and time to satisfy their passions outside the workplace and they have time for their families. Work–life balance is the norm.
Succession planning is critical for only CEOs and should be a process for identifying an heir-apparent. It is more or less a replacement process that should be a well-guarded secret.	Succession planning is a strategic intervention aimed at preparing tomorrow's leaders. It is for every critical position in an organization and focuses on creating pools of potential successors and not a single heir-apparent.

Table 2.1 A framework for paradigm shift *concluded*

Managers' paradigms	Global thinking and practices
High performance provides a sufficient basis to predict an employee's success in higher-level jobs. Promotion should be based strictly on experience and current level of performance.	High performance is an indication of competence and mastery of a particular task, duty or responsibility and does not necessarily predict success on a higher-level job. Potential is a better predictor. Performance and potential must be taken together in determining the suitability of employees for promotion to leadership positions.
Executive training is synonymous with development. The best approach to preparing employees for leadership positions is through executive training programmes, especially in reputable business schools. A series of classroom training programmes is enough to develop the leadership ability of managers for future responsibilities.	Training is only one tool in the repertoire of instruments for preparing talent for leadership positions. The more varied the tools the higher the possibility of effectiveness. Mentoring, coaching, external assignment, job rotation, etc. are potent tools for developing leadership ability.
Diversity is about fairness and equity in dealing with the diverse groups in an organization, especially minorities and women. It is compliance with quotas, implementing affirmative action, etc., and its driver is fairness, equity, justice and avoidance of conflict.	Diversity and Inclusion is a business imperative; it is strategic, reflects global orientation and gives competitive advantage. The emphasis is on creating a corporate culture that values diversity and does not merely comply with a regulation or try to be fair to a particular disadvantaged group. The driver is business success.

It is important to stress the fact that the need for a paradigm shift is not based on the tenet of the 'universalist' school of thought which contends that management is based on principles and techniques that are universally applicable to every organization irrespective of the culture. Nor is it an argument in favour of modernization or the Westernization of human resource management practices in Africa. Rather, our position is based on the rationale that while organizations need to act locally, they also need to think, plan and organize globally. In the context of globalization, the emphasis is that other countries outside Africa are different; behaviours that are regarded as normal, functional and culturally acceptable on the African continent may be viewed as dysfunctional in other countries.

Some Cultural Characteristics that Impact on Talent Management

It would be unrealistic to discuss a change in talent management without taking cognizance of socio-cultural behaviours in the workplace that tend to influence talent management, and these will be referred to in subsequent chapters of this book. It is difficult to understand organizational behaviours in Africa without an understanding of their socio-cultural milieu. Although many societal values are not formally integrated into organizational practices, some inevitably and surreptitiously find their way into social interactions between and within work teams. Therefore, it is important to comprehend *ab initio* some African cultural characteristics. They include the following:

- *High power distance*. This fosters respect for authority and dependence on bosses, demands allegiance and enhances the enforcement of rules and regulations. However, it can also stifle innovation (Hofstede, 1994).

- *Personal connections and relationships*. These generate trust, create loyalty and foster friendship and a cooperative and supportive work environment. But they can also lead to non-rational decisions that raise the question of fairness and equity, and, perhaps more importantly, the issue of leaders' integrity.

- *Ethnicity*. Most African countries are made up of many nations, ethnic groups, languages and dialects. It is estimated that in Nigeria alone there are more than 200 different ethnic nationalities, each with individual cultural identities. The workforce is drawn from these diverse cultural and linguistic groups. Sometimes the conflict along ethnic lines in the larger society is imperceptibly imported into the workplace precisely because of the struggle for scarce resources – positions and power.

- *Work ethic*. Africans have a positive work ethic, and this has the potential to enhance workforce productivity.

- *Collectivism or communalism*. This fosters group dynamics and teamwork while minimizing interpersonal conflicts (Nnadozie, 2001). However, if not properly managed, it could be a veritable source of division and conflicts because of the existence of informal subcultural groups at the workplace.

All these cultural characteristics have different effects on talent management. For instance, ethnicity and communalism are characterized by a tight social framework in which people distinguish between in-groups and out-groups;

they expect their in-group (relatives, clan, organizations) to look after them and in exchange they feel that they owe absolute loyalty to it (Hofstede, 1994). Edoho (2001) says that communalism is the 'centerpiece of African personality' and that it permeates the whole of African consciousness.

Traditional African societies care not just for their nuclear families, but also for their extended families, villages, clans and ethnic groups. Hence, Otite (1978) notes that Western individualism does not fit into the African scheme of ethics. Collectivism is epitomized by the concept that members of the in-group are their brothers' and sisters' keepers. He further explains that the African society is a system of mutually benefiting reciprocities and that it exists for the good of all its members in a system of role reinforcements.

Communalism and ethnicity affect the decisions that managers make about people in a work environment. As an organization is made up of people from diverse ethnic, national and racial groups, members of each in-group or subsystem tend to owe greater commitment and loyalty to its members than to the suprasystem or the organization. Furthermore, members of each in-group tend to seek to protect the interests of their group against those of the out-group. By implication, the interests of members of an in-group that does not have senior people in strategic positions in the organizational hierarchy may not be well protected.

Finally, employees, particularly managers, find it difficult to make rational or optimal decisions which they know are good for the organization but may hurt members of their in-group. They feel morally bound to be their brothers' and sisters' keepers. Herein lies the challenge to managers in the management of talent. Unfortunately, the losers in this scenario are the companies, the arena for ethnic competition, because their interests are sometimes sacrificed at the altar of parochial and primordial interests. The success of managing talent therefore calls for a change in the mental map of organizational leaders. The best strategies, policies and systems will fail if the mindset of the operators is not in consonance with the spirit of the strategy and policies. Success also depends on the competencies, commitment and integrity of those who conduct the process. These principles will be evident in the next chapter which examines how talent is attracted and hired.

3

Strategies for Hiring Talent

The Need to Hire Talent

If there is an asset that an organization needs most in globalization, it is talent. The reason is that international competition requires technical savvy, innovativeness, strong emotional intelligence and leadership capability. Great organizations are made by talented people. Some organizations have failed where others have succeeded. In an environment where some firms have been blown out of existence by competition, others have survived and flourished as if they operated on a different planet. The difference lies in the quality of leadership and the people they hire and retain. According to Collins, if you have the wrong people, it doesn't matter how great your strategy may be, you still won't have a great company. He declares that '[g]reat vision without great people is irrelevant' (Collins, 2001: 42). Welch (2005: 81) said that hiring good people is hard, but 'hiring great people is brutally hard'. No organization can be successful without great people no matter what other resources – technology, money, plant, land, strategy – it may possess. The path to success is not just people, but great people.

Why do some organizations succeed in hiring great people while others do not? No organization ever deliberately sets out to hire mediocre or average people. They all have great intentions to hire the best in the market. Hiring great people takes more than intention. It involves planning, expertise, commitment and integrity. It entails using the right tools for selection and demands the ability to identify and offer what prospective employees value in an employment relationship. This chapter outlines various strategies which companies can use to hire global talent successfully. Each strategy is described below.

Linking Hiring to Business Strategy

The goal of hiring is not merely to fill the holes in bench strength, but rather to develop the organization's capability to be effective today and in the future.

Therefore, hiring must be driven by an organization's business strategy through the instrumentality of workforce planning. The purpose of workforce planning is to hire, utilize, motivate, develop and retain the right number and quality of people at the right time for the right functions in the appropriate organizational units so that an organization does not have either a shortage or an excess of talent required for optimal performance. Workforce planning involves the formulation of sound human resource planning policies to guide line managers in managing an organization's most valuable asset. Unlike annual budgeting, it is strategic, holistic and oriented towards achieving the organization's strategic goals rather than the immediate annual work programme. Unfortunately, few organizations undertake workforce planning before they recruit new people or promote existing employees. Cappelli (2008) has noted that two-thirds of US employers do no planning for their talent. The consequence, according to him, is that for such organizations every new need for talent presents a serious disruption. Every employee who quits represents a calamity, and every new demand for skills represents a crisis.

Have you ever noticed that sometimes hiring is managed like an emergency situation, a firefighting, save-our-soul kind of activity, in some organizations? The reason is that the hiring which should have been done yesterday is being done today or even tomorrow. How many times have you seen people retire or resign (with an adequate notice period) and yet there was no plan for their replacement until their departure? Have you ever worked for an organization in which the number of employees involved in support services is almost as large as the number of employees in the core business? Have you ever wondered why, even without a recession or major change in strategic direction, some firms have to retrench their employees or frantically headhunt for managers or specialists to fill critical positions that are vacant? All these organizational behaviours are symptoms of a fundamental ailment – either inept workforce planning or complete lack of it.

The panel that was set up to review the Nigerian federal civil service structure in 2006 found that there was an excess of 9,839 staff at the junior grade levels (Briggs, 2007). Not only is the figure mind-boggling, but it also raises the question as to whether there was any form of workforce planning. Workforce planning encapsulates the whole gamut of an organization's talent management. Hence, lack of workforce planning culminates in the following unsavoury and organization-wide consequences:

- a shortage of talent when and where it is most needed for competition

- desperate firefighting in the bid to fill the holes in bench strength
- excess employees because no limit was set for the number of people required
- lack of succession planning, career development and employee advancement.

Workforce planning consists essentially of the following steps:

- *Estimate the number and type of skills the organization would need at each level and in each department or division within a given timeframe.* In determining the size of the workforce and the type of the expertise required, the following actions should be considered:

  a) Review the prospects of leveraging technology in the achievement of organizational objectives.

  b) Consider the possibility of outsourcing some activities or functions.

  c) Examine the organization structure and the business processes. Layers of bureaucracy may not necessarily be adding value to the business.

- *Forecast the number and type of skills that will be available to the firm, taking account of wastage, promotions and transfers.* In forecasting the future availability of human resources, it is imperative to do a wastage analysis – how many people are likely to leave through retirement, resignation, termination, end of contract, and sometimes voluntary separation? Internal movement within the organization, through transfers, international assignment, study leave, promotions or secondment to external organizations needs to be carefully analysed and built into the forecast. The analysis of future requirements will highlight the strengths and the holes in bench strength in relation to the firm's strategic business objectives.

- *Bridge the gap between the firm's human resource requirements and the actual human resources that are available through promotion, transfers and recruitment.* One of the following three outcomes (depicted in Figure 3.1) may emerge at the end of the gap analysis:

1. There may be more employees than the organization will actually require within the timeframe of its business strategy. The firm may have to shed excess weight because it is toxic and unproductive.

2. There may be adequate human resources for the firm to implement its business plan. It will have to remain trim and fit and concentrate on training, developing, motivating and retaining the workforce.

3. The firm may need more resources to be able to implement its business strategy. At this point, recruitment may become necessary.

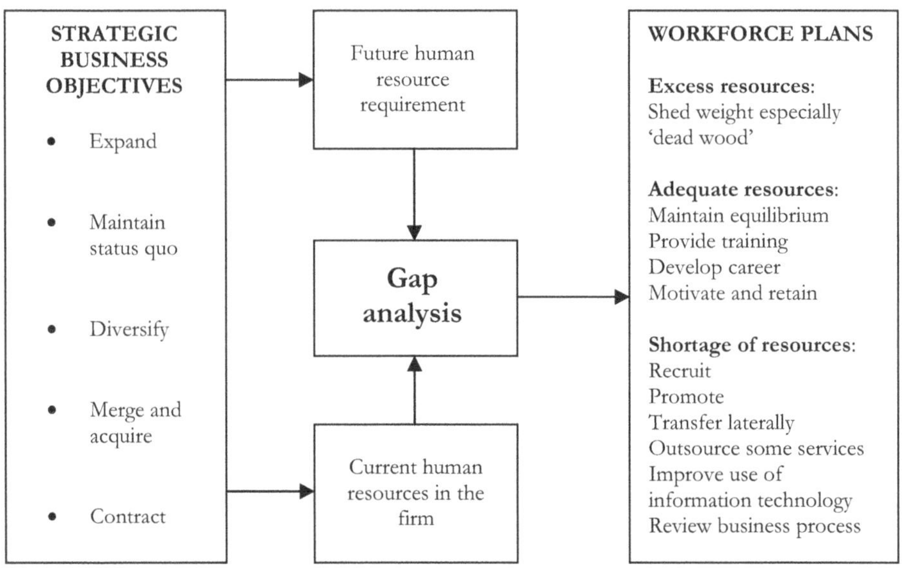

Figure 3.1 Workforce planning

Linking hiring through workforce planning to the business strategy is a critical stepts in hiring because workforce planning is about the vision of where a company wishes to be with regard to its talent capability in the future. It throws up problems that may emerge in the future and shows where a company's bench strength is vulnerable or where failure may be costly and damaging due to talent scarcity. The characteristic difference between today and 50 years ago is the rapidity of change in the information age and the stupendous risk that inheres in it. Nothing is certain except change in an increasingly uncertain environment. This is precisely the reason why hiring must be perceived from the prism of uncertainty. In view of the fact that it is a means of achieving a company's business objectives, it is only logical that if the business strategy changes in response to environmental vagaries, hiring, which is aligned to it, must respond to the change. It is the uncertainty in the business environment which poses a threat and makes demand forecasting for talent an enormous challenge.

The workforce planner is under pressure to reconcile the forecast for talent requirements fairly accurately with the destabilizing uncertainties that constantly lash out at business operations. If the company ends up hiring more than it actually requires because of an initial wrong forecast, it faces a high payroll cost or the task of how to let go the people they no longer require. If the forecast results in the recruitment of less talent than the business actually requires to meet the needs of customers, the company is in peril of losing business opportunities, valued customers, productivity, competitiveness and profitability. In a state of uncertainty, there is a constant risk of a mismatch between the demand for and the supply of talent. The greatest challenge is how to ensure that the demand forecast for talent is accurate.

It is not enough to have data about the past; rather, organizations need to identify the factors within the environment that have the greatest impact on the business. They need to identify areas of highest uncertainty. All these require deep thinking, analysis and the development of various scenarios and the varying strategies or responses to them. Cappelli (2008) advocates the use of the 'supply chain' model so that talent is delivered on a timely basis. There can no longer be one scenario in the business plan, and that implies that the workforce plan also cannot be one, since the business plan determines the workforce plan. Each business scenario must be accompanied by a separate workforce plan for the future. Many snapshots of the business require many workforce plans. Furthermore, forecasting tools such as managerial judgement, trends and time series that once served the needs of managers may no longer be adequate. A simple gap analysis is insufficient. A more rigorous approach is imperative. It is therefore important to go beyond the gap analysis by developing various scenarios of the future. More quantitative and sophisticated tools are required, and forecasting must necessarily be for shorter durations.

Finally, in planning for human resources, it is helpful to have a policy that clearly spells out the following:

- whether or not external recruitment will take place only if no employee in the organization is found suitable for the vacancy;
- a reward system that would be competitive enough to enable the organization not only to compete effectively in the labour market for desired talent, but also to retain valued employees; and
- a high premium accorded to career development and advancement so that employees can acquire cutting-edge skills and also grow in the organization.

Being an Employer of Choice

An employer of choice is usually regarded as the 'best place' to work. It is a company whose HR management practices inspire people to join and work for it despite attractive inducement by other competitors, and thus has an edge over its competitors not only in recruiting but also in retaining talent. Such employers have strategies for securing the commitment of employees. In developing the strategies to become an employer of choice, you must understand your corporate mission, vision, culture and human resources policies and practices, and decide on what message to transmit to potential hires. As a global organization, you must also take into account the diversity of needs according to countries, regions, race, cultures, age and gender. Organizations need to demonstrate sensitivity to the environment. Recruitment is like a courtship between a man and a woman; both parties try to project what is best about themselves to each other. The guiding principle is honesty. One basic truth is that no organization can be an attractive and competitive employer of choice if its human resources management (HRM) policies, practices and systems are in a state of decay, outdated, unintegrated and out of step with best practice.

What employers consider to be motivators or attractive inducements may not be what potential employees actually want. To ensure that you provide what they need and want, you have to find this out through surveys and communications during the selection process and even at exit interviews. What workers look for in an organization vary with nationality, age, marital status, gender, cultural background and level of position, but, in general, most people are searching for:

- a creative workplace characterized by challenging and interesting work;
- opportunities for learning, growth and advancement – rapid growth is highly valued by the young generation;
- good work teams and prospects for recognition and reward for accomplishments;
- solid organizations that can guarantee job security, especially during an economic downturn;
- competitive pay as well as profit-sharing, stock options and different forms of insurance cover;
- quality of life – people want to spend time with their families, have time for their passions that are not necessarily related to their work;
- an attractive culture – employees are increasingly demanding diversity and inclusion, work–life balance, a green environment, transparency, integrity and empowerment.

As noted above, needs vary according to demographic factors. The closer the conditions and terms of employment approximate the expectations or value propositions of the job-seekers, the higher the probability that the company will be successful in hiring and retaining the desired talent. The message is that a recruitment brand must be aligned with the interests of the desired talent. In the current war for talent, the mantra in organizations is to innovate by developing effective and imaginative strategies for attracting and hiring highly required or scarce skill sets. It is part of being an employer of choice to segment skills and offer different compensation packages. The most popular methods employed by organizations are:

- ***Skills premium***. Some skills are considered 'hot' in the sense that they are scarce and in great demand. There is keen competition for them. Such skills attract premiums. The problem of providing premiums within the basic salary is that it compounds the costs of regular salary increases, incentive payouts and other benefits, such as pensions.

- ***Hiring bonus***. Multinational organizations typically pay a hiring bonus which could be a percentage of the basic pay.
- ***Market pricing pay***. This could range between the 50th and 90th percentiles compared to the market.

There is a particular sphere which may significantly challenge African organizations that are going global because it touches not only on moral and religious values, but also on the fundamental traditional values of marriage in Africa. The concept of same-sex marriage or 'partner' is new in Africa; it is considered an aberration in all African countries. Africans know and believe that marriage is between a man and a woman. It is inconceivable to the African psyche for two men or two women to claim that they are a married couple. Organizations in Africa have no policies on such practices precisely because they are unacceptable. In May 2010 two male partners who wedded in Malawi were each sentenced to 14 years' imprisonment by a court in that country.

I worked for an organization that once identified a highly desirable talent based in the United States. An offer was made to him. He called me on the telephone to discuss the terms of the offer. In the course of our conversation, I realized that his so-called wife or 'partner' was a man and that his child was actually not his but a child by a previous marriage which his 'wife' had by another woman. I sought to explain that my organization's policy did not cover gay marriage and that his 'child' would have to be formally adopted by him so that it would be eligible and recognized as his child. Furiously, he told me that our HR policies were 'obsolete'. A week later, I received an e-mail message in which he rejected our offer. As African organizations move out of their familiar cultural terrain, where most organizational policies are consistent with some fundamental values, they will have to adopt a flexible and multicultural approach to talent management in order to be perceived as an 'employer of choice'.

Recruiting for the Future and the Globe

Many organizations often demand that, to be eligible for appointment, candidates must have a certain number of years' work experience because experience is assumed to be the bedrock of success. Of course, experience is definitely important. It is unimaginable that any firm would recruit a chief executive officer or a chief operating officer who did not have the relevant experience and a track record of great performance. Some organizations erroneously measure it by the number of years people have worked. Thus, individuals with many chronological years of so-called relevant work experience are considered to be the best fit even though they may actually have only three to five years of relevant and useful experience because most of their experience had been a mere repetition of the previous years.

In selecting talent for global organizations, there is a need to search for individuals with a multidisciplinary background, technical competencies and emotional intelligence, who are flexible and can move nimbly within various functional and leadership positions. In factoring experience into the selection process, emphasis should not be placed on the number of years but rather on the type, variety and relevance of experience to the position for which candidates are being interviewed. Candidates with limited work experience but who are endowed with great potential have sometimes been rejected at interviews in preference for those who have huge experience but limited potential for growth, development and advancement. The decision-makers are, in such cases, generally guided in their choice by the prosaic paradigm that an experienced candidate will be more successful than one with limited experience and do not consider their level of potential and emotional competencies. The preference for experienced candidates is also due to the desire to hire a candidate who could hit the ground running the day he or she assumes duty.

The obsession with recruiting people with several years' work experience without regard for the relevance and diversity of the experience, competencies and potential for growth in the future often results in the selection of people who cannot grow in the organization. In essence, the individuals are hired for the job not for a career and the consequences of this myopic approach to hiring rears its ugly head years later. The organization grows, but the individuals are unable to grow with it and therefore soon reach a level where any promotion would only amount to advancement into incompetence. It is the tragedy of many people that after working so hard for an organization, their career suddenly reaches a plateau because they lack the potential for higher responsibilities. Naturally, their morale declines and they react in different ways. Some may idealize the past and criticize the present for being so 'discriminatory', 'unfair' and 'failing to recognize those who built this company', whereas others may rationalize their stagnation in terms of racism, ethnicity, nepotism and 'godfatherism'. The fact is that they were recruited for a particular job at a particular time. They did a good job because of their enormous experience. The job changed, but they could not change because they did not have the capacity to move dynamically with the organization. Global organizations should be strategic and seek to recruit candidates not only for today but also for tomorrow, and not for one country but for the globe.

Mainstreaming Diversity into Hiring Process

Workplace diversity is generally considered a business imperative precisely because it provides an organization with strategic competitive advantage. It offers an organization the opportunity to maximize the potential of its human resources. In many countries, particularly in the public services, diversity has always been valued not as a business imperative, but as a moral obligation; it is about fairness and equity. Furthermore, it is usually defined in a narrow sense of balancing ethnic or linguistic representation. Organizations need to make a shift in their paradigm. It is increasingly becoming obvious that organizations that value diversity and inclusion tend to attract talent easily because most people want to work in a multicultural, rather than a monocultural, work environment. Furthermore, a diversity-oriented organization is perceived to be non-discriminatory, flexible, adaptable to change and open to diverse ideas. As Lockwood (2005: 3) rightly noted, diversity has numerous business advantages including:

- adaptability, flexibility and dynamism in a rapidly changing marketplace, and in responding to the needs of clients;
- return on investment from various initiatives, policies and practices; and
- gaining and keeping greater or new market share locally and globally with an expanded diverse customer base.

In order to achieve diversity in recruitment, global organizations must view the international labour market as its target pool for recruiting talent, irrespective of nationality, race and religion. Such an approach gives a global organization the reputation of an employer who values employee diversity.

Leveraging Information Technology

In the information age, technology is changing the way in which organizations attract and hire talent from the competitive international talent market. Although the rate of adoption and use of information technology in financial management is rapid in Africa, it is comparatively slow in human resource management. Traditional approaches to recruitment and selection are still the norm. This is incompatible with globalization and effective competition for top talent. In this section an attempt is made to outline the steps which African organizations can take to leverage information technology in hiring talent.

There is a strong business case for the use of information technology in hiring or a shift to e-recruitment. It is cost-effective and instrumental in attracting a larger and more diverse pool of candidates, facilitates communication between recruiters and candidates, reduces the cycle of recruitment, improves the quality of candidates for final selection and improves the organization's brand image. The current recruitment and selection practice in most African organizations is still traditional and consists of advertising vacancies predominantly in national newspapers, on organizations' noticeboards and in professional magazines. These media have proved effective within the national frontiers. However, they will predictably become limited in effectiveness in a talent war as organizations operate beyond their national boundaries.

The Internet has been increasingly used for recruitment over the past ten years and it is rapidly replacing the traditional approach of posting job vacancies in newspapers and magazines. Job posting on the Internet is cheaper for the employer and costs nothing to potential employees. Moreover, it is accessible for a longer time than a daily newspaper which carries only one insertion of the advertisement. The labour market is changing, and the Web is rapidly becoming an effective instrument for attracting great candidates. The argument that few Africans have access to the Internet is no longer valid. Any applicant who is good enough to be a talent must certainly be connected, one way or the other, to Internet facilities.

Hiring managers and recruiters are usually overwhelmed by the large volume of applications, some of which are not worth the paper on which they are written. On their part, applicants are often frustrated by delayed responses to their applications or a complete lack of information on the status of their applications and therefore tend to form a negative perception of the organization. However, the mutual challenge to recruiters and applicants can be resolved by installing an applicant tracking system. Table 3.1 shows the recruitment process and how each stage of the cycle could be effectively implemented by using information technology.

Table 3.1 Leveraging information technology in hiring

Hiring process	Use of e-recruitment technology
Vacancy announcement	Corporate websites, industry-specific websites, career websites, job boards and the intranet are used.
Submission of application	Application forms are designed and made available online for completion by applicants. There is provision to also attach a resumé, if necessary. On submission of the completed application, there is an automatic acknowledgement of receipt of the application form, thereby eliminating the traditional approach of sending acknowledgement by post or e-mail. The system captures and files data on each candidate for retrieval in future.
Applicant database	A central database is created for each advertised position, and data is available on each applicant. This completely eliminates the drudgery and errors of extracting information from applications into excel sheets. Any type of information required on applicants can easily be obtained provided the application form asks for the information. Furthermore, the hiring team can have online access to the same information in real time.
Applicant screening	Based on the requirements of the recruiter, applications can be screened so that those who do not meet basic requirements for the position are eliminated from the list of candidates. A letter of regret is automatically generated and sent to the applicants electronically. This is an important advantage over the traditional method of manual screening which is extremely time-consuming.
Applicant tracking	As applicants move from one stage of the recruitment/selection process to the next, their status is updated and, with a password, they can access the status of their application at no cost to them. They do not need to telephone or visit in person to obtain this information.
Assessment test	Applicants can take psychometric tests such as the 16PF online and the HR department will automatically receive the results of the test. This could also be part of the screening of candidates.
Invitation to interview	E-recruitment can be used for scheduling interviews. It provides automatic reminders when particular timelines are missed. It can also be used for inviting candidates to interviews and for giving feedback to unsuccessful candidates.
Reports	With the tracking system, the recruiter can easily produce different reports on: • number of positions filled • time it took to fill each vacancy • cost per hire • media that provided the largest number of qualified applicants, etc.

E-recruitment technology varies in complexity, depending on the needs of an organization. There is, however, some concern about its use. It could work against diversity and equal opportunity, especially in African countries where many people do not have easy access to the Internet. In addition, candidates believe that it destroys the personal touch inherent in traditional form of recruitment. Whatever the concern, it seems obvious that the business case for E-recruitment is stronger than any misgivings about its adoption. Indeed, there is hardly any large global corporation without an e-recruitment tool. They are improving their individual systems by introducing innovative solutions that can give them a competitive advantage.

An important medium which is not often used by recruiters are the social media. Social media such as Facebook, LinkedIn and Twitter are increasingly becoming effective and popular tools for sharing information about vacancies and job opportunities among people with common interests. They are a powerful medium of communication and marketing among young people who are seeking employment.

Using Appropriate Recruitment and Selection Tools

The selection of a candidate for a job is an investment decision and must be treated with care, seriousness and professionalism. It is not just a choice between suitable and unsuitable; it is not an impulsive or casual decision based on intuition; it is a commitment by an organization to enter into a mutually beneficial relationship with an individual who has the capability to contribute to the organization's effectiveness and future performance. A selection process consists of:

- gathering pertinent information from various sources (resumé, reference checks, assessment centre, psychometric tests, interviews, etc.), analysing and evaluating the information and making choices;
- marketing both the job and the organization unobtrusively to candidates; and
- demonstrating integrity and organizational commitment by selecting candidates based on their worth and suitability.

Information is critical to selection. Therefore, organizations must decide on the most cost-effective and user-friendly, yet effective, tools they can use to obtain pertinent information on candidates. Sometimes recruiters do not choose the right tools or methods for information-gathering. While, for example, an assessment centre may be an appropriate method for selecting a candidate for a leadership position, the same method will be completely out of place (apart from the enormous cost entailed) for the selection of factory operatives. Experienced recruiters know the most suitable method of selection for each position, taking account of the competences required, level of the position in the organization's hierarchy, and the efficiency and effectiveness of the method. In the following sections we examine some of the methods commonly used for selecting candidates.

SCREENING APPLICATIONS

Selecting candidates is not only about matching their skills and competencies with the current job, but also about matching their talent with the roles they would be expected to play in the future. Organizations that value talent do not recruit for a job; rather, they recruit for a career. Selecting talented candidates begins with a careful and thorough screening of the resumé or curriculum vitae. The curriculum vitae is a document in which candidates try to market themselves to the prospective employer. Sometimes, it is written by hired professionals. Managers must see beyond what they read. A cursory reading could give an impression of a great or a poor candidate, but a calm analysis could yield a totally different picture. How many times has he or she changed jobs and for what reasons? What have been his or her major achievements? Why did he or she leave a highly regarded organization for an obscure non-governmental organization with only a marginal increase on the salary he or she previously earned? Is there any discernible pattern in his or her career mobility? At this stage, a telephone reference check may prove extremely useful in obtaining clarifications of any obscurities in the resumé. For instance, from a telephone conversation, it may become obvious that the claim of capability in a particular language is not true.

The main advantage of screening is that it enables you, early in the selection process, to weed out a large number of ineligible candidates and thus reduce the cost of recruitment while enhancing the effectiveness of the selection process. This is precisely the reason why the use of technology tools is imperative. Screening is a preliminary step and must be combined with other methods of candidate selection, including reference checks, psychometric tests, assessment centre and interviews. The greater the combination of these methods the higher the predictive power of the selection process. Each of these methods is described briefly below.

REFERENCE CHECKS

Reference checks are important because not all candidates are what they claim to be in their resumés. According to the Worldatwork Newsline of January 2008, a survey conducted by Kelly Services revealed that a staggering 41 per cent of Ukrainians lie on their resumés, followed by the Russians (30 per cent), Spanish (27 per cent), Chinese (25 per cent), British (8 per cent) and New Zealanders (4 per cent) (Newsline, 2008b). I do know from my own experience of recruiting locally and internationally that sometimes applicants do not tell the whole truth. It is not that they are criminally inclined. The higher the level of unemployment the more desperate people are. Therefore there is a high probability that in such circumstances applicants will lie in their curriculum vitae.

Reference checks are a universal method of selection and consist of verifying qualifications, previous employment records, criminal record, pay, competencies, behaviours, age and so on. Organizations use reference checks at different stages of the hiring process. Some use it before interviews and others after the interview but prior to making an offer of appointment. When reference checks are done before interviews, it saves the organization money and reduces the risk of bringing to the final selection process candidates who are a total mismatch to the job. For a fee, an agency can be hired to conduct checks on potential applicants, although there are few such agencies in Africa. A major hurdle in reference checks is that those who need to provide information tend to insist on having the candidate's approval before any information is provided. The process is also time-consuming.

PSYCHOMETRIC TESTS

Ability tests and personality tests are increasingly being used for selection. The former seek to measure specific aptitudes such as vocabulary or numeracy, whereas personality tests measure the personal characteristics or values and attitudes that tend to determine an individual's behaviour. Unlike ability tests in which responses can be marked as wrong or right, in personality tests there is nothing like pass or fail. The candidate's responses are determined against the competencies required to succeed in a particular position. The utility of personality tests therefore depends on the organization's ability to determine the aspects of behaviour that are actually pertinent to success in a job. Those who use the tests must be sufficiently trained to understand how to interpret the results of the tests properly. The validity of personality tests has been questioned on the basis that candidates could fake behaviour. There is also concern about the fundamental attribution error, which means that psychometric tests tend to discount situational factors when explaining why people behave the way they do. Examples of personality tests are the 16 Personality Factors (popularly known as 16PF), Myers-Briggs Type Indicator (MBTI) and California Psychological Inventory (CPI). Personality tests are combined with other selection methods to make a final decision on candidates.

ASSESSMENT CENTRES

Assessment centres are useful for hiring into leadership positions. They are also used for the development of managers. They consist of multiple assessment methods used by trained assessors (see Table 3.2). The methods include interview, group exercises, personality inventory, in-tray exercises and presentations. Although they are time-consuming and expensive, they are known to have the highest predictive validity of all the selection methods precisely because they leverage on several methods. Furthermore, they focus on key competencies that measure the success in the job and are relatively free from bias in terms of gender or race.

INTERVIEW

The interview is the most popular and widely used method of selecting candidates for positions. It could take the form of one-on-one or a panel discussion. The reason for its popularity is probably because it involves face-to-face interaction and verbal communication. It is thus assumed, though erroneously, that managers don't need any special training or skills to use the method. Quite often, interviews are not based on the competency model for the position either because such a model does not exist or managers have not been trained to use it for talent selection.

A competency-based or behavioural interview is structured in a way that enables panellists to gather evidence from the candidate's previous or current jobs demonstrating that they actually possess the competencies required for the position for which they are being interviewed. It seeks to ascertain the actual job performance and experience of candidates. Competency-based questions require answers that are not hypothetical but clearly demonstrate

Table 3.2 Assessment centre: multiple selection methods

Selection method	How it is used	Assessor	Focus of method	Evidence gathered
Structured interview	Face-to-face discussion with candidates in form of questions and answers.	Interview panel or a single interviewer.	Required technical and emotional competencies for the position.	Responses demonstrating past experience or knowledge.
Group exercise	Group problem situation involving 5–8 candidates.	Selection panel or team of assessors.	Interpersonal/ social skills.	Leadership skills, teamwork, conflict management.
Presentation	A formal talk on a preselected topic presented by a candidate to a group of listeners.	Selection panel or team of assessors.	Communication skills, knowledge of subject-matter, generic competencies.	Self-presentation, ability to persuade and influence opinions.
In-tray exercise	A typical day-to-day routine in an office situation.	Selection panel or team of trained assessors.	Managerial competencies, organizational skills, knowledge and understanding.	Ability to work under pressure, planning, organizing, prioritizing, problem-solving and good judgement.
Role-play	Situation which allows candidates to demonstrate how they would respond to a particular situation or challenge.	Team of trained assessors.	Leadership skills or client-oriented skills.	Influencing skills, tact in dealing with people, self-confidence.

Source: Adapted from the training material of Jon Spencer Training and Consulting Ltd (2004).

that a candidate either has had hands-on experience or has not. It is not about what candidates will do if a particular situation arises; rather, it is about what they did when a particular situation arose, the result of their action or decision and the lessons they learnt from the event. A typical question might be: 'Describe a situation in which you had to deal with a difficult customer or client.'

The following factors are critical to the success of a behavioural interview. First, questions must be structured as described above and, second, all candidates must be asked the same questions with the same wording to ensure that apples are being compared with apples. The follow-up probing questions may, however, vary from candidate to candidate depending on their responses to the initial question. Third, interviewers must be thoroughly familiar with the competencies required to succeed in the position so that they can ask questions that seek to elicit information on the candidate's strengths and weaknesses in those competencies.

In 1981 an interview panellist in a steel plant asked a candidate, who was being interviewed for the job of steel melting engineer, the meaning of 'temperature inversion'. This is a term used in geography and not in steel production. The conventional knowledge is that the higher you go the cooler the temperature becomes. Temperature inversion implies that, on the contrary, the higher you go the hotter it becomes. Although the steel smelting shop is a place with incredibly high temperatures, there was practically no relationship between that question and the technical competencies required for the job and any response, right or wrong, would not have helped the panel in determining the candidate's suitability for the job. The question was completely irrelevant, and the candidate was as baffled as the panel.

What should be taken into account in constituting an interview panel? Ideally, panellists should be the supervisor of the position and any individuals who are familiar with the job and with what it takes to succeed in it. They should have the ability to listen, understand non-verbal cues or communications and be adept in asking questions that reveal a candidate's abilities, work experiences, competencies, personality traits, potential, strengths and weaknesses. Individuals with known biases against certain groups (women, ethnic or racial groups) may not be involved unless it is unavoidable. For instance, the supervisor of the position for which an interview is being held cannot be excluded. Panellists should be individuals who have integrity, an eye for smart people and no conflict of interest.

GRAPHOLOGY

Graphology, the study of handwriting, is based on the notion that an individual's personality can be determined through his or her handwriting. For instance, bold handwriting is believed to reveal an aggressive, assertive personality. Graphology is commonly used in most small French companies for the selection of managers. It is not a common method in African organizations. Research by psychologists reveals that graphology is not a valid means of assessing candidates' abilities or of predicting success in a job.

SELECTION SKILLS

The success of any selection method is contingent on the skills of those who use them. Most organizations make the erroneous assumption that every executive has the skills and experience (probably poor and inadequate experience repeated many times over) in interviewing and selecting candidates. However, not all executives have interviewing skills. Executives have to be trained on how to interview candidates using competency models. They need to learn how to adopt non-threatening and non-intimidating behaviours and also comply with a code of conduct during interviews. It is equally important for them to understand cultural differences and sensibilities, especially in an international setting. For instance, a candidate who does not look the interviewers in the eye is not necessarily timid or lacking in self-confidence. I come from a culture where it is considered rude to have a direct eye contact with elders or highly placed persons when speaking to them. You must bow your head as a mark of respect.

It is important to note that all selection methods are useful, but some are more effective than others. The three important factors that need to be highlighted, irrespective of the method chosen for selection, are as follows:

1. The user must have the skills to use the method. Although interview is the most popular method, many interviewers make a terrible job of it.

2. The selection method chosen and used must be appropriate for determining candidates' suitability. While an assessment centre may be ideal for an executive position, it would be inappropriate for the position of a factory or production worker.

3. The integrity of the user is important whatever the method used, precisely because hiring has a political dimension and is vulnerable to socio-cultural influences in both global and national environments.

Summary

This chapter has demonstrated that the effective selection of talent from a multitude of applicants cannot be haphazard; rather, it is a product of a combination of systematic and structured selection methods, tools and skills. The chapter has also shown that factors such as information technology, diversity and inclusion, and a global orientation are critical to the successful attraction, recruitment and selection of talent. The next chapter discusses the fact that it is one thing to have the right selection tools and methods, but it is another thing for the hiring manager or team to be able to manage relationships with candidates in a dynamic situation that is characterized by verbal communication, body language, subtle marketing and power disequilibrium.

4

A Guide to Talent Selection

The Cost of a Wrong Choice

When an organization decides to hire the best from the international labour market, it must recognize that it is embarking on an investment. Every financial investment requires planning, doing a feasibility study, a cost–benefit analysis, a risk analysis and a comparison of various options. Managers usually take systematic steps to gather information and relevant data to negotiate contracts for the purchase of equipment, services or technology. Hiring talent deserves a much more painstaking, systematic and prudent approach. Organizations should, therefore, take adequate time to source the best people in the market, especially if they are looking for global executives. Successful hiring requires thinking of what success would look like if a top talent is hired or what the consequences of a catastrophic hiring would be. A wrong hiring is essentially a mismatch; it is the employment of an individual who does not fit into the job or the organization because he or she does not either have the skills, competencies and motivation required for the job or holds personal values and beliefs that are at variance with the corporate culture. A mismatch significantly reduces the chances of success of the individual and implicitly enhances the probability of early exit.

The cost of wrong hiring is enormous. It includes money and time invested in recruitment; the cost of lost business; the inestimable damage to the reputation or credibility of the firm due to poor performance or blunders committed by inept employees; the impact on the morale of the team; the cost of termination; and, finally, the cost of replacement. These high costs can be avoided if recruiting managers and their teams adopt a systematic and professional approach and start the recruitment process before it becomes a crisis. Emergency recruitment or an obsession with filling a vacancy 'immediately' tends to lead to compromises that result in selecting square pegs in round holes. The guiding principle at all times is to estimate the consequences of wrong hiring on the business. This chapter provides a guide for recruiting talent in order to ensure successful and safe hiring. Behaviours and decisions during the selection process are critical in identifying and choosing the right people for the right jobs.

Managing Relationships During the Selection Process

The selection process is a social situation with dynamics that consist of power, marketing and communication in the form of verbal and body language. It requires skills to decipher some of the marketing gimmicks and body language. Some of the verbal communications may be untruths, half-truths or complete truths.

THE POWER RELATIONSHIP

A selection process is a situation of power disequilibrium between candidates and the recruiting team. The recruiting manager or team has the power to choose or reject a candidate. Candidates are generally seen as spineless individuals in search of jobs. Their fate is in the hands of the interview panel. It is therefore not unusual for panellists to unwittingly reflect this power imbalance by asking questions in a condescending or even intimidating manner, answering telephone calls during the interview and allowing letters to be brought in by secretaries for signature. This kind of display of positional power could affect the decision of a potential candidate to accept or reject an offer because it implies gross disrespect not only for the selection process, but also for the candidate. Here lies the tacit power of candidates which many panellists do not seem to recognize. Just as candidates strive to market their capabilities to prospective employers, companies must also strive to present their image as that of an employer of choice and use their power to advantage. One way of doing so is by being polite, courteous and respectful to candidates throughout the recruitment and selection process.

CANDIDATES' SELF-MARKETING

The impression which a candidate creates during the selection process influences the recruitment team's decision whether to choose or reject him or her. Candidates are aware of this fact and therefore strive to manage that impression by selectively presenting information and behavioural cues that will, hopefully, mould the opinions of the interviewers. They want to be seen as ideal candidates based on the information given in the job advertisement. In other words, some candidates may present, beginning with their curriculum vitae, highly exaggerated or partial information about their personality, motivation, capabilities and work experience. Many candidates never tell the whole truth about anything they perceive might diminish their chances of success in a selection process. From many years of experience reviewing applications and interviewing candidates I have found that while they unduly orchestrate positive achievements, they either completely downplay their failures or gloss over their shortcomings. Only a handful of candidates disclose and admit their failures without finding a scapegoat. These are authentic individuals with integrity and are likely to learn from their past mistakes. Selecting candidates is certainly not a matter of intuition; it requires tact, perceptiveness and strong interviewing skills in order to elicit pertinent information which candidates carefully seek to conceal from the interviewers because it may be damaging to them.

THE ORGANIZATION'S SELF-MARKETING

In a global war for talent organizations need to market themselves to candidates. That is why they have recruitment brands. Marketing is not only relevant at the point of advertising a vacancy, but also runs through the whole of the recruitment and selection process. Relationship marketing in hiring is a social process by which employers seek to create a long-term continuous relationship with prospective employees by identifying, developing and offering what candidates actually need. They seek to provide satisfaction through a series of continuous interactions, thereby ensuring repeated delightful experiences. Employers should focus not on the job but on the needs of the prospective employees because a market is defined not by a product but by a need. For instance, Mercedes Benz and Toyota offer not just automobiles, but also satisfy people's need for safe mobility, luxury and comfort. BMW says that it does not just make cars – it offers 'joy'. In the same way, employers should seek to meet the needs of prospective employees not just for a job, but for all those needs they value – their value proposition. This is the orientation of marketing in hiring. In fact, it is because hiring has become marketing that branding occupies a prominent position in hiring.

The paradigm that managers hold of hiring influences the way in which they treat candidates during the selection process. If they have the mindset that hiring is merely a transaction and candidates are spineless individuals who are desperately in need of a livelihood, managers are likely to treat them in a condescending manner. However, if they perceive hiring as a form of relationship management and candidates as valuable clients and an asset, they would treat them differently. A marketing orientation in hiring entails the following actions.

- Respond promptly to applicants' enquiries, particularly about the status of their applications or the outcome of the selection process. A common and frustrating but rarely talked-about practice is neglecting to give candidates information on the status of their applications. Obviously, to respond to all applications would be extremely expensive in terms of money and time. With e-recruiting, applicants can access the status of their applications, and communication can be generated to inform them of the outcome of their participation in the selection process.

- Give candidates adequate notice when inviting them to the selection process. It is irritating and frustrating for candidates to be invited to a selection process at extremely short notice ostensibly because the vacant position must be filled urgently. Such short notices send wrong signals to candidates about the organization's management style or gives the erroneous impression that the employer had already determined the candidate to be employed and that the selection process was a mere formality.

- Provide candidates with relevant information about the job, organization, and terms and conditions of employment. Some organizations deliberately starve candidates of such information on the premise that if candidates are actually keen about the job they would do some research of their own and obtain necessary information as part of their preparation. Providing relevant information to candidates is all part of marketing; lack of it can only harm the organization.

- Manage the selection process in privacy and comfort. No candidates, especially those who are highly placed and happily employed, want any publicity about their search for alternative employment.

- Conduct the selection process in a rigorous, professional and businesslike manner because this will earn you the respect of candidates even when they are not successful at the process.

Candidates should not be kept waiting for hours or days for a process that could take less time. Candidates are not on vacation in your office.

Howard, Scott and Bruce (2007) found that the following interview habits of panellists, among others, most annoy job-seekers:

- acting like they have no time to talk to the candidate
- withholding information about the position
- turning the interview into a cross-examination
- showing up late for the interview
- being unprepared for the interview
- asking questions unrelated to the relevant job skills.

The Principles of Effective Selection

An organization's ability to hire great people depends on an integrated approach consisting of three principles – namely, recruitment brand, a competency-driven selection process and managers' integrity. These principles are illustrated in Figure 4.1.

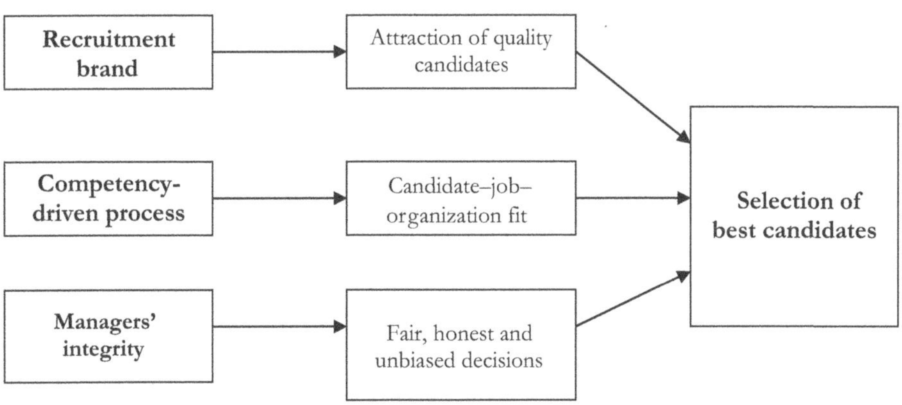

Figure 4.1 A model for hiring talent

DEVELOP A RECRUITMENT BRAND

A recruitment brand communicates to prospective employees what the organization stands for and what makes it an employer of choice. It distinguishes it from other organizations. A recruitment brand is a unique and compelling message about an organization's mission, culture, career opportunities, work environment and people management style which mark the organization out from the crowd. The purpose is to create the impression that no organization is quite like yours. Every organization needs a recruitment brand because, in the war for talent, it gives an organization an edge over its competitors. Each time I read a job advertisement, I ask: 'What is the recruitment message? How compelling is it and how is it communicated?' Whatever message you want to communicate, it must be through the medium of a recruitment brand because a brand is an attempt to create and present the identity of the firm.

After a careful content analysis of vacancies in various websites and newspapers in no less than ten African countries, I found that many organizations do not have a recruitment brand or at least do not project it when they advertise positions. In job advertisements they lay emphasis on different factors which they imagine would seduce prospective employees. Table 4.1 shows areas of emphasis, implications and probable consequences for hiring.

The main purpose of any brand is to make the organization look distinct from its competitors irrespective of the industry to which it belongs. For example, Mercedes-Benz is famous for its superior engineering and prestige brand. Google is famous as a global search brand, while Cable News Network (CNN) is an information brand. The success of any brand depends on the clarity of its message and the distinction it is able to make between it and other brands. The image presented has to be consistent and realistic all through the recruitment and selection process. Just as an excited candidate can be tempted to exaggerate his work experience profile, professional achievements and competencies, an employer that is desperate to recruit a scarce skill could oversell the organization and, in the process, compromise the truth.

A recruitment brand must be consistent with the reality of the company; otherwise, the organization would lose its credibility and would be worse off than if it never had a brand at all. This is precisely because people trust brands. Consistency in the message, at every contact with prospective employees, helps to build and solidify confidence in the organization. Candidates like to know that what they expect is the same as what they had been told to expect. It is

Table 4.1 Job advertisement: need for a recruitment brand

Employers' emphasis in job advertisement	Implications and consequences
Compensation – salary and benefits	Based on the assumption that this is the prepotent need of the African worker, it reveals the classical managerial perception of the worker as a 'rational-economic man'. This advertisement may not satisfy the needs of those in search of career development and advancement.
Qualifications and years of experience (the most popular approach)	Looks like a colonial heritage. It has no regard for the competencies and potential of prospective employees. Conveys an obsession with educational attainment and years of experience at the expense of bright minds who do not have many years of work experience. Inadequate information to attract passive applicants.
What the organization is (e.g. 'the world's largest producer of x' or 'is located in 50 countries')	The message is that we are a giant in our own right; we are successful and formidable. To work with us is a privilege. Good, but it ignores the needs of prospective employees. What do they get from this 'successful and formidable giant'?
What you would do when you join us	A detailed job description and perhaps person specification. Good information about the job but scanty or lack of information about the organization and the terms and conditions of employment. What is the attraction? Just the job?
Recruitment brand	Tells you about the organization, particularly what it is reputed for; nature of the job, not a drab job description; career prospects; organizational values; insight into terms of employment; work environment, etc. There is an employee value proposition. Naturally, prospective applicants look forward to an experience with the organization. Most likely it will be an employer of first choice. Global African organizations need to demonstrate their recruitment brand in advertising vacancies.

important to review periodically the extent to which the recruitment brand has been effective in attracting the right talent for selection.

DRIVE THE SELECTION PROCESS WITH COMPETENCIES

Successful hiring requires knowing what job is going to be performed and what it takes to succeed in it. The job must therefore be analysed to determine its main tasks and responsibilities (job description) and the profile of an ideal person for the job (person specification). The danger of failing to determine the competencies required for a job is that there is no common understanding among those involved in the selection process on what kind of individual they are seeking to bring into the organization. Failure to define the competencies required of a position affects the whole gamut of the recruitment and selection process from the job advertisement through screening of applications to shortlisting and interviews. But why are competencies important in the hiring process?

Competency models were introduced in 1973 into hiring by McClelland (1975) in response to persistent selection problems encountered by the US Information Agency (USIA) in the 1970s. A competency model provides a complete picture of what it takes to be successful or effective in each job. Competency models increase the likelihood of hiring people who will succeed in the job, minimize investment in people who may not fulfil the company's expectations and ensure a more systematic interview process. In a study of competency models for 181 different positions in 121 companies and organizations world-wide, Goleman (1998) found that 67 per cent of the abilities deemed essential for effective performance were emotional competencies such as team leadership, self-confidence, influence and achievement drive. He concludes that 'for star performance in all jobs, in every field, emotional competence is twice as important as purely cognitive abilities', and for leadership positions emotional competence accounts for virtually the entire advantage (Goleman, 1998: 31). Without a competency model there is no reliable and valid roadmap to guide those involved in the recruitment and selection process. An example of a competency model for a managerial position is provided in Table 4.2. The competencies in the model are not cast in stone. They will vary between organizations.

At an interview for a recruitment manager, the head of the HR department asked a candidate if he would recruit Bill Gates. The interviewer obviously knew that Bill Gates would never apply for any position in his firm. His point was about how, as recruitment manager, the candidate would be able to recognize another Bill Gates in the making if he submitted an application for a position or sat before an interview panel. Bill Gates does not possess a chain of educational qualifications, but he has proved that success does not depend on academic credentials.

DEMONSTRATE INTEGRITY

Even with a strong brand and a competency-driven selection process, an organization may still end up not hiring great people. Selection is a choice,

Table 4.2 A competency model for a managerial position

Competency	Description
Strategic thinking	Senge (1990) refers to strategic thinking as 'systems thinking'. Candidates with strategic thinking have a mental mode that demonstrates an understanding of both the internal and external context larger than that of the industry or country in which it operates. They are likely to have a systems perspective that enables them to clarify their role within the organization and the effect of their behaviour and performance not only on other organizational units, but also on the firm's overall performance. Candidates with strategic thinking demonstrate, a strategic intent – a competitively unique point of view about the future and also openness to new ideas and experience (Lawrence, 1999).
Intelligence	You do not necessarily need to administer an Intelligence Quotient (IQ) test to determine this. You can measure intelligence by the candidate's degree of intellectual agility – what he knows about everything around him from his field of specialization to politics, climate change, information technology, etc. The candidate does not necessarily need to have graduated from any of the Ivy League universities. A mistake often made in the selection process is to assume that those who have attended less well-known universities are less intelligent. Sometimes individual circumstances (e.g. lack of finance) have determined the educational institutions they attended; it is not necessarily because they did not have the intellectual capacity to attend an Ivy League institution. The guiding principle in recruiting great people is to seek candidates who appear smarter than you are. Unfortunately, many managers feel threatened and search for people like themselves or try to clone themselves. Smart people challenge the status quo and are creative, innovative and results-oriented. They may sometimes display a strong personality, but the good news is that they produce extraordinary results if they are led properly.
Integrity	In an age when companies that dominate the economic and financial firmament of the world have failed due to the fraud committed by top managers, it is incumbent on organizations that want to be global, great and lasting to pay attention to integrity. The fate of Enron, WorldCom, Arthur Andersen and a host of others is a classic lesson in the importance of integrity. In the recruitment and selection process, you can determine those with integrity in different ways. They tell the truth beginning with their current compensation, educational attainment and dates of qualifications and their work experience. They make clear and unambiguous statements that are not susceptible to different interpretations. There are no contradictions in the curriculum vitae. While discussing their work experience, they admit to mistakes and take responsibility for their decisions or actions.
Self-confidence	A great employee is a great ambassador of his or her firm. Without self-confidence an employee cannot effectively represent himself or herself and certainly not the firm. A self-confident individual is real, authentic, bold, decisive and able to stand by his or her convictions when there is an outpouring of criticism. They inspire confidence in others and are able to lead with authority. They have the stamina to recover from failures or mistakes and pursue a new vision or course of action with conviction. They are optimistic and persistent. Sometimes, self-confident candidates wear a garb of arrogance. The HR department and hiring managers must develop the ability to see what others cannot see in such candidates – talent, great potential and incredible self-confidence.

Table 4.2 A competency model for a managerial position *concluded*

Competency	Description
Team leadership	Every employee works either as a member or as a leader of a team at one time or another. Leading teams is an important responsibility of any leader. It involves the ability to build coalitions and collaborate across functions and departments; influence people and gain their cooperation to accomplish objectives; value diversity; and inspire and motivate the troops to accomplish goals. Candidates must show from past performance their ability to inspire mutual trust, resolve conflict positively and provide direction.
Customer focus	Irrespective of the job, every employee has a customer within or outside the firm. No employee has a job without the patronage of a customer or client. A candidate who demonstrates the importance of client-orientation to business will be proactive, produce services that give customer satisfaction and will be readily accessible to customers. They are likely to go the extra mile to please those who sustain the business, demonstrate the ability to anticipate and respond to the needs of customers and clients and demonstrate commitment to continuous improvement.
Decisiveness	Decision-making is one of the most critical responsibilities of managers and leaders. The ability to make good decisions is what defines an effective executive. Too many errors of judgement erode the credibility of leaders and can plunge a firm into great difficulties. Candidates must be able to show the sound, timely and effective decisions they made in the past; demonstrate the logical process they followed in solving problems. They must demonstrate technical savvy and an understanding of organizational and environmental realities in choosing between alternative courses of action. Finally, they should demonstrate how they made decisions under difficult conditions and situations where there was inadequate information.

a decision and a judgement. As it is subjective, those making it must be individuals with integrity, who have the interest of the organization at heart and whose actions are not driven by personal or narrow interests. They must have integrity. This is the third principle of effective selection. It works with the two preceding principles. Heineman (2009) defines integrity as the ability to tenaciously adhere to the spirit and the letter of formal rules and adopt voluntary global standards that bind a company and its employee to act in its enlightened self-interest. Multinational corporations face such enormous diversity that their success in managing talent, including recruitment and selection, will depend on their ability to explicitly pursue 'high integrity as the foundational goal of the enterprise recognizing that it should indeed be the goal of global capitalism' (Heineman, 2009: 1).

Integrity is becoming a critical competency for global executive positions, particularly in multinational corporations. A joint survey conducted by

Development Dimensions International and the Economist Intelligence Unit found that one of the leadership qualities that global executives need is integrity and ethics (Paese, 2008). Tessmann-Keys and Wellins, in their monograph, *The CEO's Guide to Preparing Future Global Leaders*, noted that 'global leaders must demonstrate the highest level of integrity' (2007: 21).

The frauds committed in Enron, Tyco and WorldCom and the various sex scandals involving high-profile political and religious leaders underscore the basic truth that leaders are no saints; they are fallible like every other employee in an organization. Political and societal pressures to recruit certain nationals or races could be strong. Without integrity, recruiting managers could succumb to such pressures with the result that recruiting in a global organization could become a scramble for positions on the basis of race, nationality, language, ethnicity or gender, but veiled as diversity. Such a scramble for spoils does not usually emphasize quality but statistical representation and thus subverts diversity. With integrity, managers are able to make fair and objective decisions in a selection process while at the same time giving due consideration to creating a culturally heterogeneous workforce. They are able to demonstrate courage and resilience in the choice of the best candidate for the job.

Pitfalls in Selection of Talent

In this section we identify mistakes that tend to plague the selection process. An awareness of these pitfalls could enhance the success in the selection of talent.

EDUCATIONAL CREDENTIALS VERSUS COMPETENCIES

In selecting a candidate for a job, managers should not be under the delusion that a chain of educational qualifications or membership of professional associations all over the globe and awards for putative excellence or leadership are valid predictors of future performance. It is normal to be impressed with qualifications from prestigious universities and work experience in blue-chip organizations. Taken together they all tell a story of the candidate, but not the full story. There is still a need to confirm the fit between the candidate and the job and organizational culture. Person–organization fit is the perceived compatibility between the personality, competencies and career ambition of the potential employee and the needs and culture of a corporation. The person–

organization fit implies person-fit because the individual has the skills, abilities and competencies to do the job. It also means that the values and personality of the individual are congruent with the culture of the firm (Higgins, 2002).

Hiring, especially at top levels and also for global positions, requires close attention to the cultural fit between candidates and the values of the organization. Do the candidates believe in integrity, empowerment, diversity, teamwork, corporate social responsibility, accountability, risk-taking and so forth? The fact that an individual was a superstar in one organization is no guarantee that he or she would be a star in the next organization because the corporate cultures of the two organizations may not be exactly the same. If the candidate's personal values do not resonate with those of your firm he is *ab initio* a candidate for failure or limited success.

Some years ago, a research organization attracted and hired a high-profile scientist from an international agricultural research organization. The scientist had an enviable track record of performance and innovativeness. He was a prolific scientist, and his scientific publications were ground-breaking and often cited by other authors. He initiated brilliant research projects within months of his assumption of duty. However, in less than one year he was relieved of his job as director of the department. His professional arrogance, lack of respect for team members and his immediate supervisor, and complete disregard for rules and authority in the name of 'thinking out of the box' were diametrically opposed to the organization's values of mutual respect and teamwork. The system rejected him as if he was a 'foreign body' in a transplant intervention because of value incompatibility or cultural misfit. You need to identify the critical cultural norms that drive the organization's mission, vision and performance, and determine the degree to which there is a match between those values and those held by candidates, if you want to hire great people.

The person–job fit should also be seen in terms of complementarity. The candidate should be an individual who is bringing into the firm a skill or capability which it direly needs but does not possess. It is a complementary match because the individual is filling a hole in the organization's bench strength, thereby making it stronger and more competitive.

INVERTED DIVERSITY

It should be emphasized that, even in global organizations, diversity could be a metaphor for internal competition for high-level positions among racial, national, regional, gender and linguistic groups. It is generally believed that everyone who is involved in the selection process has a common objective and a strong commitment to hire the most suitably qualified candidate for the job. This assumption may not be true all the time, even though it is verbalized by everyone. However, research and the experience of most recruitment managers indicate that not all managers are neutral in the selection process. Line managers and, ironically, human resource managers who participate in a selection process may have hidden agendas. Managers use diversity to pursue and legitimize their political agendas by justifying the candidates that suit their personal interests. Diversity is a myth which managers sometimes use to cover up the contradiction between recruiting the best and at the same time ensuring the fair representation of certain interest groups. This situation is evident in many countries, particularly in Africa.

According to Beugré (2004: 140), getting hired in Ivory Coast 'depends more on who you know rather than what you know'. He also noted that the tendency to hire one's fellow tribe members is due to the fact that managers feel they are under moral obligation to help their 'less fortunate relatives or tribesmen'. Aryee (2004: 127) also noted that recruitment and selection in Ghana are underpinned by particularistic rather than universalistic norms. The reason centres on the fact that when managers fail to use their position to help their kith and kin, they are criticized by their fellow tribe members. In the same vein, Muuka and Mwenda (2004) explain how rife *Wako-ni-Wako* (a tendency to hire relatives and people from one's own tribe or province) is in Zambia. According to the authors, *Wako-ni-Wako* is 'another name for tribalism, nepotism, and regionalism all rolled into one' (Muuka and Mwenda, 2004: 39). In Algeria, kinship and family bonds, driven by Islamic values, immensely influence the recruitment process. Branine (2001: 165) in fact described the process as characterized by 'bureaucratic and administrative formality and is neither systematic nor objective' because it is often difficult to obtain employment if a candidate does not have contacts within the organization. He refers to the practice as '*piston*' which he defines as 'acts of favouritism, nepotism, or bribery' (Branine, 2004: 165). According to him, a candidate must have relevant contacts to follow through an employment application; otherwise, it would be lost or ignored. The *piston* practice is not only a product of the country's indigenous culture and social structure, but also a colonial legacy.

There is also the 'as-man-know-man' phenomenon in Nigeria, which is similar to the Algerian practice. Essentially, it means influence or networking in high places. Among the Ibos it is known as *ima madu*, which is usually referred to in conversations simply as *'i m'*. It is a practice in which the applicant may not know the recruiter but knows someone who knows somebody who in turn knows somebody who can influence the recruiter. A study of human resources management in banks in Nigeria showed that the recruitment process in banks was often influenced by forces inside and outside the mandated recruiting unit. Prominent among those who exerted undue influence were board members and friends and colleagues of management staff. Furthermore, the appointment of people to positions on the boards of banks was based in most cases on political, ethnic or regional considerations, irrespective of their capacity or knowledge of the banking business (FITC, 2000: 18).

THE NORM OF RECIPROCITY

Reciprocity is veiled as corporate social responsibility. It is not unusual to hear of communities putting pressure on multinational corporations to regard them as a catchment area that should be given preferential treatment in the award of contracts and employment of people. Governments also insist on the appointment of their nationals to top positions in global firms. The general argument is simply that, as part of its corporate social responsibility, an organization should ensure that the community or country in which it is located benefits from its operations or services through the employment of its nationals. A common argument these days, buoyed by the need for a clean environment, is that because an organization degrades the environment and causes pollution and health hazards, the community must be compensated adequately one way or another for the negative impact of the organization's operations. A familiar example is the Niger Delta where communities insist that, among other things, oil companies should hire 'indigenes' or 'sons/daughters of the soil' as part of the compensation for the destruction and spillage of oil on farmlands and fishing ponds.

GROUPTHINK

Groupthink denotes a situation in which the strivings of members of a cohesive group for unanimity override objectivity and the realistic appraisal of alternative courses of action. According to Janis (1972), groupthink has the following symptoms:

- illusion of invulnerability
- belief in the inherent morality of the group

- rationalization
- stereotypes of out-groups
- self-censorship – shutting down ideas that deviate from group consensus
- direct pressure from group members to conform
- some group members serving as mind-guards
- illusion of unanimity.

A popular case of groupthink was the planned Bay of Pigs invasion in 1961. The plan was to train and equip Cuban exiles in the United States to invade Cuba and, in the process, spark off a revolution against Fidel Castro. None of President Kennedy's advisers raised a voice against the plan at the meeting where the decision was taken even though they were uncomfortable with it, particularly Arthur Schlesinger who had written privately to the president to express his concerns prior to the meeting. They were a cohesive group who did not want to upset the president or appear to be uncooperative. In reviewing the fiasco, President Kennedy wondered how all of them could have been so stupid. They were all brilliant minds, but they suffered from groupthink – an obsession with consensus.

Classic cases of groupthink happen on a less grand scale in the selection process. They are never noticed, yet they also result in disasters – the wrong choice of candidates. At interviews, panellists sometimes exhibit the symptoms of groupthink. They refrain from confrontation or disagreement with the views of colleagues or senior executives, especially if the latter have a strong personality. Panellists strive to reach consensus as if that is the ultimate goal of the interview. A candidate is either good or unfit for a job. There must be palpable excitement about the suitability of a candidate. Any doubt or strong reservation does not augur well for selection. A panel's search for a consensus is a symptom that the candidate does not fully meet the requirements of the position.

Groupthink can be overcome in the selection process in a number of ways. Senior executives on an interview panel should permit free discussion and avoid voicing their opinions prematurely so as not to unduly influence other panellists of lower status. All panellists should feel free to differ in their judgement of candidates' suitability provided such difference is expressed with respect and based on evidence. Often there is so much deference to hierarchy, characteristic of African culture, that the views and opinions of senior executives become unassailable. No manager, irrespective of status, should set himself or herself up as a mind-guard.

The pitfalls identified above are universal and not intended to suggest that every hiring in organizations in Africa is influenced by nepotism, social connections and ethnicity. Welch observed that in most state-owned enterprises in China 'most of the best jobs and rewards go to the most loyal members of the party whether they are the most talented or not' (2005: 48). Cooper, Robertson and Tinline (2003) noted that racial biases might be introduced in the interview process because of the stereotypical views interviewers have of ethnic minority personalities and background. According to the authors, there is evidence that, women who have exactly the same credentials as men get fewer jobs. The impact of social influence is strong and sometimes culminates in compromising quality in the recruitment and selection of great people for organizations.

How Do You Know Your Hiring is Successful?

RECRUITMENT METRICS

What is not measured cannot be improved. Sometimes, human resource and hiring managers become so used to the routine of screening applications, shortlisting, interviewing and selecting candidates that they forget to evaluate the effectiveness of the process and the quality of the people they have hired. There is therefore a necessity to develop recruitment metrics. In general, traditional recruitment metrics consist essentially of the recruitment time and cost of hiring. However, the metrics are changing, as shown below.

Recruitment time This is the duration it takes to attract and hire a candidate for a vacant position. This parameter not only measures the efficiency of the HR department, but also the speed at which the hiring managers respond to requests for participation in the selection process (review of candidates' resumés, availability for interview, etc.). Recruitment time also has the implication that the longer it takes, the higher the probability of losing great candidates because they are in great demand by competitors.

Cost of hiring This consists of expenses arising from the following activities:

- job advertisement, including job boards and online vacancy announcements, recruitment tours to tertiary institutions with a view to attracting young talent
- agency fees to executive recruiters
- bringing in candidates for the selection process (travel and lodging) and communication
- salary and benefits of HR manager, recruitment staff and other line managers/staff involved in any of the following activities: working with advertising agency or executive recruiters, screening applications, checking references, conducting selection tests, interviewing candidates, negotiating pay, making offers, medical examination, security check (if position is a sensitive one), creating HR records, on-boarding for new employees and relocation of new employees and their families (travel and lodging).

Quality of candidates The emphasis of hiring metrics has shifted to the quality of candidates which is examined not only from the perspective of the organization, but also from that of the new employee. This indicator can be determined at two levels. The first level refers to the quality of candidates who are attracted to the selection process. I have been at interviews where managers have literally groaned in pain because none of the candidates was good enough for the position despite their claims in their resumés. In contrast, I have also witnessed several selection processes in which many candidates were so outstanding that panellists were confused about who to select for the positions. The interview is only a means to an end and not the ultimate goal, which is the employee's performance in the job.

The second level of quality therefore refers to the actual performance of new employees in their job – being a good match for the job and for the organization. This metric is determined by the satisfaction of the supervisor. If the employee is effective in his or her role, the manager would certainly consider the hiring as a success.

Buyer's remorse Furthermore, the hiring metric also includes an employee's satisfaction with the job and the organization. Hiring is successful if an employee finds the corporate culture to be congruent with his or her personal values and also if the job and work team meet his or her expectations. In other words, the hiring is successful if there is no buyer's remorse and the recruitment brand is credible. Buyer's remorse refers to a new employee's regret following the discovery that there is a gap between what the recruitment brand portrays about the organization and the reality. The company might have portrayed itself as a place with great teams whereas in fact it is characterized by compartmentalization, turf protection, silos and Machiavellianism. It might have projected its image as one in which employees have autonomy to take decisions and risks and where the job is extremely challenging and fulfilling. The reality might be that micromanagement is the mantra, risk aversion is part of the culture, and work is routine, drab and uninspiring. A possible consequence of buyer's remorse is resignation for two main reasons. First, the employee feels he or she has been deceived and therefore may be unable to trust the organization. Second, he or she may feel that, given the reality in the organization, it is an unsuitable place to work. The buyer's remorse is a good measure of the success of hiring.

Diversity Diversity is not a commonly used metric for determining the success or effectiveness of recruitment, especially in many African corporations. However, diversity is assuming great importance in international organizations and it has to be a key metric in determining a firm's success in hiring talent. Diversity is increasingly becoming a business imperative in multi-national corporations.

EVALUATING RECRUITMENT

In determining the effectiveness of an organization's recruitment effort, it is salutary to link the evaluation to the strategic objectives of having the *right capabilities* in appropriate positions at the *time required* rather than merely assessing the parameters of efficiency. A large number of candidates may be interviewed or the cost of recruitment may be low, but none of these necessarily translates into quality or the attraction and acquisition of the needed talent at the required time. The evaluation of recruitment should be conducted along with the assessment or review of the organization's strategic objectives in order to determine recruitment's contribution to the achievement of the corporate goals.

On-boarding – Managing Transition

Organizations that value talent do not usually wait for new employees to assume their duties before providing them with information that would facilitate and accelerate their settling-in. Where there is no structured, formal on-boarding, informal on-boarding takes over. The latter is an orientation process initiated by existing employees outside the formal on-boarding framework. It is spontaneous, unstructured, personal and voluntary. It is usually initiated by an employee of the same ethnic group, religious affiliation, social club, alumni network, nationality or a colleague in the same workplace who wants to assist the new arrival. The employee who initiates the on-boarding of a new employee may take the latter home for dinner with the family or to social events in the evenings and at weekends to ensure the elimination of nostalgia which afflicts people in a new environment.

Informal on-boarding is usually popular and successful where formal on-boarding is weak, poorly organized, and inadequate. The former tends to concentrate on the politics of the organization, the unspoken rules of conduct, the landmines in the organizational terrain and the identification of the power elite or kitchen cabinet on whose toes the new employee must not step. It also helps in identifying focal points in critical organizational units that the new employee may want to contact in case of need. In addition, it accelerates learning about not only the organization, but also the social environment such as personal security, sexual morality, location of shopping malls, social etiquette and where to find local food and place of religious worship. It covers a gamut of learning. However, not all informal on-boarding is completely positive. Dissatisfied employees who believe that the organization has not been fair to them are likely to unconsciously project a negative image of the firm to new employees.

FORMAL ON-BOARDING

Formal on-boarding should begin from the moment a candidate accepts the formal offer of appointment and indicates the date of the assumption of duty. A focal point in the HR department and hiring department must be available to respond to the queries of the incoming employee by e-mail or telephone. New employees would like to know about the availability of housing, a safe area to live, good schools for children, good medical care and arrangements for the shipment or transportation of personal effects, particularly if the employer is in a developing country. They are interested and eager to know about the job, the most important and challenging ongoing projects and their work team because their future is tied to the job.

It is wrong to assume that a new employee is such a great talent or experienced person that he or she needs no form of support once operational resources have been made available to them. Such thinking is faulty because the purpose of on-boarding is to facilitate the seamless adjustment of new employees, irrespective of their position or level of maturity. On-boarding is not about fairness and kindness; it is about the integration of new employees into the work culture and teams so that they can establish an early bond with the organization. Its success or failure can influence the decision of new employees to remain with or leave an organization, because the first major impression they have about their employer is through the on-boarding process. On-boarding is aimed at achieving an early fit between new employees and their jobs and work teams. It is therefore not the same as the traditional orientation programme which essentially emphasizes the need to understand HR policies, procedures and compensation.

Organizations conduct on-boarding in different ways. In some, it consists of merely providing the 'employee handbook' and introducing the new employee to interfacing departments and work teams. Only the executives are taken to the chief executive officer on a courtesy call. Other organizations conduct a one- or a two-day orientation course which provides information on the firm's structure and functions and its HR policies – especially on compensation and benefits – followed by a tour of the organization and interesting places in the city. That is where it ends. In this template the orientation is totally the responsibility of the HR department. There is hardly any involvement of the hiring manager, neither is there a programme for the continuation of the on-boarding process when the new employee begins work in his or her department or location. Because line managers are not properly briefed or involved in the process they do not know how to gradually integrate new employees into the team and work process. Ideally, they should begin to take responsibility for managing the new hires through the on-boarding process.

An employee told me how his manager asked him to proceed on mission to represent the organization at a two-day meeting barely a week after he had assumed duty. He was just at the point of concluding negotiations for accommodation. Of course, he lost the accommodation, and the family arrived a week later without a roof over their heads. Five years later he was still recounting the pain which that single incident had inflicted on his psyche and on the family. His manager's philosophy was probably that new employees would learn faster when they are left to figure out things for themselves early in their career. Nothing could be further from the truth. Employees who are carefully and systematically oriented to the company and their jobs tend to learn faster and achieve higher productivity much earlier than those who do not have the same experience.

Leaving new employees to fend for themselves from the outset exposes them to the possibility of making costly and embarrassing mistakes. When professionally designed and managed, on-boarding shortens the learning curve of new employees and facilitates their adaptation to the work environment, thereby increasing their self-confidence, job satisfaction and productivity. This is extremely important because organizational work is becoming more complex due to rapid technological and environmental changes coupled with fierce competition and clients' ever-increasing demands and pressures. On-boarding assures new employees not only that the corporation values them and is prepared to support and give them a successful career, but also that their choice of organization is a wise and right one. On-boarding consists of a series of planned learning activities:

- *The organization's business.* This includes: mission, vision, strategic goals and values of the organization; structure and functions of each division; staffing; clientele, service providers; challenges and performance in terms of market share or the business's profitability; and how the new employee's job fits into the organization.

- *The organization's culture* – 'the way we do things around here'. This entails highlighting practices that you may not find in an employee handbook. It could range from a discussion of gender-sensitivity to the mode of dressing or mode of addressing superordinates. For instance, does the organization make a fetish of people's status or do employees address each other, irrespective of status, by first name?

- *Networking.* Employees should be introduced to internal and external clients with whom they will have to interact in the performance of their job. Networking could be formal or informal. For instance, the company's tennis club, restaurant, launching of a new product, management meeting, town hall meeting and so on are all opportunities for new employees to establish a nexus of relationships within and outside the organization. A tour of the company's plants, major departments or divisions, clients and service providers is necessary.

- *The job and resources required.* First and foremost, there must be a job description. The supervisor and the employee have to agree on performance objectives and targets so that the expectations are clear to both parties from the beginning. Managers need to be cautious at this point as new employees may not contest overambitious programmes even though they have some reservations. The last thing they would want to do is to give the impression of reluctance to accept responsibilities.

  Responsibilities determine the kind and amount of resources required for optimal performance. Organizations must provide resources to obviate initial frustration. Resources could be any or a combination of the following: people, budget, authority, office accommodation, company regulations, standard operating procedures manuals, Internet access, business cards, parking lots, computers, stationery items and so on.

- *Terms and conditions of work.* Employees need to have the employee handbook, which states the conditions and terms of the employment contract in greater detail.

- *The environment.* Employees need to be properly briefed on the security situation of the city and country where the company is located. They must be informed of any cultural peculiarities, especially racial, religious and gender sensitivity. Information about safe areas to live, medical facilities, schools and so forth would also be helpful.

- *A buddy.* Ideally, a mentor should be appointed, especially for young professional people or young managers. Linking them to friends or buddies who can take them around town is extremely helpful. These individuals will initially assist in answering questions that may be sensitive or in providing advice to ensure that the new entrants do not make costly mistakes early in their new appointment. Buddies generally facilitate the learning process, especially in understanding the organizational culture.

As leaders, line managers are in a unique position to act as organizational models, purveyors of organizational values and mentors to the new employees. They are also responsible for mobilizing the work team to support the newcomers. Sometimes, a new employee is viewed by peers with suspicion. In other cases, they may be rejected outright if, for instance, their peers thought that an internal candidate should have been promoted to the position. In such circumstances, managers have to support the new employee and subtly impress on peers that management has a good reason for its choice and that the new employee enjoys management's confidence and full support.

It should be obvious at this point that selecting talent should be a serious business in multinational corporations. It is one of the most important decisions that managers make and certainly has a significant impact on the future of their corporations. Consequently, hiring decisions must be driven by integrity, a careful analysis of available information about candidates, an entrepreneurial view of the business and a commitment to organizational success.

5

Managing Employee Engagement

Now You Have Talent: What Next?

The reason why organizations go to great lengths to search for and hire talent is because great people deliver great products and services, provide customers with immense satisfaction, give their companies a competitive advantage and, in summary, make organizations great and effective. The mere acquisition of a talent or great people does not spontaneously produce these awesome results. Extraordinary ability alone does not yield extraordinary performance. Hence, company executives must answer the question: 'Now that you have talent, what next? How do you ensure that they are actively engaged so that you can derive optimal benefits from their capabilities?'

Since Elton Mayo's study of Hawthorne Works at the Western Electric Company in Chicago between 1924 and 1927 (Brown, 1954), managers and social researchers have been preoccupied with either explaining why some workers are more productive than others or postulating what motivates workers, gives them satisfaction, makes them productive or inspires them to remain with an organization despite opportunities elsewhere. Theories of motivation are essentially about employee engagement or commitment. Different writers have defined 'employee engagement' in various ways: the level of employees' commitment towards their organization, values and job; emotional connection to an organization; organizational identification; affective attachment to an organization's goals and values; willingness to go the extra mile or make discretionary efforts; and commitment to act in a way that meets team and organizational goals and interests.

Employee engagement is based on the philosophy that employees can only give the best of their abilities and remain with an organization if the latter is able to meet their individual needs, such as a challenging job, an enabling, social work environment, competitive total rewards and rapid career development.

When these needs are satisfied, employees become fully involved in, and enthusiastic about, their work and the organization (Seijts and Crim, 2006). They are inspired to and will go the extra mile to provide satisfaction to customers. Engagement is manifested in a positive attitude towards the organization and its values, and a commitment to collaborate with others to achieve agreed objectives and improve performance.

In contrast, the symptoms of low engagement or disengagement include the following:

- slow or tardy reaction to challenges
- gradual failure to meet deadlines, lack of drive for creativity, innovation and effectiveness
- ceasing to give customers' concerns the priority attention they used to receive or deserve
- lack of drive, enthusiasm and low energy – burn-out
- consistently only doing enough to get by
- reluctance to make discretionary effort due to lack of emotional commitment to the job and the company
- lack of cooperation in working with team members
- finding fault in virtually every policy, system, procedure, initiative, programme and behaviour in the corporation.

Employee engagement relates to employee commitment, motivation, attitude and behaviour. It is reflected in personal sacrifice made for the sake of the organization and shows persistence in achieving desired goals and preoccupation with the organization (Wiener, 1982). Employee engagement may be inferred where an employee remains with an organization even though he or she has better and more attractive career opportunities elsewhere. The challenge that organizations face, therefore, is how to induce the attitudes and behaviours that will produce desirable outcomes. Such outcomes could take the form of performance, continuing to stay with the organization, innovativeness, creativity and discretionary efforts. These behaviours are instigated by drivers that not only create the enabling environment, but also meet the needs of employees.

Employee Engagement Drivers

Engagement drivers consist of policies, practices and managerial behaviours which satisfy the needs of employees and thus generate or reinforce their motivation and engagement. Helping employees to become engaged is about getting rid of behaviours, policies, practices and systems that block the motivation and commitment to perform and also push employees out of an organization. Figure 5.1 and Table 5.1 show the determinants, outcomes and indicators of employee engagement. Management literature tends to lump employee engagement drivers together without demonstrating their respective impacts on the desired outcomes. Here, engagement drivers have been analytically separated into three categories – instrumental, normative and professional engagement – so that managers can understand the kind of outcomes each category of drivers can induce in workers' behaviour. However, they are not mutually exclusive.

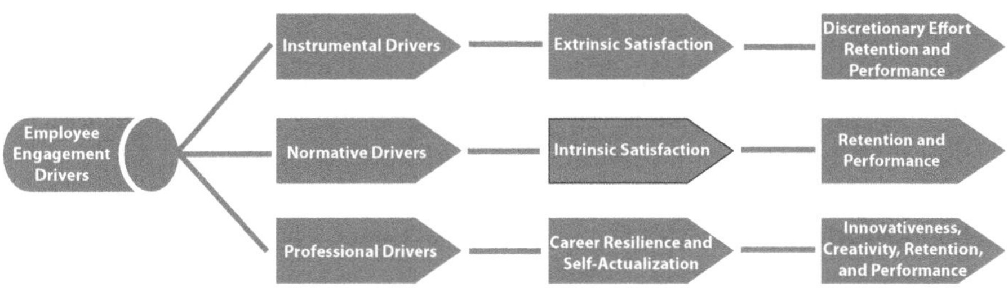

Figure 5.1 Employee engagement drivers

Instrumental Engagement Drivers

Instrumental or utilitarian engagement is rooted in the exchange perspective typified by the equity and expectancy theories. The basic formulation of these theories is that individuals will contribute to an organization in exchange for valued rewards. Their continued performance and stay in the organization are guaranteed only as long as the valued rewards are also guaranteed. Implied in the exchange perspective are two main tenets. The first is expectancy, which is the probability that performance will lead to desired outcomes, and the second is valence, which is the value an employee attaches to the reward for

Table 5.1 Employment engagement drivers

Form of engagement	Engagement drivers	Outcomes	Engagement indicators
Instrumental driver	Compensation (salaries and benefits)	Extrinsic satisfaction	Discretionary effort Retention Performance
Normative drivers	Vision Social work environment and work–life balance	Intrinsic satisfaction	Retention Performance
Professional drivers	Job characteristics Empowerment Career development Career advancement	Career resilience Self-actualization	Innovativeness Creativity Retention Performance

performance. Furthermore, people compare their contributions and the rewards that they receive to the contributions and rewards of comparable others. Membership and performance, as noted by Scholl (1981), continue if there is a balanced ratio between contributions and rewards when compared to those of others. Imbalance causes the individuals to either change their contributions or leave the organization.

The driver in the instrumental engagement category is compensation which comprises salary and benefits and excludes other forms of psychological incomes, such as career development and advancement.

COMPENSATION

To understand how compensation drives employee engagement, it is important to know the social meaning of compensation for employees. Employers, compensation experts and motivational theorists engage in an endless debate as to whether pay is a motivator or a satisfier. Employees are not bothered about what it is; rather, they are concerned about what compensation can do for them. Compensation (pay and benefits) which organizations provide to employees has a deep social meaning that goes far beyond the conceptualization or imagination of employers. To employers, compensation is a reward for performance that is characterized by internal equity, fairness and external relativity or competitiveness. It is also an instrument for driving productivity and reinforcing desired behaviours.

To employees, their compensation is a symbol of their social status in the organizational hierarchy and the value of their job to the organization. They also perceive rewards as segmenting the organization into classes as evidenced by, for instance, not only the pay structure, but also differential benefits such as a restaurant exclusively for management with better food and services. Outside the organization, rewards have an even deeper social meaning for workers in that they determine their social status in so many ways in their local community. Compensation defines what social privileges workers can afford; where they can rent or purchase a house; the social clubs they can belong to; the schools their children can attend; the kind of wedding ceremonies they can afford; the kind of funeral ceremonies they can organize at the death of their parents; the type of car they can drive; the stores in which they can shop; the class in which they can travel by air when undertaking a personal trip; the restaurants in which they can eat; and even the kinds of clothes they can wear. To the African worker, compensation largely determines the degree to which he can assist members of the extended family, perform religious obligations and contribute to the development of his village or community, all of which tend to affect his social standing or esteem in the community.

Instrumental engagement shows that high engagement can only be sustained if the organization is able to consistently provide valued rewards for performance, and such rewards must not only be valued, but also be seen to be equitable. Compensation per se may influence employees' choice of organization to work for, but it may not sustain their engagement or retention in the long run because it creates entitlement mentality. However, performance-related pay, results-based bonuses and profit-sharing pay may stimulate engagement. Furthermore, differential merit increases, based on individual performance, must be significant to justify individual efforts. Usually, individuals will either quit their organizations or reduce their level of performance and contributions if rewards are perceived as inequitable, the value of rewards declines or expectations are not met. If employees continue to remain with an organization despite dissatisfaction with pay or inequity in pay, the reasons must be rooted in some other factors. Scholl (1981) believes that there could be three possible explanations: namely that the employees experience other valued rewards associated with continued employment; have re-evaluated their expectations, or have made perceptual changes in either outcomes or inputs. Finally, they may not in fact have a better choice of organization. There is therefore a compelling reason to examine other drivers of employee engagement.

Normative Engagement Drivers

Normative engagement is driven by congruency between the values of the organization and those of the employees. There is thus a person–organization fit. Like instrumental engagement, normative engagement may produce high performance and retention in organizations. However, whereas in instrumental engagement the individual's motivation is driven by a nexus of relationships between input and outcomes and rewards, in normative engagement the individual derives an inherent, intrinsic satisfaction from working in an environment that supports or promotes the norms, beliefs and values that he or she cherishes. In other words, organizational values and practices, such as trust, cooperation, teamwork, diversity, good leadership, mutual respect, regard for family life and the ideals and mission of the organization, are seen to be consistent with the values that the employee holds very dearly. These values connect employees to their organizations. Lack of value congruency results in alienation because of a mismatch between the individual and the organization. The drivers of normative engagement include the vision and values of the organization, work–life balance and social work environment. Each of these drivers is discussed in detail below.

AN EXCITING VISION

Where there is no vision people can hardly make progress. Just as individuals have dreams of what they would like to be in the future, so organizations have visions of what they would like to become by a given time in the future. A vision is a desired future state. Covey (2004: 70) defines it as 'applied imagination', the beginning of the 'process of reinventing oneself or of an organization reinventing itself'. It consists of desires, aspirations, hopes or dreams but not of fantasies. All great transformations in organizations or society have been the product of visions – the creation of a mental picture of a desired state of the organization or society in the future. In essence, without a vision there is no change and, without change, an organization cannot make progress; it will sooner or later suffer atrophy or be a casualty of environmental change over which it has no control. How does a vision engineer employee engagement and result in high performance? A vision appeals to emotion, experience and noble ideals without losing credibility. When understood and internalized, a vision stimulates, energizes and mobilizes people to a noble cause. It is performance-driven. Quite often organizational leaders develop great visions and strategies and yet fail woefully at actualizing them for the simple reason that the dreams belong to them and not to the employees.

When Martin Luther King said 'I have a dream', it was not a dream of how he would single-handedly free the black people in the United States of America from oppression, discrimination, humiliation and racism but of how all the black people would work together with white sympathizers to attain equality. Freedom is not only a universal human right, but also a universally accepted, cherished value. Hence Martin Luther King had massive support. He was assassinated, but his vision survived him because his followers shared and owned the vision; they were normatively engaged not because they expected any pecuniary rewards, but because the vision synchronized with their cherished personal values and beliefs.

There is a popular story of three men who were cutting stones at a building site. A man asked each of them what they were doing. The first stone-cutter said he was cutting stones, the second said he was working for his livelihood, while the third said he was building a cathedral. Although the three men were performing the same task at the same location, the job had different meanings for them. The first stone-cutter was undertaking a frustrating routine and boring job while the second needed the job to earn money and provide for his family. The third was significantly different. He had a big picture of what the stones would be used for and he saw himself as contributing to the great mission of building a great place of worship. Organizations need to help workers to become cathedral-builders above all else. It is a source of high engagement.

In general, the potential for such an impact exists in employees' work, but they are unable to see it because it is not clearly and consistently defined and communicated to them by their managers. Vision drives performance and moves the source of motivation from pecuniary rewards to intrinsic rewards. This is particularly important during a recession when organizations do not have the financial resources to reward workers for their performance. What buoys their motivation and high engagement in such a situation is the intrinsic mission of the job – its contribution to the strategic goals. Jobs should therefore be designed in such a way that each employee can see what they contribute to the achievement of the organization's vision.

SOCIAL WORK ENVIRONMENT

The environment in which people work also influences their motivation and level of engagement. Every organization has two types of internal work environment – the physical and the social – which can make or mar employee engagement. The physical environment must be safe, free from extremes of heat and cold and toxic substances, and should be properly lit and ventilated to create comfortable conditions for optimal exertion of efforts. An uncomfortable physical environment is palpable and can easily be felt through the various senses. This is not exactly the case with the social environment. You have to be observant, perceptive and sensitive to discern any discomfort in the social environment, although it has a more pernicious effect than the physical environment on employee engagement. When the social environment is not conducive to work, it adversely impacts on employee engagement.

When people join organizations they bring with them certain values which are part of their personality. The values include teamwork, trust, dependability, honesty, integrity, cooperation, fairness, equity, diversity and affection. They are products of the individual's personality which has been moulded through childhood experiences in the family and at school, and in associations and religious organizations. Consequently, practices and behaviours at work that seem to resonate with those internalized values are considered acceptable and conducive to work and the employee's continued stay in the organization.

Most organizations are a melting-pot of people with different capabilities, personalities, cultural backgrounds and idiosyncrasies. This is even more pronounced in global or multinational enterprises where there is diversity in race, language, colour, gender, ethnicity and nationality. Certain values that are normal to some nationalities or races may be anathema to others. What ultimately binds people together in such a global environment is a common mission and commitment to achieve corporate goals. As individuals with clearly defined responsibilities, they cannot succeed without the collaboration and cooperation of other members of the group or team. However, this bond can be destroyed by the behaviour of each individual in the work environment. Interdependence is imperative. Any attempt to pursue individual self-interest tends to destroy trust and create a toxic social environment. Below are two remarkably typical examples.

First, consider a situation in which a colleague deliberately withholds the vital data that you need for an important presentation to senior management or an important client. Despite several reminders and emphasis on the urgency and criticality of the data to your presentation, you receive the data, with flimsy excuses and apologies, only one day before your presentation. Or the information arrives early but with a warning that it was hurriedly put together for you. On close scrutiny, you discover that it is full of inaccuracies. It is difficult not to smell the toxic odour of a careful plan to ensure that your presentation will be a failure. Second, consider the classic example in which you share an innovative idea in a draft proposal with a colleague in confidence and within 24 hours he has escalated it to a top executive of the company or to your boss as his own idea before you have even had a chance to finalize it. This is an idea that could enhance your career in the organization. It could propel you to new heights. When your proposal finally reaches your boss a week later, he looks at you askance, suggesting that you have plagiarized your colleague's original idea!

This kind of work environment is a fertile ground for conflicts, because some employees will invariably extract revenge as soon as they have the opportunity. You are constantly walking on a minefield. It poses a challenge to executives and managers because no employee can be fully engaged in an environment characterized by distrust, disharmony and back-stabbing. Individuals who play the kind of games described above generally lack self-esteem and integrity, and suffer from insecurity. The motives behind such behaviours could be any or all of the following:

- the need to be recognized by the boss or top management
- ethnic/racial competition for power and positions
- inordinate ambition for advancement to higher status
- turf protection which results in the creation of silos and the destruction of communication and team spirit
- envy of high-potential colleagues – those who are envious of them adopt the tactic of besmirching their image and undermining their success and effectiveness with a view to portraying them as unfit for higher responsibilities
- a belief that belittling colleagues enhances their ego, self-worth and popularity
- 'kicking the ladder' – an attempt by managers to frustrate the advancement of their reports to higher positions by portraying them in a bad light to top management.

It is not only team members who could pose a problem in the work environment. Paradoxically, managers who possess poor leadership skills and lack integrity or commitment to organizational values could also constitute a challenge. Imagine a situation in which even though your high performance and great potential are widely acknowledged in your division, other less capable people are being promoted over and above you. The only reason for this – although it cannot be acknowledged – is your race, ethnicity or gender. When employees leave organizations, it is often because of their supervisors. Managerial behaviours that can create disharmony and employee disengagement include:

- *Implicit discrimination*: against subordinates in performance appraisal, career development and promotion on the basis of race, colour, ethnicity, gender, language or nationality.

- *Micro-inequities*: Stephen Young, Senior Vice President for Corporate Diversity at JP Morgan Chase in the United States says that micro-inequities consist of micro-messages that are small, subtle and sometimes unspoken, which are capable of discouraging and impairing performance and lead to damaged self-esteem and withdrawal. Micro-inequities are used consciously or unconsciously against women, minorities and people of less prominent cultures. They could result in the disengagement and turnover of such targets.

- *Lack of trustworthiness*: to be credible, managers must 'walk the talk'. Managers' actions must be consistent with their words, promises and organizational values.

- *Taking credit and allocating blame*: taking credit for the ideas, achievements and contributions of subordinates but blaming them for errors in order to cover their own weaknesses and look good before their bosses.

- *Lack of respect*: for subordinates through the use of abusive language, lying and displaying racism, nepotism or ethnicism.

Managing multiculturalism is one of the greatest challenges facing organizations. Global organizations need to build teams out of diverse groups and cultures. The first step is to help employees to accept cultural differences and reject the notion of the superiority or inferiority of any race, religion, language or national or ethnic group. They are all equal. An awareness programme reinforced by role-modelling by organizational leaders is imperative. Furthermore, employees must be assisted in developing interpersonal skills that will enable them to interact and work with colleagues with mutual respect. This process leads to understanding and adjustment to cultural differences. Finally, to achieve full integration there has to be an internalization of the values of diversity and not mere compliance with organizational rules. Team-destroying games and conflict must be confronted and resolved in a firm, but win–win and non-threatening manner. As Covey (1998) noted, self-mastery and self-discipline are the foundation of good relationships.

Organizational leaders should seek to generate trust by being trustworthy. People must be loyal to others, even behind their backs. To be trustworthy, people need to be faithful to their word. Individuals working in a team have to do little things to support and help one another. Elephants do not bite, but mosquitoes do. It is not usually the big things that hurt friends and colleagues but little acts or uncomplimentary remarks that convey lack of care, respect and support. Finally, communication is perhaps the greatest challenge in maintaining harmony and good relationships. Most of the time employees do not have the patience to listen to and understand their colleagues. They hear only what they want to hear. They are deaf to every idea that contradicts what they believe in or have in mind. Although the advent of e-mail technology has made communication easier, it is not as effective, in certain circumstances, as a face-to-face meeting or the spoken word. The choice of media of communication has to be appropriate to forestall the misinterpretation of good intentions.

WORK–LIFE BALANCE

The family is universally accepted as an important institution. Yet the policies and practices in many organizations appear to undermine its importance in the life of workers. One of the challenges workers face today is how to reconcile the demands of work with those of the family. This conflict in roles is a dilemma with costly consequences resulting from whatever choice the worker makes. Many marriages have been ruined by the fact that one partner or the other had no time to meet marital obligations because they are implicitly made, by their organizations, to choose between their job and their families. Company policies that do not provide for flexible working hours have inevitably compelled some parents to devote so much time to their job that they have little or no time for their children. As a result, cases abound of children who have resorted to antisocial behaviours or have completely dropped out of school as a form of protest against parental neglect. The increasing number of women in the workforce, particularly at managerial levels, as well as the difficulties women face in combining the three conflicting roles of wife, mother and employee have led to an increasing awareness of, and demand for, work-life balance. Of course, this is an issue for men, too; they also need to spend adequate time with their children and wives.

In Africa such difficulties have been exacerbated by the weakening of the traditional family support system. In the past, working-class women usually had sisters and nieces who gladly lived with them, taking on the role of caring for the children, cleaning the house and cooking meals for the family. They managed most of the domestic chores and were not paid any wages because they were regarded as members of the family and were treated as such. They were provided with food, clothing and medical care, and sometimes were allowed to acquire a skill in tailoring, hairdressing or catering so that they could live an independent life later. The desire for every child to be educated has changed this situation. Sisters, cousins and nieces are no longer available; when they are, it is at a high cost. They have to be at school most of the time. Initially, the use of paid house-helps was an attractive option. However, apart from the prohibitive cost for families on lower incomes, issues of disloyalty, the inhumane treatment of children, theft of property and lack of integrity have become a concern for families. It must also be noted that, in the past, most women worked as teachers, nurses, midwives and clerks in government offices – occupations that offered fairly manageable working hours that gave them scope for personal life.

As most women took up employment – especially at professional and managerial level in highly demanding industries such as banking, insurance, telecommunications, and oil and gas – the conflict between work and family life became an ever greater challenge. The challenge faced in this regard by single women with children even looms larger than what other women experience. In Africa, the number of single parents has increased as a result of wars and the plague of HIV/AIDS, and some single-parent employees may have as many as 4–6 children. What is evident is that the workforce, whether in the United States, Europe or Africa is composed of numerous married women and single parents, and their individual circumstances put incredible psychological pressure on them. In a survey conducted by Career-builder.com of 880 women who were employed full-time and with children aged below 18 years, 43 per cent of the respondents were willing to take a cut in pay to enable them spend more time with their children. Furthermore, 51 per cent of them said they would quit their jobs if their spouses earned enough money to support the entire family (Newsline, 2008c).

Many organizations operate in a way that robs employees of their life's passion – health, music, sport, games, charity, religious activity and so forth. These passions give meaning to people's lives because such people do not define life necessarily in terms of status, salary or power but, rather, in terms of what they give to society and the joy they bring to others through particular talents that cannot be tapped by their organizations. They have a compulsive quest for meaning of life. The actualization of innate potential is itself a form of self-fulfilment, an achievement valued beyond money and promotion in the workplace. Organizations that recognize the importance of the family and individual passions can easily drive employees' engagement through policies and practices that put a high premium on work–life balance.

The starting point will be for organizations to change the prosaic mindset that employees' devotion to their individual families and passions outside the workplace results in a loss of productivity to the employer. It is not a zero-sum game. Not only is the mental map inappropriate for employee engagement and retention, it is also anachronistic in the modern global environment. It must be understood that a win–win philosophy, rather than the traditional win–lose approach, characterized by trade-off, is mutually beneficial to all parties. Friedman and Greenhaus (2000) noted that, in family-friendly organizations, employees feel less compelled to make trade-offs between work and family; they are more satisfied with their personal growth and development; and they feel they perform well as parents. Work and personal life are complementary. The authors have spelt out how this could be achieved.

Managers and their reports need to agree on organizational and personal priorities in an atmosphere of trust. The old paradigm that for an employee to have a passion for an activity (sports, singing, religious or community activity) outside the workplace suggests lack of commitment to the organization must give way to the recognition that the employee could have personal passions for other activities along with a passion for their work. Gone are the days of the organization man. Whyte (1956) described the 'organizational man' as an individual who worked long hours – 50 to 60 hours a week – but didn't feel that it was a burden. According to Whyte, we have, in sum, a man who is so completely involved in his work that he cannot distinguish between work and the rest of his life and is happy that he cannot. Nowadays, the organization man is an anachronism. The organization's emphasis should be on agreed deliverables and not on how much time the employee spends at work.

Furthermore, managers should know their employees as whole persons. That means knowing their passions – their commitment to taking care of elderly parents, commitment to their nuclear family, commitment to a philanthropic cause or commitment to a religious or sporting activity. Merely knowing their age, educational qualifications, marital status and previous employment record is not enough. Without knowing the whole person, managers cannot understand their subordinates' needs, interests, concerns and what ultimately motivates them to perform at work. Without knowing the whole person a manager has no valid idea of how to support the talent he has taken so much time and pain to hire. Showing interest in the whole person, without necessarily intruding in the individual's private roles, enables managers to develop a strategy that enhances employee job performance and still allows them to effectively meet their commitments outside the workplace.

Finally, managers need to continually review the way in which work is done because research shows that it is not lack of time that is responsible for the conflict between work and personal life, but the inability to manage time and work. They should review business processes and eliminate those that have no value, take advantage of growing information technology such as telecommuting and teleconferencing, outsource certain activities where necessary and so on. Introducing flexible working hours is also helpful. When employees' work enables them to find meaning in their life, they feel a strong commitment to the organization. Consequently, they double the energy they invest in their work and their loyalty to the organization, and performance improves for the benefit of the organization. Employees need empowerment to be able to manage their work and time effectively.

McDonald's confirmed that the passion for individual hobbies or interests does not necessarily harm job or organizational performance when in 2006 it organized the 'Voice of McDonald's' competition. It was such a success that the company decided to hold it every two years. McDonald's commitment is to show off the talents of its employees (Martin, 2008). Great companies that want to be employers of choice encourage and support their employees in developing their talents and interests in areas that are not necessarily or directly related to their jobs. Such encouragement and support result in higher employee engagement, greater job satisfaction, higher individual productivity and better organizational performance.

Professional Engagement Drivers

Professional engagement is based on the philosophy that job-related aspects which result in recognition, growth and career progression are strong drivers of employee engagement. This form of engagement is probably stronger in Generations X and Y who do not have loyalty for any specific organization but focus instead on their career. The main drivers of this engagement are: job characteristics, empowerment, and career development and advancement. Its focus is on individual growth, progress, recognition, status and self-fulfilment.

THE JOB

In my experience of working with managers, I find that most of them have no idea whatsoever about job design. Their emphasis is primarily on the size of a job; hardly on its enrichment or its capacity to provide intrinsic satisfaction to whoever would perform it. Jobs differ in many ways. Some jobs are varied, stretching and replete with challenges while others are merely routine and therefore boring; some jobs have an inherently inspiring mission while others are just mundane; and some jobs are so large that the performers are perpetually struggling to cope with them while others barely provide the job-holder with enough to do. Although the above descriptions show the differences between jobs in a kind of binary comparison, jobs may also be seen on a continuum. The way in which a job is designed can either enhance employee engagement or frustrate it. In this section we examine the various intrinsic aspects of a job that are germane to employee engagement.

Employees are excited by a job that is varied, challenging and stretching, and that provides an opportunity not only to use their current skills and competencies, but also to increase their knowledge, hone existing skills and acquire new ones. Repetitive, routine and monotonous jobs are not stimulating; they are a daily drudgery and do not motivate workers. If anything, they result in what sociologists call 'alienation' – a situation in which work has no meaning. Think of a job in which the employee is involved in daily routine – shuffling papers, churning out statistics, tending the conveyor belt at the factory, attending meetings at which he or she cannot make any decisions or compiling reports that nobody uses for decision making. The consequence is decline in employee engagement. In a research study on the motivation and performance of health workers in Mali, the researchers discovered that the workers, particularly doctors, could be better motivated if they had greater responsibility and were held accountable for their work (Dieleman et al., 2005).

There are certain basic facts which managers ignore when placing employees in jobs. One is that employees have different capabilities, versatilities and learning agilities. Second, a large volume of activities does not necessarily translate into a challenging job. Finally, because people vary in abilities and competencies, job descriptions should not be static. While the former incumbent of a position might have found the responsibilities of the job enormous to cope with, a new incumbent may find it so light that he could take on additional responsibilities. Top talent easily outgrows a job. Job descriptions may be static, but the incumbents are not. They learn fast, gain mastery of virtually all aspects of their work and psychologically yearn to move on to bigger or new challenges to 'conquer'. It is at this point that managers need to demonstrate their sensitivity and capability as leaders by identifying and differentiating high-achieving employees from the laggards or average people and redesign their jobs according to their needs. Merely increasing the volume of work without building in challenges is not only unproductive, but also stressful and frustrating for the employee. There must be what Hertzberg (1966) calls 'vertical job loading' – that is, job enrichment and not merely job enlargement. If employees grow and their jobs do not change, there is a mismatch between them, and that incompatibility impacts on their motivation and engagement.

When in search of employment, especially in a recession which is usually characterized by a high rate of unemployment, people tend to pay less attention to the mission or purpose of the job they are applying to do. Their primary concern is how to earn a living or be gainfully employed in a financially strong organization. On assumption of duty, they soon realize that there must be *task significance* or a purpose of the job other than just earning a living. Employees have a clearer line of sight about their job when they fully comprehend the vision of their organization. Understanding the vision gives them a sense of purpose, a need for achievement and a desire to make history. When I worked in a steel plant, most of the candidates we interviewed were excited about the opportunity to work for the first steel plant in sub-Saharan Africa. In an international agricultural institute the story was the same. Candidates had read about the extraordinary research contributions our institute had made to knowledge about cassava and plantain production and wanted to be part of the great team.

Whether or not the candidates were sincere in their professed commitment is irrelevant. What is significant is the common denominator of wanting to contribute to a lofty mission or make an impact on the future of some amorphous population. The lesson for organizations is clear. Line of sight or task significance means that employees are able to see the value and impact of their contribution on society, organizational performance or on the internal and external clients.

EMPOWERMENT

Empowerment is a ubiquitous construct that is found in politics, community development, psychology and organizational behaviour. The surfeit of interest in the subject suggests its relevance to society and organizations. It has been defined by different people in different ways. To some, empowerment is the delegation of authority to employees for the execution of their tasks or responsibilities. To others, it is the involvement of employees in the decision-making process. And to yet others, it is the process by which employees have control over their lives and achieve personal goals.

Empowerment is a process of providing information, responsibility, knowledge, skills, authority and resources to the appropriate employees who need them to serve the customers/clients or get their jobs done efficiently and effectively. Lack of empowerment effectively deprives workers of their rights as 'citizens' of the organization. It makes them slaves because they have only obligations, duties and responsibilities and no right to be involved in decision-making, no access to information and no opportunity to exercise their creativity. Lack of empowerment implies management's lack of confidence in employees' character, competence and sense of judgement. Empowerment obliges managers to encourage and permit employees to take personal responsibility for managing and improving the way in which they do their jobs in order to contribute to corporate goals. In addition, it requires the creation of a culture that encourages people at all levels to feel they can make a difference and enables them to acquire the confidence and skills to do so (Clutterbuck and Kernaghan, 1994).

In many multinational enterprises, power and resources are concentrated in the hands of top management at the headquarters or home office with the result that those who actually do the job or directly deal with customers or clients in external operations have no capacity to make decisions and provide services and products in a timely fashion. The hoarding of authority by managers is based implicitly on the assumptions of Theory X which postulated that people dislike work and would avoid it if they can; therefore they must be controlled and coerced to perform their assigned tasks. By holding on to authority, top management implies that the executives are unable to take the right decisions.

By giving power to employees, organizations move the power of decision-making from the top to the level where action is usually taken. As a consequence, decisions are made faster and on time, and customers and clients are delighted by the quick response to their needs. This is precisely the reason why Welch (2005) said that if organizations want to get the benefit of everything employees have, they have got to free them – make everybody a participant. Everybody has to know everything, so they can make the right decisions by themselves. Empowerment is therefore about liberation from fear and liberation of creative potential so that employees can have control over their destinies. Employees are also happier, more committed, more innovative and more productive because they have little or no constraints in serving the customer.

The delegation of authority to employees does not necessarily result in empowerment, even though it creates the climate for it, because authority without the information, personal efficacy, resources and ability to influence the outcome of one's performance is not really empowerment. Empowerment means the individual has authority, resources (including information), competency and ability to influence his or her work or take whatever action that is necessary to meet a client's needs on the spot without having to seek clearance from the supervisor on every action. It is the foundation of customer service. Despite this reality, most top managers still conceptualize empowerment in terms of a zero-sum game. It is what Spreitzer and Doneson (2005) call the 'moral hazard' for the manager. Empowering subordinates does not result in a corresponding loss of authority or control over the subordinate. Empowerment is accompanied by accountability. In the final analysis, subordinates must give an account to the manager of how they used their authority, resources, competency and information. The phobia of losing control is more imaginary than real, and can be reduced by building trust.

Quality control circles (QCCs) which began in Japan and gradually evolved into total quality management (TQM) are a typical example of a programme based on empowerment. TQM was extremely popular in many African countries, especially in Nigeria, in the 1980s and early 1990s. In TQM, workers are trained, constituted into teams and provided with resources, including the authority to identify and solve quality- and productivity-related problems.

The lesson from QCCs and TQM is that if employees are empowered, they can contribute significantly to the achievement of organizational goals. But the paradox of empowerment in African organizations is that while, in principle, responsibility and authority inhere in the position of every employee, in practice employees are not allowed to make decisions or take risks without the permission of their superordinates for fear that they might make wrong decisions that could ruin the manager's career or even the entire organization.

Most managers do not realize how much their organizations lose through micromanagement and risk aversion. General Electric, under Jack Welch, sought to reduce apprehension about mistakes and to create a risk-friendly workplace because punishing failure discourages risk-taking. There was a story about product developers in General Electric whose new lamp design did not function as designed when it was time to test it in front of the CEO. Resources had been invested in the project. They naturally felt embarrassed, yet the company gave them television sets for their efforts and innovativeness. A study in Botswana showed that the high productivity of nurses and midwives were due to, among other factors, their involvement in decision-making (Fako, Forchen and Balogi, 2002). Workers are highly engaged when they believe that management has confidence in their capability to make the right decisions

An important African cultural characteristic is high power distance identified by Hofstede (1994) in his study of Africa. This characteristic is copiously demonstrated in the form of respect for, and loyalty to, authority and also considerable dependence of subordinates on managers. It is therefore postulated that in a culture characterized by high power distance, African employees are most likely to expect and respond much better to an authoritarian leadership style. In other words, they may not value empowerment. High power distance is not unique to Africa. Countries like France, Spain and Mexico are also high power distance countries. Nevertheless, empowerment is valued, pursued and practised in organizations in these countries.

African culture is changing; so must their global organizations. Many young workers and managers are university graduates who have acquired democratic values. In fact, their education and work experience in countries like the United States, France, the United Kingdom and Canada have reinforced their personal desire for empowerment and dislike for micromanagement. Empowerment is a critical element in the job satisfaction of new-generation workers. A young, talented telecommunications engineer said at an exit interview that he was leaving his employer because the bureaucracy was 'overwhelming and choking'. He had no authority to experiment with his ideas as every proposal took months to be approved by the general manager in charge of Operations. To implement empowerment, a paradigm shift is necessary. Managers must move from suspicion to trust, from micromanagement to employee involvement, from information and authority hoarding to information-sharing and delegation of authority, and from risk aversion to tolerance of mistakes arising from experimentation and genuine creative efforts. On the other hand, employees need to move away from overdependence on supervisors for direction to self-reliance and independence (without necessarily compromising interdependence), from avoiding challenges to accepting them, and from waiting to be directed to seeking responsibility.

CAREER DEVELOPMENT AND ADVANCEMENT

It is a truism that people don't work for only the money. They also work for growth, development, self-actualization, status and advancement. Development and advancement are important drivers of motivation and engagement. Although organizations recognize this fact, their approach sometimes fails to resonate with talent's conception of development and advancement. They have the mindset that, barring termination or organizational collapse, employees will work for them until they retire or at least stay several years before moving to the next organization. A successful career is therefore defined in terms of long tenure and vertical progression within the hierarchy. This mindset is not consistent with reality and therefore cannot enhance employee engagement. The new generation of knowledge workers, especially those belonging to Generations X and Y, has a set of values that are significantly different from this conception of career success. They are mobile and have no long-term commitment and loyalty to any particular organization. They have no plans for long tenure in any organization except those that can continue to meet their divergent and changing expectations. The paradigm of employers and that of the young generation of knowledge workers are therefore incompatible.

As organizations begin to operate in the international marketplace they will find that a common denominator among talent is the need to remain employable, not necessarily within their current organizations but, rather, within the international labour market. Because organizations cannot be trusted to provide lifetime tenure in the context of acquisitions, mergers, buy-outs and so forth, their preoccupation is career resilience. Therefore, they yearn to acquire skills and abilities that give them a cutting edge in their specializations. They want organizations in which they have opportunities for networking that will enable them to have global connections and to be able to ferret information from diverse sources. In essence, they want their organizations to provide them with the kind of experience that will equip them to become global executives. Because they have a high need for achievement, they are driven by the desire for responsibility, personal achievement and recognition.

However, they are not desirous of growth for its own sake. A major source of frustration and disengagement is the fact that after undertaking educational and leadership training programmes in reputable business schools and also development programmes within their companies, they do not have appropriate opportunities to use their knowledge and skills. Often there is no defined career path, leaving them uncertain as to their future career progression. No talented individual likes to be stuck in a cul-de-sac. Such situations produce frustration, disengagement and turnover. Chapter 12 describes the pathetic case of a steel plant in Nigeria which attracted some of the most brilliant young minds, carefully selected and trained in Austria and India in steel technology. Within a couple of years most of them were gone – poached by competitors.

Sustaining Employee Engagement in a Recession

Nothing affects high employee engagement during an economic recession more negatively than anxiety and fear of job loss because it impacts on the individual's livelihood and future career. The main antidote to employees' fears and concerns is trust, communication and transparency. During a recession, the rumour mill usually has a field day if management does not communicate clearly, honestly and realistically about the financial situation and future of the firm. Workers, staff associations and the unions want to be realistically assured that their jobs will be there tomorrow and the day after when they clock in for their day's work. They want to be assured that although they may not receive any bonus, there will be no cut in pay or reduction in their valued benefits. If for any reason the reduction in the workforce is inevitable it should be done quickly, transparently, fairly and in compliance with necessary labour laws, once and for all so that 'survivors' could move on with their work without any fear of another impending separation exercise. Formal and informal communication is imperative.

Measures that could be taken to sustain the high engagement of talent during a recession include the following:

- Involve the organization's talent in the development or implementation of strategies and tactics that would lead to a rebound or repositioning of the firm for competitiveness in the aftermath of the recession. Not only is this a positive challenge; it also channels the efforts, energies and capabilities of the talent in the workforce in preparing the organization for tomorrow. The mere thought and hope that the organization has a future is inspiring and engaging.

- Orient the workforce towards the more humanitarian and altruistic values and mission of the organization, which go beyond financial rewards. Workers must be encouraged to see the joy they bring to humanity through delivering the organization's products and services.

- Involve staff in creative thinking and problem-solving. The economic environment is changing dramatically with the current economic crisis. Businesses, especially financial institutions, will not operate the way they did prior to the downturn. Organizations have to figure out what the nature of competition will be in the aftermath of the recession. The talent in the organization can be constituted into think tanks in their specialized areas with a view to generating new ideas about processes and technologies for the creation of new products, services and solutions for their business.

Intergenerations and Employee Engagement

There are four main generations of workers, namely: veterans (1922–1945), baby-boomers (1946–64), Generation X (1965–1980) and Generation Y (1981–2000). The generations have different values, expectations and needs, and those needs and expectations may largely influence their individual level of engagement, productivity, teamwork and commitment to the organization. Identifying the needs of the different generations of employees therefore enables organizations to develop policies and implement practices that seek to satisfy them. More importantly, it helps organizations recognize that a one-size-fits-all approach is inappropriate and ineffective in achieving high employee engagement.

The responsibility of managers is to be proactive in identifying the value propositions of their employees and use them to develop employee engagement drivers. However, where this has not happened they need to have the sensitivity to detect symptoms of gradual disengagement and nip the problem in the bud. Employee disengagement and low level of engagement are an indication of frustrated workers, and the cause has to do with policies, practices, the job, the work environment and the way in which they have been treated by managers. Some may have been abused, others may have had no training and a few may have been denied promotions despite their perceived contributions and many years of service to their organizations. Yet others may have had low pay increases, are overworked, have no life of their own and constantly live in fear of being fired. Managers need to reverse this situation because it risks a decline in the productivity and contribution of disengaged employees.

More importantly, like a bad apple, disengaged people may sow and spread seeds of discontent, frustration, tension and negativity among highly engaged team members. Furthermore, they become increasingly uncooperative, unreliable and unpredictable in their behaviour. The overall effect on organizational performance and morale of other employees is incalculable. Unfortunately, most managers fail to react quickly to symptoms either because they cannot recognize them or they do not know how to tackle the slow but inevitable process that leads to the loss of employees that were once star performers.

The first step in dealing with employee disengagement is to identify the cause of the problem. The manager could do this by having a private discussion with the affected employee. A discussion is imperative because it is preposterous to assume the cause of the decline in engagement. The manager should seek to understand the root cause of the change in performance and behaviour by asking open-ended questions, probing, listening actively, commending the employee where necessary, explaining issues that the employee does not seem to understand and, above all, avoiding defensiveness. Both parties must agree on what can be done immediately to reverse the situation, and plan what will be done in the future. Some solutions, such as career advancement, may not be within the manager's authority. If this is the case, he or she must say so and avoid making a commitment. The meeting must demonstrate to the employee that the organization cares about him or her and that it is committed to reversing the decline in engagement.

6

Getting the Best Out of Talent

It is one thing for an organization to identify and hire great people; it is another thing for it to channel their expertise and competencies appropriately to achieve organizational effectiveness. Talent alone cannot produce effective outcomes. It requires some catalytic action to enable it generate tangible results. Performance management is therefore about how organizations use the talent they have painstakingly acquired to achieve innovativeness and high productivity to outperform their competitors. Armstrong (1991) defines performance management as a systematic approach to the management of people, using goals, measurement, feedback, performance and recognition as a means of motivating them to realize their maximum potential. Performance management enables an organization to achieve its strategic business goals, increase productivity, drive organizational effectiveness and enhance the development of its human asset. It is a potent tool for building and sustaining a culture of performance.

Managing performance is one of the critical responsibilities of organizational leaders because it provides a basis for managing the business of today and for developing it into the future through the performance of its people (Williams, 1991). Ironically, because it is the basis for reward, organizations place so much emphasis on performance appraisal that most managers and employees tend to be completely oblivious of the performance management process. Sometimes, it is even confused with performance appraisal. However, performance appraisal is just one of the components of performance management. The latter is a system and a process, which consists of strategic business plans, objective-setting, training, coaching, feedback, performance appraisal, performance-related pay and identification of training and development needs. This process is shown diagrammatically in Figure 6.1. As a system, its various components are interdependent, and the failure to effectively manage one component inevitably impacts on other elements.

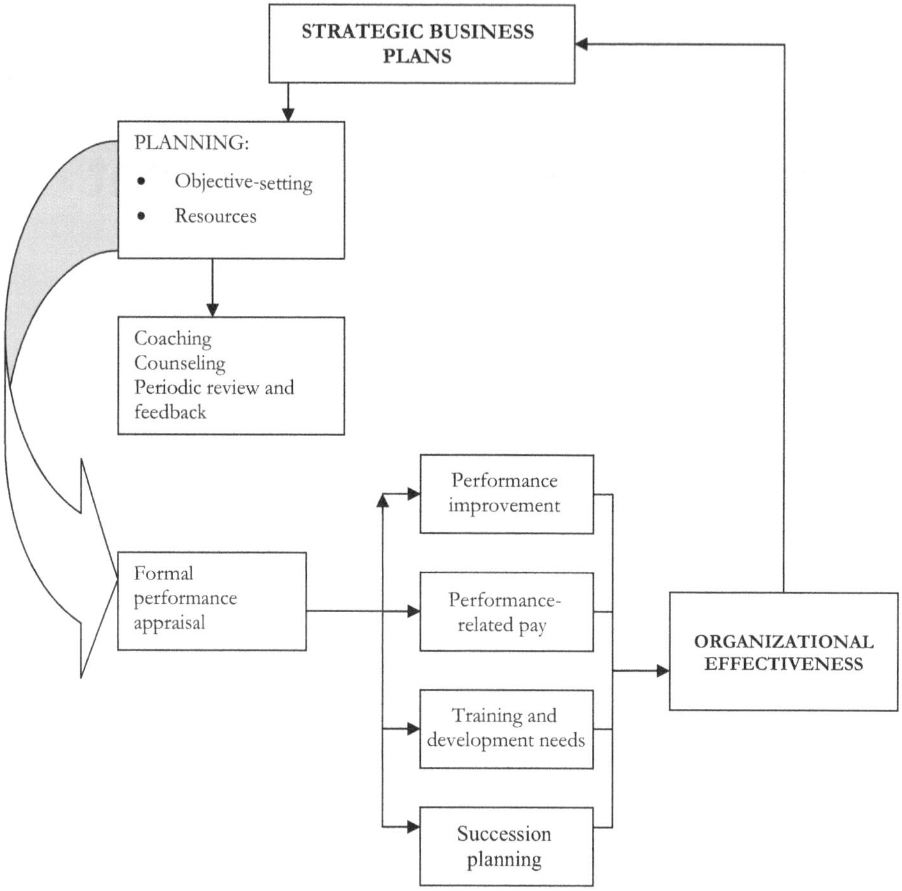

Figure 6.1 Performance management system

What managers fail to do or do inappropriately is largely responsible for the ineffectiveness of the utilization of talent. This is precisely the reason they need to deftly manage each and every component of the performance management system.

Aligning Performance Management with Business Plans

The purpose of performance management is to ensure effective utilization of resources, particularly talent for the achievement of organizational goals. Therefore, it must be aligned with the corporation's strategic business plans. Such an alignment provides managers and employees with the appropriate line of sight – how their contributions impact on corporate performance and effectiveness. Corporate business goals are defined and communicated by top management to the heads of the various divisions at the beginning of the year. The corporate goals are then disaggregated into divisional objectives, which cascade down to departmental, sectional and individual employee objectives. Corporate objectives essentially provide the direction to organizational units and individual employees regarding what they should aim to achieve during a particular year. This is important because, quite often, employees wonder how their little tasks could affect the bottom line of a whole mammoth organization. Certainly, they do, because the combined efforts of individual employees produce a synergy that results in extraordinary organizational performance.

Performance Planning

Every organizational unit plans what it has to achieve at the beginning of each year. Budgetary provisions are provided on the basis of the plan. It is people that make the plan happen. Logically, each employee must have clearly defined objectives at the beginning of each year – what is to be achieved and the timeframe within which the objectives have to be achieved. Employees need to be involved in defining their performance objectives precisely because they must understand what they have to do, why they have to do it and how success will be measured. Planning for performance should take account of employees' individual abilities, competencies, experience and specific circumstances. For instance, is the employee new on the job or does he or she have any physical disability that makes him or her less mobile or less capable of responding promptly to the needs of internal and external clients? Planning must include the provision of the resources that are required for optimal performance. Planning for performance is a leadership role for which managers are accountable.

Performance objectives are necessary because they define the results that are expected from employees within a given timeframe and provide them with direction and focus on their jobs. Objectives also provide an empirical basis for measuring employees' performance, their contributions to the achievement of corporate or divisional objectives, and for differentiating them on the basis of their individual performance during a given period. Performance objectives are not meaningful if they are not stretching, measurable, attainable, realistic and time-bound (SMART). A typical example of an objective is: 'By 31 December 2009 achieve a sales turnover of $5 million.' Setting quantitative performance objectives is problematic for some managers and even draws the ire of others who argue that, despite the importance and usefulness of SMART objectives, they should not be applicable in service organizations. Their argument is predicated on the assumption that services cannot be measured. They often ask: 'How do you measure the performance of an accountant or a human resource manager?' However, performance objectives for services can be measured in qualitative terms.

The claim that objectives cannot be set for service-oriented jobs implies that their output cannot be determined and that there is no way in which organizations can determine the effectiveness and efficiency of the incumbents. Where objectives are not set, it is tempting for organizations to merely state the activities that should be performed by an individual during the year and thus avoid the rigour of providing an objective basis for measuring employee performance. What cannot be measured certainly cannot be improved. There are performance indicators or metrics for every job – they are either quantitative or qualitative. They vary from job to job, but generally include quality of product or service, quantity, timeliness, cost-effectiveness, customer satisfaction, accuracy, market share, net income, sales volume and so on. It is true that measurement may be easier in some jobs than in others, but that does not vitiate the fact that objectives and performance indicators can be set for each job.

Performance objectives should meet all, not some, of the criteria for SMART objectives because each criterion plays a role in enhancing performance. 'Stretching' means: providing a task or project that challenges the skill, knowledge, intellect, and creative and innovative potential of employees. When a job is 'measurable', it is susceptible to improvement, and employees can move from good to excellent performance. If an objective is too easily 'attainable', employees may not experience a great feeling of achievement. By the same token if it is too difficult to achieve, it is not 'realistic' and therefore becomes a source of frustration and stress. Finally, objectives have to be achieved within a certain 'timeframe'; otherwise, organizations cannot meet their commitment to stakeholders. Setting objectives is the first significant step towards the optimal utilization of talent.

Ideally, an employee should not have more than six objectives during the review year. All objectives may not have the same weight in terms of importance and contribution to the overall goal of the department or division. Objectives are not static because both the organization and its environment are dynamic and continually changing. As the business environment changes, the organization's business plan is likely to change. Since individual objectives are directly or indirectly linked to the business plan, any change in the business plan impacts on the objectives of individual employees. Objectives are therefore intended to be flexible and responsive to changing conditions.

Objective-setting is usually a joint activity between managers and subordinates. Unfortunately, few managers actually adopt this approach and, instead, tend to unilaterally determine what their subordinates must do. Experience shows that when employees have the opportunity to participate in jointly setting their annual performance objectives with their managers, they usually tend to set objectives that are more stretching than those that their supervisors would have normally imposed on them. When objectives are mutually agreed, it is like entering into a compact. The great advantage of a compact is that employees are driven by a sense of honour, commitment and accountability to live up to their word. Joint objective-setting sends strong signals to employees that managers recognize their abilities, trust their competencies and commitment and acknowledge that they have a stake in the organization and the right to be involved in matters affecting their job. The way in which managers set performance objectives reflects their talent mindset.

Joint objective-setting is one aspect of performance planning. The other is the provision of operational resources for the accomplishment of the objectives. Resources include people, money, time, office space and authority. Of these resources, the authority to carry out responsibilities is so highly valued that some managers make a fetish of it because, by definition, it is legitimate position power. It can be in short supply if it is hoarded, jealously guarded and used for turf protection. Yet, this resource is so critical for achieving results that, without it, employees' performance is seriously limited because they are unable to make on-the-spot decisions and respond effectively and in a timely manner to the needs and wants of customers. The achievement of great results by talent then becomes a mirage. Granting authority means empowering people, effectively utilizing them and growing them to become tomorrow's leaders. Employees grow if they have the opportunity to learn, and they learn better if empowered to experiment, take risks, and sometimes make mistakes and learn from them.

Without standards, individual performances cannot be easily differentiated, and managers will be unable to determine outstanding, average and mediocre performers. Typically, organizations use performance standards such as the following for evaluating the level of performance of employees:

- *Exceptional performance*. The employee's performance exceeds set targets or expectations in all respects; the performance is excellent or outstanding.

- *Superior performance.* The employee's performance exceeds expectations in most respects, especially in critical objectives.
- *Solid performance.* The employee meets performance expectations.
- *Minimally satisfactory performance.* The employee does not meet most of the performance expectations and needs to improve.
- *Unsatisfactory performance.* The employee does not meet minimum performance expectations.

Communication and Feedback as a Managerial Imperative

Effective utilization of talent cannot be achieved without effective two-way communication. Managers and their teams cannot operate in silos. The way in which leaders communicate can inspire employees into extraordinary performance or completely destroy their morale. It is not enough to set objectives with subordinates and provide necessary resources. Managers' sensitivity and ability to quickly identify a problem before it escalates into a crisis are important to performance management. Managers need to know that, in managing performance, they are managing not only jobs, but also whole individuals – their fears, concerns, values, interests, aspirations and drives. One of the reasons why managers fail in managing performance is because they pay attention to one and neglect the other. Both are organically bound together, and communication is critical to managing them.

Regular feedback is a two-way communication that helps employees understand how well they are doing and how effective and acceptable their behaviour has been. It also enables employees to inform managers about their individual aspirations, difficulties, working relationships with colleagues and how best the manager could assist them to be more effective. Feedback is a continuous process and is important to the performance of talent because it keeps the channels of communication between them and their supervisors open throughout the year. It banishes the element of surprise at the annual performance evaluation and, more importantly, provides an opportunity for the early detection of barriers to performance and individual inadequacy before they degenerate into a performance crisis. Monitoring and feedback create a culture in which the periodic review of performance is accepted as part of the normal process of managing talent. As Welch (2005) aptly noted, employees cannot achieve better performance if managers do not provide candid and consistent feedback through a system that is characterized by integrity.

Unfortunately, in many organizations feedback is generally lacking and the usual reason is that managers are challenged for time. In many cases, communication begins and stops with objective-setting. It only occurs again when mistakes have been made or the manager needs to issue further instructions. Feedback does not always have to take the form of a formal review. A brief meeting at the end of the week or after an incident with a view to reviewing performance and lessons learnt are forms of informal feedback. When necessary, it could be documented to ensure that there is no controversy when managers make any reference to a particular event during the annual performance appraisal. However, documentation should not degenerate into record-keeping of minute daily events and it should also record great achievements.

Without regular feedback between both parties, managers are ill-informed about the difficulties or challenges faced by subordinates, the kind of assistance they need and even what great competencies they possess that are not being tapped in the current assignment. Equally, subordinates are unaware of the supervisor's expectations and of how well they are doing. Sometimes, it is only during the annual performance evaluation meeting that employees hear for the first time, of a weakness that the supervisor noticed but never mentioned to them throughout the whole review period. I was at a review committee meeting when a line manager stated that his direct report conceptualized his ideas in his native language and translated them mentally into English. The employee's writing skills consequently posed such a challenge to the supervisor that he had on several occasions rewritten feasibility and other reports that were prepared by the subordinate. In tears, the appraisee screamed in frustration: 'You have never, never told me of this, have you?' Such surprises are symptomatic of a lack of candid two-way communication and they tend to destroy mutual trust and instil lasting suspicion.

Managers' failure to provide employees with regular feedback could be due to several factors, including: lack of skills to enact this role; procrastination owing to overwork; a desire to avoid confrontation; inability to recognize the importance of feedback; or a deliberate attempt to assemble enough evidence or alibi to settle a score at the end of the year. Whatever the reason, failure to provide continuous feedback is unhelpful to both parties because, on the one hand, employees live in ignorance and therefore are unable to make necessary changes in behaviour and, on the other hand, their supervisors persistently agonize over the difficulty and frustration caused by their employees' weaknesses.

Managers need to provide feedback as soon as the activity takes place because proper timing enhances its benefit. Feedback has to be specific and based on actual results or observed behaviour and not on vague generalizations. Managers need to limit it to important matters which have a bearing on behaviour and performance and should not focus on every little event, as that would amount to micro-management. Like any other human activity, too much feedback destroys its value. Feedback is more effective when it is not judgemental but presented in the form of a description of an actual occurrence. All feedback is an opportunity to assist and support employees in doing better; it should not destroy their morale by focusing on mistakes and giving only negative and damaging criticisms. In addition, it should be restricted to issues over which employees have control and on which they are capable of improving. Feedback becomes counterproductive if it is limited to criticisms or areas of improvement alone; instead, it should also focus on what employees have done well and which must be sustained. It must aim at encouraging them, boosting their self-confidence and inspiring them to greater achievements.

Finally, managers cannot provide feedback and build trust if they work in a silo. A silo is built out of concrete material and is airtight and tall; it has no windows, and vents, and so communication between a silo and the environment is more than a challenge. Because it is airtight, it is also capable of exploding. Sometimes managers witness such explosions during performance evaluation discussions when employees react violently to the fact that they have a weakness that has never been mentioned to them throughout the performance review period. They are learning about it for the first time because the manager has been operating in a silo. Communication has to be free, candid, frequent and, above all, conducted with mutual respect to have meaning and create trust. As feedback is a two-way interaction and communication, managers must seek feedback from employees if they do not come on their own initiative to express their views, concerns and ideas. However, employees cannot give feedback in a culture characterized by intimidation and threat of sanctions – a culture in which managers want to hear only good news or do not want subordinates to disagree with their views. In such a culture the natural tendency is to tell managers only what they would love to hear, even if it is misleading and untrue.

Coaching: Improving the Performance of Talent

One of the skills managers must possess to be able to effectively manage people and get the best out of them is that of coaching. Coaching equips individuals with the skills and knowledge they need to perform the current task better or to provide leadership at a higher-level position. Managers and executives have diverse opportunities each day to coach their direct reports, but sometimes fail to identify these occasions because of their mindset. Many managers take the view that it is not their responsibility to train or coach employees and that if employees do not have what it takes to do their jobs, they ought to look for other jobs elsewhere. Every individual in an organization has a learning curve; it is coaching that accelerates the process and ensures easy mastery of the job. As with mentoring, most managers recognize the importance of coaching, yet very few find adequate time to coach their subordinates. The usual reason is lack of time – too many meetings, deadlines and so forth. But lack of time is not the only barrier to coaching. Many managers do not have the skill and feel uncomfortable about taking on a responsibility for which they feel ill-equipped. Furthermore, those who have never benefited from coaching may find it hard to comprehend its value or appreciate what the organization loses when managers fail in their responsibility to coach their reports.

Coaching is about learning – thinking, reflecting and behaving differently. It consists of a structured interaction in which the coach does not exercise any formal authority, but operates as a partner seeking to assist a subordinate or peer in overcoming a performance problem. Unlike training, coaching takes place within the work environment and deals with real issues that are directly related to the performance, interpersonal relations, productivity and job satisfaction of individuals or teams. It is therefore practical, problem-oriented and focused on change in skills and behaviour. Although coaching focuses on the individual or team, it has enormous multiplier effects on the organization. For instance, when a manager improves his leadership capability as a result of coaching, the improvement immediately impacts on subordinates and peers and, ultimately, on the team's performance. Coaching provides an opportunity for more frequent communication and feedback between supervisors and their teams, accelerates the development of high-potential managers and enhances the retention of valued talent.

With rapid changes in technology and the business environment, jobs are becoming increasingly complex. Employees consequently face greater challenges than ever, and coaching has proved to be a potent instrument for coping with those challenges. The following are examples of situations that call for coaching:

- A new employee in an organization does not understand procurement procedures, operations procedures, values, business ethics or certain practices that are not documented. Coaching will be helpful.

- An executive has just been posted to another country on an international assignment. Coaching can be used to ensure a seamless transition and success in the new business and cultural terrain. He needs to understand the culture of the host country, the way of doing business and how to establish relationships with customers, suppliers and government functionaries.

- A newly promoted manager continues to behave like the shop-floor supervisor, a sales supervisor or a quality control technologist that he has been for several years. He has to be coached to make the transition from a supervisory to a managerial/leadership role. Being a manager and leader of people requires a different mindset – a different approach to work – to ensure that results are achieved.

- Sometimes a manager has a maverick in his or her team – a talented individual who is versatile and smart, with high potential and performance. Unfortunately, he or she is arrogant and disrespectful, treats other team members with disdain and displays impatience and occasional temper tantrums in interactions with clients and colleagues. Coaching is necessary to integrate the individual into the team.

- An executive with high potential and incredible performance has been promoted to chief operating officer in a plant or a division that has experienced declining performance. Coaching could be required to help the new executive make significant changes in the plant's operations.

The above list is not exhaustive, but it does suggest the numerous and diverse situations that call for coaching and which managers and executives cannot fail to recognize if they change their paradigm. Situations such as those identified above affect performance in an unproductive way. Therefore, the first step in coaching is to discover or identify a problem. No problem, however, can be effectively resolved if its cause is uncertain or unknown. Care must be taken to ensure that managers focus on behaviour rather than on personality. Supervisors' have a duty not to seek to change employees' personalities. Employees want to be accepted the way they are. Because of the power disequilibrium between supervisors and their reports, it is not unusual for managers to inform an employee of the problem they have identified, decide unilaterally that change is inevitable and present a proposal of actions that both the employee and the managers have to take in order to change the existing situation. This approach is doomed to failure from the outset, because it is paternalistic and demonstrates lack of respect and regard for the employee's views and commitment. The solution to a behavioural problem cannot be imposed; it requires ownership and commitment.

The process of coaching an employee may initially be fraught with difficulties for a number of reasons. The employee may be defensive and attribute his behaviour or poor performance to the supervisor's leadership style, the uncooperative attitude of his team or factors beyond his control. He may refuse to take responsibility for his failures. He could even be suspicious of the motive behind the supervisor's initiative and therefore deny the existence of a problem or refuse to state the actual cause of the problem if he accepts that one exists. Any of these situations will pose a huge challenge to managers. These defensive mechanisms or rationalizations may be due to fear of, and lack of trust in, the supervisor. Coaching thrives in a nurturing, trusting, non-dictatorial and non-intimidating climate.

First, managers have to demonstrate genuine interest in the performance and career development of talent. Second, they should seek to build mutual trust so that their reports can be open and transparent. Third, they should seek to define the existence of a problem which is hurting the performance of both parties at a meeting with the employee. For instance, the manager could say, 'I have noticed that in the past month you have missed three agreed deadlines.' This is a fact; it is incontrovertible because the deadlines were agreed upon and presumably documented. The manager should not express any judgement about the failure to meet the deadlines; instead, he should highlight the negative effect of the failure on the business by saying, for instance, 'The monthly report could not be delivered to the Central Bank as scheduled and our bank was penalized for it.' This statement demonstrates the gravity of the failure to meet the deadline. Any attempt to apportion blame may result in defensiveness or cause the employee to switch off. Then the manager should ask the employee about what he thought was the cause of the failure to meet the deadline and also add, 'Is there anything I can personally do to accelerate early delivery of the report in future?' The question is likely to create some relief, and the employee will be inclined to offer explanations about the cause of his failure. The manager should then examine this cause with the employee carefully and empathetically. The objective is to prevent future failures and not necessarily to penalize the employee.

The next step is to search for possible solutions to the problem. The employee should be encouraged to take the lead in proposing realistic measures for eliminating the barriers confronting him. This is to ensure his commitment to, and ownership of, the implementation of whatever measures may be agreed upon. Where the employee is unable to propose a solution, the manager should propose options for him to choose from. A solution is the state desired in the future, and this should be clearly defined in terms of quality, quantity, accuracy and timeframe. The employee should be asked to develop the plan, which must be agreed by both parties. It must be realistic, achievable, time-bound and challenging. The action plan essentially defines the results to be achieved, and when and how they would be measured. It must also be made clear and agreed that the employee is responsible for taking the action that will bring about the desired result and that he will be held accountable for the result. The supervisor will be held accountable for providing the guidance, resources and learning needed by the employee.

An action plan is only effective if it is followed through by the coach. While the employee is accountable for achieving a change in behaviour, the coach is accountable for ensuring that the plan is implemented as agreed. The plan should have milestones for determining what progress has been made along the journey. Periodic review of the status of change is imperative. Coaching is terminated when the employee has mastered the required skill or eliminated the behaviour that negatively affects his performance.

The coaching process can be summarized in the following seven key elements provided by Larson and Richburg (2004: 311):

- *Context*. The coach must understand the organization's business environment, culture and competitive demands to be able to provide the kind of guidance and support needed by the employee.

- *Clarity.* Objectives, expectations for change and coaching process are clearly defined to avoid ambiguity, confusion and disagreement.

- *Commitment.* The coach and the individual to be coached are committed to producing change.

- *Coachability.* The performance challenge and the employee it affects must be seen to be amenable to coaching. Not all performance issues can be dealt with through coaching.

- *Courses of action.* The coach and the employee agree on an action plan with clearly stated objectives and realistic strategies for making the employee more effective.

- *Confidentiality.* This is critical for building mutual trust.

- *Chemistry.* Compatibility between the coach and the employee is essential for a successful relationship.

The effectiveness of coaching depends largely on trust, the coach's communication skills and the commitment of both the coach and the employee. Trust depends on the extent to which the coach is esteemed for his or her technical competence, integrity, leadership capability and genuine interest in the career advancement of his or her subordinates. Daily interpersonal relations with the team have to be strong and not characterized by intermittent conflicts and rivalries.

The employee also needs to have the motivation to participate in coaching. Motivation is a function of not only what the employee hopes to gain from it, but also the timing of the process and the positive attitude of the coach. Coaching is about communication and professional support to improve performance. What the supervisor says daily at work and during coaching is just as important as how he says it, both in words and in body language. The employee may be enthralled by the prospect of learning new skills and by the apparent commitment of the supervisor, but paternalistic and condescending behaviours could smother the employee's enthusiasm to learn. He deserves to be listened to because he has the right to express his views and even defer in opinion with the coach. Mutual respect and a spirit of partnership are crucial to the business of successful coaching.

Not all performance problems can be resolved through coaching. For instance, an employee who is on drugs or who has just gone through a divorce is an individual in a traumatic situation whose low performance may largely be a function of his or her present circumstances and not due to lack of skills or knowledge of the job. Here, coaching is certainly not the most appropriate remedy. The following section provides guidelines as to what an organization could do in such circumstances.

Counselling: Helping Talent to Be in Control of Their Lives

The causes of poor or low performance are many and varied. Some are job-related whereas others are connected with factors external to the workplace. The problem is that managers rarely delve into the root causes of low performance. Within the workplace, lack of promotion, inability to fit into a team due to racism or ethnic discrimination or a supervisor with incompatible ethical values and leadership style could affect performance. Beyond the confines of the job and workplace there are other factors that can affect performance. They include: drug addiction; alcoholism; death of a spouse, parent, sibling or child; divorce, particularly when the employee was unprepared for break-up; financial distress; debilitating illness, such as cancer or HIV/AIDS, of a family member, poor performance of children at school; and relocation resulting in separation from the family. Unlike job-related factors, these are challenges over which supervisors do not have any control. In fact, they may not know of the existence of some of these problems because they are not informed by the affected employees who may fear that information about such problems may be used against them. Supervisors must have excellent rapport with their subordinates to have the privilege of being entrusted with such personal information.

In Africa, employees who are afflicted by the kind of problems listed above will typically go first to their religious adviser – a pastor, a Catholic priest, an imam or traditional medicine man. The reason is not hard to find; employees are seeking a theological explanation of the cause of their problems. The illness, divorce, poor performance of children and so forth must be the handiwork of some diabolical forces that can only be appeased by some supernatural, divine intervention. The solution is seen to be beyond human wisdom and expertise, and that is the reason why employees may not bother to discuss it with their supervisors. Going to a professional counsellor may be the last resort.

Employees who are mired in personal problems over which they have no control need empathy, not sympathy and least of all a manager's authoritarian advice on 'what to do to save your job or career'. What such employees need is counselling. The purpose of counselling is to help them adjust to changes and be in full control of their life without feeling helpless. Counselling also provides them with a vehicle for implementing their own solutions to the problems (Neale, 1992). It represents the caring and human face of an organization and makes employees feel valued. What can managers do? Besides the fact that managers do not have counselling skills, they may not want to get involved in employees' personal lives. In addition, it is sometimes difficult for them to know where to draw the line between official help and interference in individual privacy, even if they want to help. Finally, managers do not have the time for counselling because they are busy managing one crisis or another.

However, managers can be trained to do basic counselling. It requires creating the right rapport and a confidential environment. The manager's role is to listen patiently, help the employee define the problem and also identify the causes of the present situation without any criticism or apportioning of blame. The manager should lead the employee to generate various solutions. If the solutions are not realistic or practicable, the manager could make suggestions and encourage the employee to evaluate the feasibility of each solution before making a choice. Milestones for periodic evaluation of progress are then jointly agreed. Finally, the manager monitors and evaluates progress jointly with the employee until a stable condition is attained and the employee is fully in control of his or her life again.

Depending on the severity of the situation and the attitude of the employee, an external counsellor could be retained by an organization to provide necessary assistance. Employees may feel more at ease with an external counsellor than with an internal manager or human resource specialist. Organizations should also take account of cultural sensitivity. For instance, in Africa few employees would want to visit a psychiatrist, as such visits carry a social stigma. The general, though erroneous, belief is that only 'mad' people need a psychiatrist. However, such views are changing. Some multinational corporations provide counselling services through psychologists and psychiatrists as an integral part of their healthcare system. Like relationships with doctors, discussions with the psychologists and psychiatrists and therapy are treated with confidentiality. While the use of such services may not be mandatory, organizations usually insist that those who are in need of help but refuse to take it, with the result that their problem persists, may not be retained any longer.

The Performance Appraisal

Performance appraisal is the annual review or evaluation of the employees' performance. It is the culmination of the foregoing processes in performance management, beginning with performance planning. A formal performance review encourages a systematic, joint stock-taking and planning for the future. It does not merely summarize the past; it helps determine future performance. During the course of the day-to-day work, managers ideally give informal feedback to their employees regarding their performance. However, time pressure often limits the value of this informal feedback. Thus, employees have limited opportunities to hold regular and profound discussions with their supervisors. Hence, some organizations, hold a formal mid-year review during which managers and their reports are compelled to meet formally to review the work programme, past performance and any concerns arising during first six months of the year.

Managers and employees don't generally look forward to the performance appraisal because it puts the former in the uncomfortable situation of sitting in judgement, as it were, on their subordinates while the latter have to defend themselves against the 'accusations' of the 'appellant' who is also the 'judge'. Yet, it is crucial to individual performance and organizational effectiveness. The objectives of the performance appraisal are usually as follows:

- Review the performance of the past year with a view to identifying factors that have enhanced or militated against performance. Consequently, an action plan can be agreed between both parties to sustain facilitating factors and also to reduce or completely eliminate blockages to performance.

- Review the employee's training and development needs with a view to implementing appropriate programmes to enhance career advancement in the organization.

- Agree on the work programmes and set objectives and performance indicators for the next review period.

- Reward performance through performance-related pay.

Quite often, managers and their reports become so mired in the controversy of performance rating because it determines merit pay that the whole essence of the review is lost to them. Controversy usually emanates from the different perceptions of the employee's achievement and competencies and differences in perception are due to the following factors:

- mutual distrust during review period
- lack of chemistry between the two parties
- disagreement over objectives and/performance standards agreed during the year under review
- the employee's inability to accept the concept of being considered a 'poor' or 'average' performer
- an element of surprise due to lack of feedback and open communication
- insensitivity of the manager as manifested in his or her choice of words and body language during the discussions
- the employee's unpleasant experience during the previous performance appraisal discussions
- the manager's failure to understand the employee as a whole person – his or her needs, concerns, fears and aspirations.

Other important factors which affect performance review are managers' lack of preparation and lack of skills to conduct a discussion on a highly emotive subject. For instance, if managers do not review the agreed performance targets, gather evidence about their employees` performance during the year to justify their rating and have no documentation on formal feedback sessions during the review period, they cannot conduct a credible performance review. The review will be equally ridiculous and pointless if they do not have ideas or plans on how to assist both the high performers in sustaining performance and underperformers in improving their performance. Managerial gaffes such as these frustrate employees, destroy morale and accelerate their exit from the organization.

AFRICAN WORKERS' PERSPECTIVE OF PERFORMANCE APPRAISAL

It is important to note how societal values stealthily filter into the behaviours of managers and employees, sometimes without their awareness. For instance, the average African worker does not believe that his performance is a function of only his ability, resources, motivation and work environment. Other factors in his radar screen, which may not be mentioned officially, include supernatural forces over which he has no control. They are generally God, witches/wizards and gods of his village. An African is generally modest in stating his achievement; but modesty alone does not explain the reason why he begins the story of his success or performance by attribution to God. Just as he attributes his success to some supernatural powers, he also believes that his failure should not be attributed solely to his inability but rather to the transcendental forces that invisibly manipulate and mangle all his efforts to achieve great performance. It is humorously referred to as 'home trouble' in Nigeria.

Rewarding Talent for Performance and Contribution

Differentiation through performance appraisal is necessary for determining who to reward and for what level of performance and contributions. Reward generally takes the form of a pay increase. Pay is one of the most important reasons why people work for organizations. Because of its importance, it has the power to influence employees' behaviour and performance. If properly administered, it can affect productivity, quality of work and most importantly, retention.

PERFORMANCE-RELATED PAY

If you ask managers and employees what they consider to be the main purpose of performance appraisal, most of them would probably say that it is to provide a basis for a salary increase or a bonus as a reward for their previous year's performance or achievement. This is so central to the way in which employees perceive performance management that the appraisal is almost meaningless if it is not linked to pay. In fact, it is one of the most powerful ways by which an organization can communicate how much it values the achievement of an individual or group. Performance-related pay means that employees are rewarded on the basis of differentiation – their level of achievement of the agreed performance objectives.

The implication of performance-related pay is that there is a direct correlation between the performance of employees and the rewards they earn. When an organization provides annual salary increases irrespective of the level of performance of individual employees, such largesse becomes an entitlement. A cardinal value of performance-related pay is that it seeks to eliminate 'entitlement mentality'. Although organizations use merit pay with a view to creating and sustaining a performance-oriented culture, it is a moot question as to whether it actually motivates employees to higher productivity. Motivation is a function of complex factors, the most potent of which could be non-pecuniary. Be that as it may, with performance-related pay, organizations are able to demonstrate that reward is contingent on performance and contribution.

Pay-for-performance programmes may, however, fail for the following reasons:

- All employees essentially receive the same increase regardless of their achievements.
- The differentiation in salary increases is insignificant.
- Employees do not understand the programme and suspect some unfairness in its administration.
- Pay-for-performance programmes are not linked to the organization's strategic business plans.
- Employees do not have a clear understanding of the relationship between their performance and their reward (Loucks, 2006).

The amount of salary increase which an employee receives is a function of the performance rating on a continuum of exceptional to unsatisfactory performance. Usually, employees who have a rating of 'exceptional' performance earn an increase that is higher than those with a lower rating such as 'solid' or 'minimally satisfactory'. Generally, those with an unsatisfactory rating do not earn any increase. Performance rating is a way of differentiating levels of employees' performance because they do not all perform at the same level. Table 6.1 shows the relationship between performance rating and pay increase on the one hand and the relationship between the position on salary grade and percentage pay increase on the other. This is important because, as the table shows, some employees have a 'minimally satisfactory' rating and do not earn any salary increase. The rationale is that they are already earning over and above the reference market and, although they are doing similar or even identical jobs as new employees who are at the minimum point of the grade,

Table 6.1 Merit increase matrix

Position in salary range	Performance rating/percentage pay increase				
	Exceptional	Superior	Solid	Minimally satisfactory	Unsatisfactory
Minimum (80–88%)*	6.0%	4.5%	2.5%	1.5%	Nil
(88–96%)	4.5%	3.5%	2.0%	1.0%	Nil
Midpoint or market reference (96–104%)	3.5%	2.5%	1.5%	0.5%	Nil
(104–112%)	2.5%	1.5%	1.0%	Nil	Nil
Maximum (112–120%)	1.5%	1.0%	0.5%	Nil	Nil

* Percentages indicate the individual employee's point in the salary range. For instance, 80–88% indicates that the salary is very close to the entry point of the salary range, while a location between 111% and 120% indicates proximity to the salary ceiling.

they earn a much higher salary than them. There is thus an inequity in pay that would be perpetuated if the rate of increase were to be the same.

As noted above, performance-related pay has been criticized for different reasons. It is generally believed that the amount of increase is usually so small that it does not sufficiently distinguish between high and low performers. This is true as evidenced by the marginal pay increase between those whose performance is rated 'exceptional' and those whose performance is rated 'solid' in Table 6.1. The difference is 4 per cent, 2 per cent or even 1 per cent in one case. There is a weak causal link between performance rating and the merit increase with the result that this kind of performance-related pay may not send a strong signal to employees about the extent to which their contribution is actually valued. Thus, it is regarded as inequitable. Besides inequity, the paucity of salary increase has low valence and therefore may not meet the expectations of high-performing employees. The risk of low employee engagement and loss of talent thus becomes high. Other forms of performance-related pay include bonus and achievement pay:

- *Bonus pay*. This is a one-off ad hoc payment to employees or teams in recognition of extraordinary performance in terms of either meeting highly challenging goals or exceeding such goals. Bonuses and incentives are not added to basic pay in order to avoid the compounding effects on pension and other benefits usually based on basic pay. It is argued that incentives and bonuses are more effective as motivational tools than the basic pay or even merit pay because the latter is usually small and makes insufficient differentiation between high and low performers.

- *Corporate achievement pay*. Achievement pay essentially recognizes the ultimate impact that employees have made on the organization's bottom line. It is an attempt not only to direct the focus of employees to the ultimate goal of profitability, but also to send a strong message that their final well-being also depends on the financial health and performance of their employer. In addition, it gives employees a sense of ownership because this type of pay takes the form of profit-sharing, stock options and so forth.

The effectiveness of pay-for-performance depends largely on how the organization designs and implements it. Furthermore, it has to be a part of a sound compensation policy that is integrated into a human resource strategy in order to support and reinforce behaviours that are critical to the achievement of corporate goals. A sound compensation policy requires the following:

- A proper analysis and evaluation of jobs, as well as grading of positions. Jobs in any organization do not have the same value or worth because they differ in responsibility, complexity, skill requirements, competencies and criticality to the core business of a firm. Logically, the greater the value of a job the higher is the grade and the pay that is attached to it. A job that requires hot or scarce skills will equally attract higher pay than jobs for which the skills are in abundance.

- A policy based on a philosophy which clearly spells out the organization's commitment to position its compensation at a certain point of its market reference with a view to attracting, hiring, motivating and retaining talent. The purpose of a compensation philosophy is not necessarily to be the highest-paying employer, but rather to ensure external relativity and enable it to effectively compete for talent in the international labour market.

- Salary increases that are strictly linked to the level of individual performance and contribution to organization's objectives.

For a compensation policy to serve as a tool for employee engagement and retention, it must guarantee internal equity and external relativity. Management has the responsibility for communicating it effectively to employees. Sometimes, the perceived inequity in rewards may not be real; it may be due to lack of adequate communication by management. As Trahant (2007) rightly noted, if a compensation package is relatively competitive, better communication can actually be more important as an employee motivator and engagement device than the objective worth of an individual employee's pay and benefits package.

Summary

This chapter has highlighted that it is one thing to hire talent but a completely different thing to obtain optimum value from it. The ability to derive value from talent and also retain it depends on the way in which their performance is managed and rewarded. It is not just the performance or work of the talent that has to be managed, but is the totality of the individual. In the next chapter we examine how talent can be differentiated for the purpose of ensuring that corporate investment is made in the right calibre of people. The chapter also looks at factors that tend to vitiate the validity of differentiation.

7

The Challenge of Differentiating Talent

'All animals are equal but some are more equal than others.'

George Orwell

The above quotation is from George Orwell's (1946) famous satire, *Animal Farm*. The pigs believed that although all animals were equal, but when the importance of each animal's contribution to the community was considered, some animals (the pigs) should be regarded as more equal than the others. It was a clear case of differentiation. A major outcome that should emerge from any performance management is the differentiation of employees according to their performance and potential. All employees and managers can never perform at the same level. Axelrod, Handfield-Jones and Welsh (2001: 9) noted that the best 20 per cent or so of managers raise operational productivity, profit and sales revenue much more than average performers do. In one manufacturing company they found that the best plant managers increased profits by 130 per cent.

Differentiation is inherent in performance management because, by its very nature, it demonstrates that while some employees meet and even exceed the performance standards of their jobs, others do not meet the same standards. Differentiation is the outcome of the evaluation of the workforce; it provides a basis for fair and equitable reward and is also a means of identifying the respective training and development needs of employees. Jack Welch (2005), former CEO of General Electric, was a strong advocate of differentiation. In his book, *Winning*, he explains its importance and admits that it influenced his approach to managing talent.

Although not exactly the same, the underlying principle of differentiation is similar to that of Pareto analysis, a concept developed by a nineteenth-century Italian economist, Vifredo Pareto. He observed that 80 per cent of wealth was owned by 20 per cent of the population. This concept has been applied to quality improvement where it is observed that 80 per cent of customer dissatisfaction stems from 20 per cent of defects. Also, 20 per cent of customers account for 80 per cent of sales. By implication, marketing and sales departments prudently invest more time and resources in meeting the needs of the 'vital few' than meeting those of the 'trivial many'. Client- or customer-focused organizations segment their markets so they can pay greater attention to those clients or customers who contribute significantly to their profitability.

By the same logic, differentiating employees enables an organization to develop the ethos of how to manage people according to their worth. Differentiation is therefore about the prudent manner in which an organization allocates its scarce resources to activities that will bring the highest return on investment. That also includes investment in people. In a competitive environment, such as organizations face in globalization, differentiation is imperative for survival. This is precisely the reason why, in evaluating employees' performance, organizations have to distinguish between star performers, solid performers and underperformers. Without differentiation organizations have no valid basis for determining their most valued employees and for taking necessary actions to ensure their retention. Through differentiation, management is able to determine who gets rewarded and by how much, who gets trained, promoted and groomed for future leadership positions, and also, of course, who has to be shipped out.

How to Differentiate the Workforce

Despite these benefits there are those who believe that differentiation is cruel, susceptible to favouritism and culturally inappropriate. It is also argued that it tends to create unhealthy rivalries among employees. A popular approach to differentiation is forced ranking – essentially, identifying the best performers who are usually in the top 20 per cent of the population, solid performers who constitute about 70 per cent and the remaining 10 per cent who constitute underperformers. This latter category, according to Welch, has to be moved out so that better talent can be brought in.

Welch (2005) defends differentiation by stating that it is based on the principle that the team with the best players wins and that it does not mean 'rank and yank' the poor performers. In fact, the poor performers are given an opportunity to improve and, in some cases, they leave the firm on their own accord.

The limited effectiveness of many performance management systems lies in the failure to make an objective and honest differentiation in the performance of the workforce. Differentiation involves hard decisions. Some employees are more talented and perform much more effectively than others, and so organizations need to invest in them accordingly. Organizations that operate with this ethos are likely to retain their most valued people and are likely to be more successful than those that do not. The parameters for differentiating employees must be objective, clear and transparent. This is important to ensure that the system is not abused by managers, considering the fact that racism, ethnicity, gender, nepotism are real challenges that sometimes force managers into compromising rational decisions.

Whereas performance relates to the achievement of predetermined targets and objectives, potential refers to the high probability that an employee could assume higher leadership responsibility within a given timeframe. Whereas performance is the basis for reward such as merit increase and bonus pay, potential provides the basis for development. The combination of performance and potential parameters produces a clear differentiation between the various categories of employees and, on that basis, management can determine how each category can be effectively managed for the mutual benefit of both organization and employees. The categories that could emerge from the performance/potential matrix are shown in Figure 7.1. With this kind of differentiation, organizations are able to identify the leadership talent they need for sustaining current performance and for leading the business in the future. Furthermore, they are in an advantageous position to determine who to invest in.

Assessing Potential

The Sound of Music is a classic movie in which Maria, a novice nun, is expelled from the convent and sent to an army officer who is a widower. Her job is to help him take care of seven difficult, motherless children. Amazingly, Maria's versatility and creativity are initially lost upon Captain Von Trapp who cannot see the potential of this beautiful and caring lady simply because she does not fit into his military way of thinking and managing his children. At one point he threatens to fire her for having the audacity to think out of the box and also stand up to him – challenging his authority and regimented approach to bringing up his children. All he sees in her is eccentricity and stubbornness. Ironically, Von Trapp's children are more perceptive in recognizing the talent in Maria than their father. When he finally changes his mindset he sees the gem in her and cannot resist taking her for a wife, even at the expense of a rich fiancée.

Like Von Trapp, many managers are unable to see the 'gold mine' or talent in their employees. Some see only the technical competencies and capabilities for the current job and no more. Worse still, others see only the minor deviant behaviours that do not even impact on performance: unconventional mode of dressing, poor timekeeping, lack of docility and the courage to differ in opinion on practices that have no basis or logic. Such managers are thus blinded by these putative 'delinquent' behaviours with the unfortunate consequence that they cannot see the huge potential, core character and competencies of these individuals. The challenge in determining potential could be due to the fact that, by its nature, it is a prediction of another person's success in a job which he or she has never performed. Even the assessor may never have performed the job. The dynamic nature of jobs in a rapidly changing organizational environment further complicates the assessment of potential. Some managers find it threatening to their survival and advancement, while others feel that it will create a culture of unnecessary rivalry that may destroy team solidarity. Nevertheless, potential assessment is critical because it enables an organization to differentiate talent from average or mediocre employees.

According to Berger and Berger (2004), potential assessment consists of the following three mutually-related domains of leadership: how managers set their business agenda; how they take others along; and how they present themselves. Barner (2000: 155–157) offers a methodology consisting of three factors for evaluating executive potential. They are:

- *Learning agility* This consists of the ability to: quickly and skilfully adapt to new work; seek and respond to feedback; perform well under tough conditions; cope with complexity and ambiguity; take a creative approach to problems; and seek new learning experiences. Learning agility is an indicator of an individual's ability to grow and advance in his or her function.

- *Scope of competencies*. This refers to the possession of a broad range of leadership and technical competencies that will enable the individual to advance within his or her current function.

- Time required to advance. This is the amount of developmental support an employee would require to advance two or more levels within the next five years.

Based on potential and performance indicators, a matrix (Figure 7.1) showing the potential of each manager can be developed.

	HIGH FLIERS High Potential/High Performance	**SOLID PERFORMERS** Low Potential/High Performance
Performance	**PROMISING TALENT** High Potential/Low Performance	**UNDERPERFORMERS** Low Potential/Low Performance
	Estimated Potential	

Figure 7.1 Performance/potential matrix

LOW PERFORMANCE/LOW POTENTIAL

Employees in this category need to be managed out because their contribution is less than the organization's investment in them. They do not produce enough, as it were, to attain break-even point. However, such employees should be terminated only after training and coaching have failed to produce any positive results. About 5–10 per cent of the workforce population falls into this category. Coaching should be provided with the aim of helping the employees do what they cannot do or what they are not doing well. Regular feedback should be an essential component of the coaching strategy.

LOW POTENTIAL/HIGH PERFORMANCE

Employees in this category have generally achieved a career plateau and therefore have very limited chances of being promoted to higher-level positions. Promotion to a higher level may result in incompetence; the Peter Principle would then come into operation. Generally, these employees are unable to cope with the challenges and requirements of a higher leadership position, but need to be given interesting jobs to maintain good performance in their present position. A lateral move could also enhance their motivation. This category of employees constitutes the bedrock of organizational performance because they are solid performers. About 70–75 per cent of the workforce belongs to this group. With training and development, a small percentage of the people in the category may rise one level above their current position. There is also the possibility that a small percentage may also fall into the category of underperformers. Employees in this category should be sent on training programmes aimed at sustaining their solid performance in their current jobs. Because of their strong technical competencies they should be allocated to projects that resonate with their development needs, such as learning to work as team leaders or managing a project.

HIGH POTENTIAL/LOW PERFORMANCE

As in all cases of low performance, the cause must be identified by the supervisor. The cause could be any of the following: wrong job placement, uncooperative team members, lack of pertinent experience, lack of proper guidance and supervision, and newness on the job or in the organization. Individuals in this category may not be immediately ready for leadership positions, but they are worth saving because they could be tomorrow's superstars or 'high fliers'. They are likely to rise above their current position because of their high potential. If not properly managed, they could leave the organization for a more conducive environment where they could become high fliers. Their performance could be enhanced through appropriate job placement, coaching, job redesign, mentorship and change in the work environment. They usually constitute less than 5 per cent of the workforce.

HIGH POTENTIAL/HIGH PERFORMANCE

About 15 per cent of the workforce falls into this top-performing category. They are superstars, high-fliers, and consistently outperform their counterparts. They have helicopter qualities: self-starting, highly motivated, and full of energy and initiative. They could rise about two, three or more levels above their current position because they have high learning agility and a broad range of both technical and leadership competencies. They need a plan for development and advancement. They are also high-risk talent that can be poached by competitors – which is precisely why efforts must be made to invest in and retain them.

Such employees need to participate in executive development programmes to enable them to acquire important perspectives in financial management, marketing, corporate strategy and environmental factors that affect the firm's business. This kind of training is particularly essential for those who do not hold MBA or management degrees. As they have high learning agility and broad technical and leadership competencies, their development should include an international assignment or a highly challenging cross-function project such as starting a new division, turning around a troubled division or managing an organizational change project. They will benefit from important and high-profile projects. Participation in a project is a form of action learning. Participation does not necessarily emphasize results, but rather the lessons learnt in gaining an insight into the types of challenge facing the organization, in working or leading a team, and in gaining self-awareness.

Sources of Subjectivity in Assessment

Differentiation is based on the following fundamental assumptions:

- that those who assess performance and potential clearly understand what the parameters stand for;
- that managers are responsible individuals who will usually and strictly comply with the organization's laid-down principles of fairness, objectivity and honesty when evaluating the performance of their work teams, even though, by its very nature, performance appraisal is subjective.

However, as this section shows, assessment conducted by managers is sometimes compromised for various reasons. I have met managers who recounted how they had, on occasions, inflated or deflated their subordinates' performance ratings for a variety of reasons, ranging from a desire to maximize subordinates' merit increase, avoid confrontation and facilitate the promotion of a good subordinate to a commitment to save a loyal subordinate's career or accelerate the exit of a problem team member. What was evident is that managers justify their inflated or deflated ratings of subordinates by a selective choice of events, behaviours, successes and failures that constitute an alibi serving to validate and legitimize their decisions. In other words, managers sometimes make a deliberate attempt to distort the facts for self-serving purposes. Performance evaluation is therefore plagued by a number of pathologies which not only destroy its objectivity and credibility, but also compromise it as an instrument for differentiating talent from non-talent. Common sources of subjectivity include the following.

CENTRAL TENDENCY

Central tendency is used in performance evaluation as a practice whereby supervisors concentrate their performance rating scores at the midpoint of the scale, usually at the average score, regardless of the differences in employees' performance. This approach is usually adopted by managers who want to avoid confrontation. Central tendency defeats the purpose of differentiation and puts at risk management's ability to reward and develop talent equitably.

HALO/HORNS EFFECT

The halo effect is a cognitive bias whereby supervisors tend to carry over the great impression they have about one aspect of an employee's performance to other aspects of his or her performance. It is a kind of managerial delusion that is not based on any empirical facts. Thus, if an employee has strong analytical ability, the manager assumes that he or she is also a good communicator, decision-maker and team leader. Of course, this may not be true. The horns effect is also a cognitive bias and the opposite of the halo effect. Managers assume that an employee who is weak in a particular competency must be weak in other competencies. Thus, a temperamental person is assumed to be uncooperative, inefficient and deficient in communication skills and team leadership. Again, these assumptions may not be correct because they are not based on any factual data. In both cases, the outcome of the differentiation is not valid because the actual strengths and weaknesses of the employee have not been correctly assessed.

LENIENCY/INCONSISTENT EVALUATION

Some managers are mean in the way in which they rate employees' performance while others dole out high ratings to employees like Father Christmas. A study conducted by Personnel Decisions International found that employees who were rated outstanding by one manager were rated lower by other managers 62 per cent of the time (Sammer, 2008).

PERSONAL BIAS AND CHARACTERISTICS

Studies show that physically attractive people are evaluated more positively than are unattractive people (Ugwuegbu, 2001). Sex-role stereotypes held by managers also influence the way in which they rate performance. Result- or task-oriented supervisors tend to be less lenient in their performance rating scores than people- or relationship-oriented supervisors.

SOCIO-CULTURAL FACTORS

In Africa there are additional pathologies: namely, ethnicism, religion, racism, language and nationality. Ugwuegbe (2001: 207) noted that managers with greater social distances from their workers 'tend to evaluate employees who are different from ethnic groups more negatively than employees from the same ethnic group'. Writing on human resource management practices in the Ivory Coast, Beugré (2004) noted that managers tend to positively evaluate the performance of employees who are their protégés, while Aryee (2004) noted that, in Ghana, cultural norms influence the process and outcome of performance assessment. Kamoche *et al.* (2004) noted that, in Kenya, appraisals in organizations are sometimes manipulated by supervisors in order to pursue a personal vendetta against appraisees and that employees who belonged to the same ethnic group as the manager could expect to have a good performance assessment. They also noted that the high level of job insecurity, unemployment, as well as the socio-cultural and economic context, put pressure on managers and compelled them to grant favours, even though they presented a veneer of fairness and objectivity.

These pathologies are universal – they are found in virtually every country and organization irrespective of size, industry and ownership. They are not peculiar to any culture, and their consequences can be far-reaching. First, talent is not correctly differentiated on the basis of performance and potential. Second, top management is misled into making wrong decisions on reward and development because the information available to them is inaccurate and distorted. They may never have a way of knowing the truth because managers justify their unfair and subjective evaluation by selectively choosing events, incidents and documentation to support their seemingly rational and objective assessment. Finally, unfair and inequitable evaluation of performance may result in employee disengagement and the loss of talent.

A fundamental question is: why do apparently responsible managers sometimes misrepresent the performance of their subordinates to top management? Do managers recognize the harm they do to their organizations and the careers of highly valued talent when they appraise their performance unfairly and subjectively? It all has to do with personal values and socio-cultural influence. In a work environment there are different webs of relationships. Some are ethnic, religious and professional while others are political, and, in a typical African society, they impose on a manager the obligation to be his 'brother's and sister's keeper'. For instance, how can a manager give an employee from his village a performance rating that would harm his or her career? How can he rate as 'unsatisfactory' the performance of his 'Christian sister' who worships with him in the same church? These are individuals whose interests he is socially expected to protect! Socio-cultural relationships are never dropped at the gates of the organization. They intrude and impact imperceptibly on the emotions and decisions of managers.

Managing the Imperfections of Performance Management

Subjectivity and unfairness have led to loss of confidence in performance management in many organizations. Employees have made many scathing criticisms of performance management. These include:

- its subjectivity and unfairness due to non-job related influences;
- its failure to improve the future performance of employees;
- its inability to reward high performers significantly, even though it is compensation-oriented;
- its failure to enhance the growth and development of employees;
- its failure as a tool for effective succession planning;
- its inequitable distribution of rewards; and
- its poor integration with other human resource systems.

These criticisms call into question the extent to which performance management can be used to differentiate talent. An intervention to make performance management credible could be two-dimensional. The first should consist of a fundamental approach that treats performance management as an organizational development intervention. This means doing first things first by adopting a change management methodology in the installation and operation of performance management. The second dimension is what we refer to as 'control mechanism'.

FIRST THINGS FIRST

The limited effectiveness of performance management is often due to the fact that first things were not done first. Quite often organizations seek to achieve effectiveness by fine-tuning, revamping or installing a new performance management system. Any such intervention is like motion without progress because it misses the point. Performance management systems can be made effective if managers take into consideration the preconditions for success described below.

Define and communicate your vision Every organization has a reason for its existence – its mission. But not all organizations have a vision. A vision consists of not only what the organization stands for – its mandate, its identity – but also its dream – where it hopes to position itself in the global market in the future. A vision also describes the values by which an organization intends to conduct business with its customers, suppliers, employees and the larger society. It provides a framework for developing corporate strategy and culture. Within this framework, performance management can be used as an effective tool for driving the strategy and culture of the organization to achieve effectiveness. The importance of a vision is that, if vigorously and consistently communicated to all levels of employees, it can propel the workforce to high performance. The core values of an organization are embedded in its vision. These core values – such as creativity, risk-taking and tolerance of failure, empowerment, optimizing opportunities to use talent, individual growth and development, and teamwork – enhance an organization's ability to institutionalize its unique way of doing business. When performance management is aligned to the values of the vision, it has a high probability of success, provided that both management and employees understand and own the vision.

Focus on people, not on systems Most literature on performance management describes it as a process of setting performance objectives, monitoring, giving feedback, coaching and, finally, evaluating performance. The impression is that if a performance management system is well designed (aligned with corporate strategy) and sufficient training is provided to the operators, success is almost guaranteed. Strategy, structure and system are important and, in fact, necessary for the effective implementation of performance management, but they do not guarantee change in behaviour or in the organization's culture. Many organizational interventions that were once promising have failed in the past because of the neglect of the human side of managing change. A typical example is total quality management (TQM).

TQM was regarded by many as the bastion of the Japanese miracle in the 1980s. In its original conception people were the centrepiece. But as TQM gained universal acclaim for its effectiveness, there was a gradual shift of emphasis by firms in Europe and America from people to ISO 9000 and BS 5750. And that was the beginning of the decline in the effectiveness of TQM. Performance evaluation has suffered the same fate in many firms. People make organizations effective; yet in the design of performance appraisal there is more emphasis on how the system is designed – the structure, the evaluation forms, rating scales, evaluation methods, performance standards and legal requirements – than on the people who will appraise and be appraised with the system. Although structure, system and standards should not be ignored, people need to be at the centre of the change process.

Demonstrate ownership Some years ago, a multinational corporation redesigned its performance management system. A top-notch consultant in human resources designed and installed the new system. All managers were trained for one day, while other employees were briefed for a couple of hours about the new system. During the first year of its implementation, top management noted with disappointment that managers still evaluated performance the way they did in the past. Some were extremely lenient in their performance rating; others did not even hold any appraisal discussions with their subordinates; and yet others did not pay any attention to the training and development needs of their reports during the appraisal discussions.

What the top management of the firm did not understand was that middle managers did not own the new system. The management was also oblivious of the fact that changing human behaviour takes time, and people always initially resist change. In the past, managers had the autonomy to rate the performance of their subordinates strictly against agreed objectives. They were not required to compare the performances of their subordinates with those of their colleagues on the same pay grade or in other departments. They were not amused by the restriction imposed by the new system, which introduced forced ranking. Managers considered forced ranking an unfair system that would destroy teamwork because it could create unhealthy rivalry.

Have a talent mindset For performance appraisal to be effective, all levels of management must have a mindset that accepts talent management as their responsibility. A talent mindset is based on the philosophy that:

- organizational effectiveness is a corporate responsibility, and all employees are capable of contributing to it if they are provided with an enabling environment;
- attracting, hiring, training, motivating and developing talent to achieve their potential and organizational goals are the most critical responsibility and legacy of any manager;
- employees have a reservoir of relevant knowledge, skills and competencies which can be tapped through their involvement, reward and recognition; and
- effective engagement and retention of talent are not fortuitous – managers have to eliminate all toxic practices that can push talent out through the gate to competitors.

Have an integrated human resource management system Are you puzzled by the fact that when managers resign or retire, it takes a firm so many months to find a replacement and usually from the outside through a recruitment process? Yet there may be capable people within the same organization who can do the job. The answer to this question lies in the lack of integration of the performance appraisal system into other human resource management systems, such as training, development, promotion and succession-planning systems. The only system that is commonly linked to performance appraisal is the reward system. Performance appraisal is at the heart of other HR systems because it generates data for decision-making in those systems. It highlights the training and development needs of individual employees, reveals employees with great potential who need to be groomed for future leadership positions, validates previous hiring, provides a basis for merit pay and provides data for succession planning and for determining who is fit or unfit to remain in the organization.

Build trust Many well-designed performance appraisal systems have been ineffective owing to the fact that employees did not trust their managers. Trust means confidence or lack of suspicion. It is a function of two things: character and competence. Character consists of integrity, motive and intent with people. Competence includes capabilities, skills, and results – your track record. And both are equally important (Covey, 2006). No matter how competent managers may be, employees can never trust them if they do not have integrity or 'walk the talk'. Integrity is about honesty; it is about character. The inability of employees to trust their managers to be objective and fair is borne out by daily experience. For instance, who is put on an important project or who accompanies the manager on frequent business missions?

Opinions about managers are formed from daily activities that appear miniscule and of no significance to managers, but they are of great importance to those who feel disadvantaged. Covey puts it succinctly: 'It's the little things – a day at a time, a weak or dishonest act at a time – that gradually weaken and corrode credibility' (2006: 47). The best designed performance appraisal system will achieve only limited success if there is no mutual trust because the credibility of the main operators is at stake. Therefore, the first thing is for managers to build trust. It is a leadership responsibility. A trusted army general easily mobilizes and effectively engages the troops because they believe in his ability, judgement, skills, leadership and integrity.

Ensure corporate culture fit Business process re-engineering (BPR) was intended to be an effective tool for business and organizational improvement. It failed. Want's argument against BPR is that, by itself, it was not a bad programme, but its implementation tended to ignore existing organizational cultures (Want, 2006). One of the reasons why performance management systems are less effective than required is because of corporate cultural misfit. An off-the-shelf system cannot work. It must be tailor-made. Corporate cultures that value people, individual autonomy, risk-taking, tolerance of failure, continuous improvement, teamwork, trust, individual growth and development provide an enabling ambience in which a performance management system can thrive. This is because the fit between the organizational culture and performance management system is inspiring to employees because they perceive it as reinforcing existing values.

CONTROL MECHANISMS

There must be control mechanisms to ensure that differentiation is real and fair during the annual performance appraisal. Although such mechanisms serve as a means for regulating managers' behaviours, the most effective system is internal control exercised by individual managers. This is precisely the reason why top managers must model the way and consistently communicate with managers on the need for differentiation. Initially, sanctions would be inevitable to ensure that those who infringe the principles are duly penalized. In the final analysis, the internalization of the norms of fairness, objectivity and equity will culminate in fair differentiation.

The multi-rater system The multi-rater system – also known as 360° feedback – is designed to mitigate the imperfections of a single rater, as catalogued above, and correct the anomalies of the conventional appraisal system in which only the supervisor pronounces judgement on the performance of an employee. It is a multi-source process whereby an employee's performance is evaluated by those who are familiar with his or her performance and contributions within a given period – usually a year. Besides the fact that it is a potent tool for development, it offers employees a great opportunity to see themselves through the prism of different people. Raters include the immediate supervisors, peers, project team members and customers. It also provides for self-assessment by the employee.

The system has the advantage of enhancing objectivity and fairness in the performance appraisal of subordinates. Furthermore, it is comprehensive and inclusive in the sense that information on employees' performance is gathered from different sources and levels of the organization. Each rater or appraiser provides a different perspective on an employee's performance, competencies and skills, resulting in a more complete and reliable picture of employees' achievement and capabilities than the assessment of only one manager could have presented. Finally, it increases organizational communication and effectiveness and could lead to the institutionalization of a culture in which feedback is accepted as the norm.

Despite these advantages, the multi-rater system is not common in African organizations, apparently because of some inherent challenges. While it is seen as a system that could address the problems of a single rater, the logistics of operating it are often a source of discouragement to many organizations. First, there is the risk that it could easily become a mutual benefit system in which employees informally agree to give favourable reports on one another. Second, both managers and subordinates have practised a system in which managers have always dominated the performance evaluation exercise. It is a system in which managers have demonstrated the power disequilibrium between them and their subordinates, and they are unlikely to want to give up this cherished resource. Finally, managers and those whose performance they appraise already consider the annual performance evaluation a difficult exercise. To introduce a system in which managers can be evaluated by their subordinates and peers poses an even greater challenge fraught with the fear of vendetta, victimization, nepotism and male chauvinism.

For a multi-rater system to succeed, top management has to lead the implementation of the system, define clearly what the organization and employees stand to gain and provide adequate training, especially to middle managers. Change initiatives are quite often killed by middle managers, usually for personal reasons. Some degree of confidentiality will be required to protect raters and ensure that their role does not create unnecessary tension and conflict between team members.

Consistency calibration Another form of control mechanism is consistency calibration (Sammer, 2008):

- First, managers present their subordinates' performance ratings for discussion to their own colleagues in the same organizational unit, who are presumed to have a general appreciation of the performance of the employees whose ratings are being presented. The peer review meeting is presided over by the head of the division, who is the supervisor of the managers or raters. A rigorous review of ratings is undertaken by the team, and each rater provides a justification for his or her rating and compares achievements with agreed objectives. There are interdivisional comparisons of ratings of employees on the same grade.

- Such a review has a number of advantages. Firstly, to a large extent, consistency is achieved. Secondly, the basis for employees' rating is justified and, if colleagues are not satisfied with the justification, the rater is requested to review the rating. Thirdly, at the end of the consistency calibration process, the rater feels more confident in discussing the rating with employees, as the rating has the blessing of the management team. Finally, the fact that managers have to justify their ratings at a joint meeting of their colleagues and supervisor may compel them to be fair and realistic, as they could face embarrassment if they were deemed to be unduly subjective.

- The consistency calibration control mechanism can be time-consuming where there are a large number of employees in an organizational unit. Discussions may therefore focus on outliers such as 'outstanding', 'minimally satisfactory' and 'unsatisfactory'. The consistency calibration team must uphold integrity and avoid the risk of a mutual benefit practice by which managers share a tacit understanding not to be overly critical of one another and to support their respective ratings.

- A critical aspect of the consistency calibration mechanism is that the review of performance rating does not begin with individual performance. Rather, it begins with the review of organizational performance, and the review cascades to divisions, departments and the individual, as in objective-setting. Each division or operation has a point rating which cascades down to the level of the individual. If a division's performance rating is 4 on a scale of 1–5, based on its contribution to the achievement of corporate goals, none of the departments that comprise it can have an average that is higher than 4. The same principle applies to individual ratings, with the result that the average of all the performance ratings for a division will not be higher than the 4-point rating.

Performance management training A third control mechanism is training. When consistently and continually provided to managers, it is the most effective antidote to unethical behaviours in performance appraisal. Unfortunately, the emphasis in most performance management training programmes is on compliance and not on the commitment to do what is ethically right and what inspires the confidence and trust of subordinates. Fair and objective performance appraisal cannot be achieved in the absence of character or integrity. As both managers and subordinates need to understand the performance management system, training should focus on the following areas:

- the business case for performance management

- the firm's strategic business objectives so that managers and employees can understand how their contributions impact on corporate performance

- how to set individual objectives with performance metrics and performance standards
- how to seek and give regular feedback
- responsibilities of managers in talent development – training, coaching and counselling
- the philosophy and principles of performance appraisal
- self-awareness and the possible impact of personal values in performance appraisal
- performance review – its purpose and how it should be conducted, and consistent calibration of rating
- how to assess performance and potential
- performance rating – linking performance to merit pay
- how to identify training and development needs.

Summary

Differentiation creates an environment in which employees seek to achieve excellence and also improve their skills. It is a way of building a culture of meritocracy and constantly pursuing high performance as a lifelong journey and not as a one-off event. Furthermore, differentiation allows an organization to reward deserving employees according to their individual performance and contributions, to invest on their development in alignment with the needs of the business and to prepare tomorrow's leaders who will have responsibility for ensuring the sustainability, competitiveness and effectiveness of the business. Finally, it is an antidote to the bias and socio-cultural pathologies that plague performance rating.

8

Succession Planning and Management

Succession planning has become more imperative than ever because great leaders are scarce and competition for them is strong and almost vicious. The turnover rate of business leaders is so high, particularly among chief executive officers (CEOs) that organizations which do not plan for succession may face a crisis when they lose their executives unexpectedly. According to Paese (2008, 19), 'over the last decade, CEO turnover has increased by over 50 per cent, and performance-related departures by over 300 per cent.' Many organizations recognize the gravity of the situation. Research conducted by the Society for Human Resource Management (SHRM) Foundation in 2007 revealed that three out of four executives in the United States said that succession planning was their most significant challenge for the future. Furthermore, about 71 per cent of the respondents also said that the next most pressing problem was providing leaders with the skills they needed to be successful. Paradoxically, few organizations seem to be taking appropriate actions towards addressing these challenges.

On 4 November 2007 Charles Prince resigned as chief executive officer of Citigroup. The precipitating event was the loss of over US$8 billion related to sub-prime mortgages. One month after his departure, Citigroup was still searching for a successor. After five weeks without a substantive corporate leader, the bank finally announced the appointment of Mr Vikram Pandit who had been, until then, head of Citigroup's investment banking division, as CEO. He had worked for the bank for only eight months at the time of his appointment (NPR, 2007). The state of affairs in Citigroup exposed the bank's lack of readiness with a successor for its most high-profile position as evidenced by the length of time it took to identify a successor even though it was eventually an internal candidate.

When Mr Stanley O'Neal was also forced to resign on 30 October 2007 in circumstances similar to those of Charles Prince, it took Merrill Lynch two weeks to appoint a successor on 14 November 2007. The successor was not from within the organization: the new CEO, John Thain, was appointed from the New York Stock Exchange Euronext. When the position of CEO became vacant in Siemens in 2007, it hired Peter Loescher, not from within Siemens, but from Merck. On 1 December 2009 Fritz Henderson, CEO of General Motors resigned (Krisher and Thomas, 2009). He had been appointed only in March 2009 when he took over from Rick Wagoner. The chairman of the company, Ed Whitacre, was immediately appointed as interim CEO because there was no potential successor in the company. He became substantive CEO and held the position up to August 2010 when he announced that he was stepping down and would likely be succeeded by Dan Akerson. The fact that the chairman of the company took over the leadership of the company for eight months seems to suggest that succession planning is a challenge in the company. In the space of only one year, General Motors appointed a third CEO, thereby confirming the high turnover rate of CEOs. These examples, which are by no means exhaustive, underscore the business imperative for succession planning. In an organization where there is no succession planning, the sudden departure of a leader becomes a crisis.

The advantages of succession planning are obvious and easily recognizable by any management team, yet it is puzzling that many of them cannot either see the obvious benefits of succession planning or fail to avoid the inevitable consequences of the failure to plan for succession. A survey conducted by the Institute of Corporate Productivity revealed that less than 45 per cent of respondents had a formal succession plan in place (Amble, 2008).

The Business Case for Succession Planning

Succession planning is 'an effort designed to ensure the continued effective performance of an organization, division, or work group by making provision for the development, replacement and strategic application of key people over time' (Rothwell, 2005: 10). It is a process which aims at creating a pool of high-performance leaders to meet the strategic needs of an organization. So important was succession planning to Jack Welch, former chairman and CEO of General Electric, that he declared, as he was approaching retirement, that choosing his successor would be the most important decision he would make and that it would occupy a considerable amount of his thought every day. This statement captures what should be the disposition of all CEOs, because succession planning is a business imperative and not merely one of the activities in human resource management.

THE CONTEXT

A critical element in succession planning is to understand the context in which future successors are likely to operate. With globalization, many companies from the emerging economies are becoming a formidable force to reckon with in the international markets. Twenty years ago Russia, China, India, Brazil and South Africa were not great players in the world economy. Today the story is different. China's economy has become the second largest after the United States, thereby pushing Japan into third place. American and European companies are facing fierce competition from these countries and the Asian tigers. In the not-too-distant future there may also be competition from a group of emerging countries which Boshyk (2009) refers to as N-11: namely, Bangladesh, Egypt, Indonesia, Iran, Mexico, Nigeria, Pakistan, the Philippines, South Korea, Turkey and Vietnam.

Technology is changing almost at the speed of sound due to increasing innovations. There is growing pressure for the regulation of financial sector in order to protect consumers from the greed and unethical practices that led to the 2008–2009 global economic and financial crisis. Governments are asking industries to go 'green' as part of their social responsibility to protect the planet and, more importantly, forestall the catastrophic consequences that may befall poor countries as a result of climate change. Finally, shareholders are demanding more returns on their investment, diversity and inclusion, and high ethical standards in business deals. All these variables create the context which should inform corporations of the criticality of succession planning and the calibre of leaders they need to develop for tomorrow's business.

THE RATIONALE FOR SUCCESSION PLANNING

All the factors listed above lead inescapably to the following conclusions.

- A company that is successful today may not succeed tomorrow because the current technology, products, processes and systems which are the basis of its success may become obsolescent. Constant innovation and adaptation to environmental changes are not only imperative, but also inevitable. There is a compelling need to develop innovative and transformational leaders for tomorrow's challenges and competition.

- The competencies that are required for managing an enterprise in a stable environment are not the same as those that are critical in fast-changing circumstances. Furthermore, the competencies that have been useful in managing a national enterprise are not necessarily the same as those required to drive cutting-edge innovations and change, penetrate new markets in a multicultural environment or manage an acquisition or merger. As each business situation changes, the competencies and capabilities required for effectively responding to it must also change. Therefore, employees who demonstrate the potential agility to lead in each situation must be equipped with leadership capabilities. The practice of acquiring the right leader through head-hunting or even leaving it to chance might have worked in the past and within national frontiers where competition was not fierce, but these approaches may no longer be effective – as many corporations have already sadly learnt. Organizations must systematically identify and prepare high-potential employees for key positions.

- In organizations that fail to plan for succession, managers tend to groom successors who are remarkably like themselves in appearance, background and values. The inherent risk is that the background and values that worked for an organization in the past may not work for it in the future (Rothwell, 2005). In the absence of succession planning, managers could unscrupulously recruit or promote those from their country or ethnic group, thereby eliminating the possibility for diversity and multiculturalism. urthermore, there could be succession by seniority – a common practice in African organizations – with the result that although there is no 'interregnum' between successive leaders, an average or mediocre person may, by default, be appointed as a successor to a critical leadership position.

Beyond Replacement Planning

It is commonplace to equate replacement planning with succession planning. However, they are two distinct talent management practices. Replacement planning happens when an organization has a back-stop plan to replace an incumbent of a position in case of death, resignation or disability so that there is no break in continuity. Its objective is essentially risk management. In contrast, succession planning is aligned to the strategic direction of the organization. It involves a systematic and dynamic programme of development of the talent pool for future strategic leadership positions. Replacement plans focus on current needs whereas succession plans focus not only on today's needs, but also on those of the long-term future. While the career path for replacement planning is usually within the function, succession planning is cross-functional and goes beyond geographical boundaries. Managers generally own the replacement plan whereas the succession plan is owned by the top management team, and the plan is reviewed as part of the organization's development plan.

The approach to succession planning has changed even though its objectives and necessity have remained the same. In the past, it was restricted to the top positions of a company, particularly the CEO. Today, succession planning is done for all key leadership positions in an organization. A key position is regarded as one which, if it becomes vacant and is not filled immediately, the business of the organization could be hurt with far-reaching consequences. Previously, succession planning was wrapped in secrecy like the election of a pope. You would never know the heir apparent until you saw the 'white smoke'. The rationale for the secrecy was to obviate unnecessary rivalry and back-stabbing if the 'crown prince' were known. It also avoided demoralizing unsuccessful aspirants who were not regarded as candidates for the anticipated position. Secrecy also gave senior management the flexibility to review its decision if at some point they thought the heir apparent was no longer the best match for the job. Today, organizations create talent pools from which a choice can be made. Rarely is one specific individual designated as an heir apparent.

One of the criticisms of succession planning in the past was that it was managed independently of the business strategy. There was hardly any link between the succession plan and the business model. In contrast, the current approach is driven by the organization's strategic direction for the next two to five years – acquisition or merger, diversification of products, growth, establishment of new plants in low-cost countries, expansion of markets into new regions, acquisition of new technologies and so on. All these strategic decisions impact on workforce planning in general and on the organization's leadership capability in particular.

The main characteristics of succession planning are as follows:

- It is a planned activity.

- It is strategic and enhances organizational continuity and effectiveness.
- It is led by top management.
- It targets those holding critical and key leadership positions in an organization.

The framework of succession planning and management consists of the following components:

- top management commitment to succession planning and management
- competencies required to implement future business strategies
- talent review – analysing the gap between what is desired and what actually exists in the firm
- development and implementation of a succession plan.

Top Management Commitment

Without the ownership of top management, any effort by the HR department to plan for succession will predictably fail. In fact, it is not the responsibility of the HR department, but of top management. To elicit the commitment of top management, there must be a clear demonstration of the consequences of failing to plan for succession. The scenario of what the future would look like with or without a succession plan needs to be developed and shared with top managers in order to provide them a basis for understanding the importance, urgency and enormity of the challenge that faces or may confront the organization in the future. Every innovation brings about the need for learning or change. Hence, succession planning may have its protagonists and antagonists. Some members of top management may be cynical while others may be resentful or pay mere lip service, especially where an organization has a history of poor human resource management. Resentment and resistance are usually born out of a hidden agenda, ignorance, insufficient information, fear of change or lack of consultation and involvement in decision-making.

Top management will have to demonstrate their commitment in a number of ways. They need to hold middle managers accountable for a credible performance evaluation, assessment of employee potential and systematic training and development of the talent pool. Monitoring and evaluation of the plan is also top management's responsibility in order to ensure that the plan is implemented as it was originally intended. Finally, they have the responsibility to communicate lucidly and constantly their commitment to excellence and to the development and advancement of any employees who can contribute to the success and competitiveness of the firm.

Determining Leadership Competencies

As organizations become global or are affected by globalization those who manage them must have competencies that will enable them to succeed in the global environment. Experience has shown that appointing CEOs or top management staff merely on the basis of seniority, length of service, experience or track record of performance, without regard for the competencies of the position, is wrong because none of these is a sufficient and valid predictor of success. Competencies that make managers effective within their national boundaries or in their current position may prove ineffective in the global environment or in a higher-level position. Therefore, succession planning should begin by identifying the competencies that future business leaders must possess to be able to cope with global business challenges and sustain the competitiveness and effectiveness of organizations. Without a set of clearly defined competencies it is difficult to determine the bench strength and also who have the capabilities to fill the holes in the bench. In determining the competencies that will be required of future successors, it is pertinent to have a global and strategic business outlook. Hence, the competencies required are those of global executives.

'Global' refers to a mindset that takes into account the complexities of doing business anywhere in the world. Fulkerson (2002: 304) defines a global executive as 'a business leader who is effective regardless of where in the world the executive may focus attention or energy'. Pucik (1996) defines global executives as 'executives who perceive global competition as an opportunity, have a hands-on understanding of global business as well as an ability to work across organizational, functional and cross-cultural boundaries, and are able to balance simultaneous demands of global integration and local responsiveness'. Both definitions imply that the global executive transcends geography and physical location and has a mindset that drives the actions that in turn help businesses and organizations to succeed irrespective of where the executive is located. It also means that operating across international borders is more demanding of executives than operating in one country in terms of political savvy, executive maturity, people management skills, diplomatic skills, cross-cultural sensitivity and knowledge of international business and local trade regulations. Global executives must have the ability to manage diversity, innovativeness and risk-taking, and an ability to manage change.

In addition, global executives must have the ability to think strategically and see the business from a multidisciplinary and systemic perspective such that they can easily establish or forecast the probable impact of an occurrence in one country on their business in another country. That means that they must be sufficiently connected to relevant sources of information, using appropriate and up-to-date technology to garner and analyse information, and be able to establish appropriate relationships or networks in order to perceive situations holistically and take effective decisions. In cultural terms, they need to develop a sensitivity that enables them to perceive things not only from their own cultural prism, but also from the cultural perspectives of other people, particularly the stakeholders, without losing the global perspective.

Talent Review

Talent review is a top management audit of leadership positions with a view to determining an organization's leadership strengths and weaknesses in relation to its strategic plan. It involves bridging the gap between existing and required capabilities. From a pool of potential successors, top management decides on those who are immediately ready and eligible to fill the holes in the bench strength and also on those who would be ready to assume higher responsibilities in the next two or three years. Top management agrees on recruitment plans for positions for which there are no suitable internal candidates and also on the development plans aimed at grooming potential successors for future leadership positions.

BENCH STRENGTH

Bench strength refers to an organization's capacity to meet its leadership capability needs from within. In other words, it has such high-quality people that it is capable of filling key positions without resorting to recruitment. In determining the bench strength, management has to decide whether the review will be limited to senior and top leadership positions or be extended to middle managers and some specialized, key professional positions that are either difficult to fill or could cause great harm if the incumbents were to leave the organization without potential successors. The review of bench strength usually reveals holes in the bench. A hole refers to a position that cannot be filled from within because no manager is currently qualified to fill it now if it becomes vacant either immediately or in the future. The formidability of the bench strength is determined by the number of holes in it. The higher the number the weaker is the bench strength.

Turnover tends to deplete the bench strength. Although a certain level of turnover is desirable, it hurts the business when those leaving are the best or most valuable people. In assessing internal capabilities there is a need to have reliable information about turnover so that the organization can forecast from the past trend how many managers and incumbents of critical positions it may lose each year or during a given period. A retirement chart for the next two to five years can easily be generated from the database. Retirement is an unavoidable element of turnover and has to be planned for. What may not be certain is how many critical employees will leave through resignation, termination or death. Assessment of turnover should also focus on those who are 'retention risks' – key positions where incumbents could be poached by competitors or where there is discernible evidence that incumbents are no longer committed to the organization.

The essence of a talent review is to craft a strategy or plan for bridging the gap between bench strength and leadership requirements. Without an adequate inventory of skills and competences, it will be futile to determine the gap between what is required and what is available. There is a compelling need for multinational enterprises (MNEs) to have an integrated human resources information system. Software such as PeopleSoft or Employee Resource Planning (ERP) is necessary to maintain comprehensive data on employees. Data on career history, performance evaluation, training, skill set, competency profiles, career goals and preferences and level of potential may exist in personal files or in different HR functions. Collating the data from different sources and integrating them into a comprehensive database when required for decision-making could be a challenge.

The following scenarios could emerge from a talent review:

1. The organization may have the right number of managers, but not the right quality in terms of required competencies.

2. The organization may have the right number and quality for today, but not for the years ahead because a significant change may be required in the competency profile of future leaders.

3. The organization may not have both the right number and quality of leaders required today and even in the future. Many of the managers in critical positions may have outdated skills and are unable to cope with rapid technological and business changes.

4. The organization may face the paradox of being in short supply of critical skills while suffering from a surfeit of skills that are no longer relevant to its business in the future.

The Succession Plan

A succession plan for a multinational enterprise provides information on the holes in the bench strength of each function, subsidiary, division and external operation. It outlines the steps that will be taken to fill the holes and also the timeframe within which the actions would be taken. Various strategies for filling the holes, depending on the nature of the challenges identified in the gap diagnostic, will also be examined. Usually a major decision is whether to bridge the gap through the promotion or transfer of existing managers, recruitment of the required talent, or a combination of both strategies. While recruitment injects 'new blood' into an organization's circulatory system for greater vitality, it carries the risk of demoralizing existing managers who have patiently waited in the wings to fly to higher positions. It therefore could result in a high turnover of good people. External recruitment is usually an option only when no suitable internal candidate can be found to fill a leadership position.

A strategy for filling the holes in the bench strength through internal promotion to the exclusion of recruitment may, however, culminate in in-breeding and lack of opportunity for fresh thinking, new perspectives, and the injection of valuable ideas and best practices from diverse sources. An integrated approach seeks to strike a balance between recruitment and internal promotions and thus ensures a win–win situation for both the organization and the existing talent. Ultimately, the greatest beneficiary is the organization because this approach creates a basis not only for employee engagement and retention, but also for enriching and diversifying the talent base of the business. A multinational company would also have to decide whether external recruitment or internal candidates for positions would have to be from a third country, the home country or host country, irrespective of where the executive positions are.

A succession plan provides not an heir apparent to each position, but a pool of potential successors who need to be groomed and developed for final selection. As illustrated in Figure 8.1, a pool of talent is created for the position of Managing Director/CEO. The process cascades down all the managerial positions. No single individual is identified as *the* successor for any position. All the people in the pool have equal chances of succeeding to the position. They could also be rejected if, ultimately, they do not meet the requirements of the position. The plan should pay attention to the individuality of the pipeline of potential successors. It should indicate: name, age, performance level, potential level, readiness for promotion within a given timeframe, specific nature of development required (training, coaching, mentorship, lateral mobility as part of job rotation, international posting, or assignment to a special project), timeline for the implementation of development programme, and responsibility for the follow-through to ensure that development programme is implemented as required by top management. The plan must be reviewed periodically. Managers may not be informed that they are being groomed for a specific position in order to avoid a 'horse race' or disappointment if management's plans change later in the course of plan implementation. However, it is important to give potential candidates a strong signal that the organization values them and is committed to their development and advancement.

In the past, the succession plan period used to be five years or more because the financial, socio-economic and political environment was relatively stable. Nowadays, change is occurring so fast that such a period is generally no longer tenable and realistic. A succession plan is a living, dynamic document that has to be reviewed in accordance with changes in the leadership pool. It should also be reviewed according to changing business strategy.

Software systems such as PeopleSoft, WisdomNet Integrated Talent Management System and Enterprise Resource Planning (ERP) are useful tools for managing data on succession planning. They have the capacity to generate reports that will enable top management to see, at a glance, the talent pool for the entire organization. They can also provide for early warning signals, such as a turnover map. The objective is to have in place an early warning mechanism so that the organization can have enough time to prepare for any eventuality.

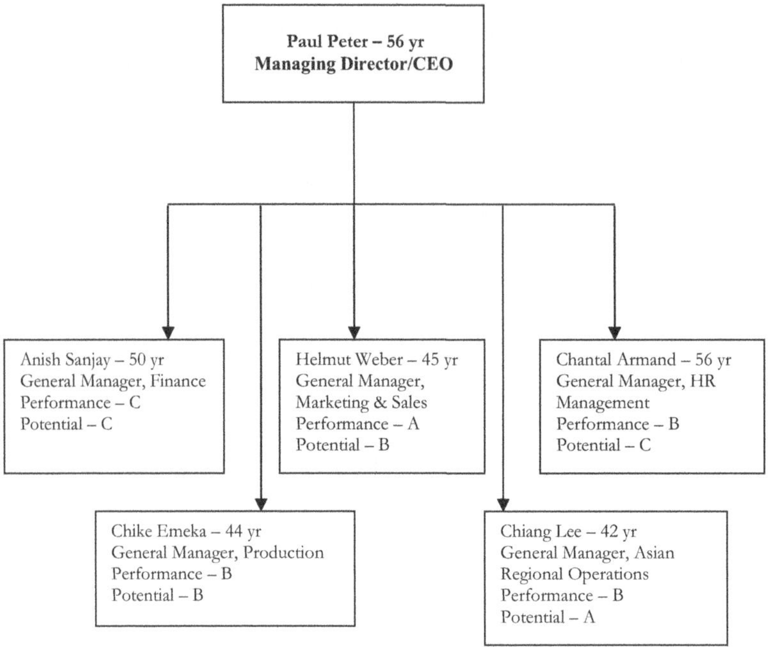

The talent pool will consist of the following General Managers: Weber, Emeka and Lee. Sanjay's low levels of performance and potential make him ineligible for the talent pool. Armand is also ineligible for two reasons: she is retiring in the same year as the Managing Director and her potential is limited. (The names do not represent real people.)

Figure 8.1 Succession planning: succession chart

IMPLEMENTING SUCCESSION PLANS

Implementing a succession plan is more challenging than the exercise of talent review because many of the actions in the plan are either difficult or time-consuming to implement. One of the commonest problems with succession planning is the lack of follow-through by top management. More often than not, the responsibility is placed squarely on the HR department which has no authority to compel top executives to implement decisions in the succession plan. Furthermore, although top managers may agree on a plan, individual agendas may derail its implementation. Hence, there is a need for top management to be guided by the following principles.

Boundarylessness Talent is a corporate asset and not the possession of any organizational unit. Top management should therefore adopt the concept of boundarylessness and flexibility in order to ensure cross-functional, geopolitical and gender mobility of talent with no impediments.

Integrity versus organizational politics Objectivity, fairness, candour, courage and commitment to excellence are critical to implementation so that decisions are not unduly influenced by parochial national, ethnic or personal interests.

Diversity and inclusion Diversity is a business imperative. While succession planning is not an allocation of plum positions on the basis of national, ethnic, linguistic or racial groups, there should not be a glass ceiling for any talented people, irrespective of nationality, gender or race.

Talent mindset Top managers shall recognize and accept that talent management is their respective and collective responsibility and that it cannot therefore be abdicated to the human resource management department.

Dispensability No manager or employee shall be considered indispensable to a division or an operation. Therefore, top managers should not stall the mobility of any high-performing manager to another function, division or external operations as part of the development plan for him or her.

Potential versus seniority While seniority should not be ignored, it cannot be the driving criterion for development or promotion; rather, each manager's performance and potential shall be the primary consideration. This is the essence of differentiation in performance appraisal.

Monitoring mechanism There must be a monitoring mechanism for providing the CEO with information on the implementation status of the plan on a regular basis.

Generally, the implementation of a succession plan will focus on the following critical actions:

- *Development programme.* Development is based on the principle that success in every managerial position requires the possession of certain leadership competencies and that, if a gap exists between what managers can do and what they will be required to do, a development programme must be crafted to bridge the gap.

  Quite often, managers conceive of development in terms of a series of classroom training sessions, especially at prestigious institutions. However, development is a process and not an event. Top managers need to understand that development for career progression consists of a number of integrated learning experiences, such as leadership development programmes, coaching, job rotation, assignment to a special project, international posting and mentorship. The reason is that development aims at producing a well-rounded individual for the position to be occupied.

- *Promotion.* Promotion should be based on readiness, willingness and ability to perform at the next higher level (Rothwell, 2005). Readiness means that the individual already has a mastery of most of the responsibilities of the position, while willingness is the acceptance and motivation to take on new responsibilities. Ability refers to the possession of what it takes to do the job. Sometimes, willingness is taken for granted by top management because of the usual belief that every manager is always excited by an opportunity for career advancement. However, there could be exceptions or outliers, especially in R&D departments where, for instance, professional scientists prefer their specialized research work to managerial responsibility. This is why there is a need for a dual career path – one for management-inclined people and the other for technocrats or specialists.

- *Smooth transition.* Succession management must be characterized by a smooth transition or continuity. In September 2006 the United African Company (Nigeria) announced the appointment of a new Group Managing Director/Chief Executive Officer (GMD/CEO) from within the organization. The effective date of the appointment was 1 January 2007, when the outgoing GMD/CEO would retire. An interesting aspect of the succession process was that, with effect from 1 November 2006, the incoming GMD/CEO was made responsible for the new strategy and long-term plan process which would be presented to the board before the end of the year. He was also responsible for running the business, but with the assistance of the outgoing GMD/CEO. The arrangement was to ensure not only a smooth transition and continuity, but also, apparently, confidence-building of the new GMD/CEO.

9

Developing Talent for Business Leadership

Understanding Talent Development

Talent development consists of planned experience, training and guided growth provided by an organization in order to ensure an uninterrupted supply of competent leaders who are sufficiently equipped and ready to manage the vagaries of the business environment. It is not a one-off learning event; rather, it is a continuous process. The ultimate goal of talent development programmes is therefore to improve the leadership capabilities of those who perform managerial functions and enhance the future performance and effectiveness of organizations. Although every organization appears to appreciate the criticality of talent development, not all organizations actually 'walk the talk'. There are therefore concerns that lack of leadership development may threaten the performance of many multinational corporations not only in Africa, but also worldwide. A study of Fortune 500 and Global 2000 companies by Corporate University XChange in 2007 revealed that commitment to leadership development was weak and not supported with adequate financial investment. Furthermore, only 3 per cent of respondents were confident in their firms' ability to develop future leaders to ensure the long-term success of their firms.

In a global online survey of 412 executives conducted jointly by Development Dimensions International and the Economist Intelligence Unit, '55 per cent of respondents said that their firms' performance was likely or very likely to suffer in the near future due to insufficient leadership talent' (Paese, 2008: 1). This perception was found to be common amongst most executives irrespective of company size or geographical location. The implementation of any succession plan is imperilled without leadership development. Certainly the future of an organization is programmed for ineffective performance and decline where leadership development is on the backburner. The good news, however, is that many executives have made talent management part of their core business strategy and in fact consider talent management to be as important or even more important than other business priorities (Paese, 2008).

The most critical element in talent development is to understand the context in which the firm operates or is likely to operate in the future – namely, 'the strategic issues, business realities and environment' (Delano, 2008: 1) – and how these circumstances are likely to evolve in the future. It is therefore logical that talent development must be congenitally aligned with the business strategy. Any change in strategic direction should result in fundamental changes in the talent development agenda. If the necessary changes are not made, the agenda will lag behind the strategic shift and there will be a disconnect between them. The consequence is predictable: the strategic advantage that inheres in the alignment of the executive learning agenda with the business strategy is imperilled, if not lost.

Comprehensive and systematic development for leadership is more critical now than three decades ago not only because of the impact of globalization and rapid technological changes, but also because younger people (Generations X and Y) are taking up global executive positions previously occupied by baby-boomers. Although the younger generations sometimes think that intelligence, academic credentials and technological savvy can be substituted for experience, the truth is that they need to be guided, in a planned and systematic sequence, in learning, acquisition of knowledge and experience from different sources. This is precisely the reason why a multidimensional and integrated approach is certainly more productive than a one-dimensional approach, which comprises only executive training programmes or international assignment. In the past, development focused essentially on preparing managers to climb the career ladder; today, development concentrates on providing managers with a resilient career and transforming them into global executives. Therefore, development should be designed in such a way that it has the capacity to remould managers into individuals who are sufficiently equipped and confident to take on the awesome, but intrinsically satisfying, leadership challenges of making their companies great.

One tool is inadequate to provide the variety of experiences required of a leadership role. Talent development is therefore more successful where there is a mix or blend of tools for providing learning experiences.

Table 9.1 Tools for the development of talent

Development tool	Contribution to leadership development
Executive training	Bridges the gap in knowledge and skills, particularly in the spheres of leadership, people management, language capability and corporate strategy.
Mentoring	Useful for the development of political awareness, diplomatic skills, ability to navigate in difficulty terrain, networking, building technical and leadership capability, and acquiring a holistic picture of career opportunities.
International assignment	Instrumental in acquiring the skills of a global executive: learning cultural sensibilities; developing a flexible paradigm; acquiring negotiating and diplomatic skills; and developing a global view of the business and understanding international competition.
Action learning	Useful in developing skills in problem-solving, decision-making and leading teams, and also for the acquisition of competence.
Job rotation	Necessary for acquiring technical skills and knowledge in different functional areas; produces a well-rounded specialist and leader.

EXECUTIVE TRAINING IS NOT TALENT DEVELOPMENT

There is a tacit assumption that with executive training programmes managers could be sufficiently prepared for the global leadership challenges in business. However, it is important to underscore *ab initio* the important fact that executive training programmes are only one component of the integrated package of learning experiences, planned and guided growth and continuous learning in the development of talent. Talent development cannot be effective, therefore, if executive training programmes are its primary instrument. It is necessary to make a distinction between training and development.

Training is the process of bridging the gap in knowledge, skills or attitude which is believed to affect the performance of an employee. Development, on the other hand, is regarded as a process of acquiring leadership skills or preparing managers for leadership responsibilities. Training is tactical and linked to immediate performance gaps while development is strategic and focuses on preparing for tomorrow's leadership in organizations. Whereas training improves performance, development enhances potential. Because the outcome of development programmes is not immediate and the development process is continuous, it is usually difficult to measure the success of each event on its completion whereas the outcome of training may be measured within three or six months of the completion of the learning event. Although training, in the form of a leadership or executive development programme, is a component of talent development, it is not the same as talent development.

There is no gainsaying the fact that executive leadership training is imperative for talent development because of the extremely fast rate of change in technology and the business environment, and consequent obsolescence of knowledge and skills. Obsolescence of skills, ideas and knowledge negates innovations and creativity and this could translate into an organization's incapacity to cope with change and competition. In fact, Tannenbaum (2002: 15) noted that the US Department of Labor estimates that, on average, 50 per cent of an employee's knowledge and skills become outdated every 30–36 months compared to an estimated 12–15 years in the 1970s. Managers and leaders are therefore constantly challenged to keep abreast of changes in business and technological knowledge. Hence, in the following section we describe the various tools that an organization can deploy to effectively foster the learning and development of talent.

Executive Development Training Programmes

Executive development training programmes are planned learning experiences designed and delivered to enable executives perform their current jobs effectively by increasing their business skills, while also preparing them for effective leadership in the future. The purpose of executive training is not only to prepare talent for higher level positions, but, more importantly, to equip them sufficiently to meet the challenges in the rapidly changing international business environment. Sometimes organizations send their managers on executive training courses in business schools lasting one to three months, in the hope that they will return as competent business leaders. However, many of such programmes are usually generic and are neither aligned to the business strategy of the participant's company nor aimed at bridging any specific gap in skills and leadership capability. They scarcely cater for the participant's individual development needs. The training is usually just an event and not a process within an integrated learning agenda. It is no wonder that managers return with a lot of knowledge but with no visible change in their leadership behaviours.

For executive training to serve as a developmental tool there must be a shift from generic to customized executive training that is designed and delivered to meet the specific needs of the target individuals and their organization. This gives two advantages: first, a customized approach leads to a change in culture in the development of talent; and, second, the company can clearly see a return on its investment in the form of better leadership capability and organizational effectiveness. In designing a customized executive training course, the business school or consultant recruited for the purpose needs to seek to understand the organization's context – its strategic direction, business realities and environment. It is equally fundamental to understand the development needs of the target managers and how meeting those needs would translate into meeting the strategic needs of the organization. Most executive programmes focus on leadership, strategy, financial management, marketing and sales strategy, negotiating skills, business ethics and a host of other topics. These generic topics are no doubt critical to the development of leadership capability, but perhaps more critical are the specific strategic issues or challenges which the organizational leaders have to deal with. Equally germane are specific challenges relating to the socio-cultural dynamics, politics and economics of the regions where the participants' company does business. It is the understanding and internalization of such particularities that tend to make the difference between the effectiveness and ineffectiveness of an executive development programme.

Even when an executive training programme has been customized and the specific developmental needs of managers have been identified and used as inputs in the design of the programme there is still the compelling need for other tools of talent development. Mentoring, job rotation, international assignment and action learning reinforce training. All the tools are mutually reinforcing. In fact, the greater the number of tools carefully selected and used for development, the higher the probability of success. Each of them is examined below.

Mentoring

The word 'mentor' originated from Homer's epic poem *The Odyssey*. In Homer's story, Odysseus, King of Ithaca, had gone with his army to the Trojan War. Prior to his departure, he had put his son, Telemachus in the custody and care of his friend, Mentor. Odysseus asked him to take good care of Telemachus and give him good education, apparently with a view to grooming him to succeed his father. The war lasted ten years and Odysseus' return trip took another ten years. Mentor faithfully carried out his friend's wishes, and his efforts were evident in the development of Telemachus. Originating from this tale, the word 'mentor' became synonymous with loyal and trusted friend, adviser and teacher.

Barner (2000: 97) defines mentoring as a method for providing employees with structured opportunities to develop competencies and address career roadblocks, through personal guidance by exemplary performers in an organization. It is a tool that organizations use to nurture and grow their people, and is particularly important in developing employees for leadership. Kunich and Lester elegantly describe the criticality of mentoring to leadership development:

> *Through mentoring, the wisdom and experience of the senior is passed to the junior … Mentoring provides a framework to bring about a cultural change in the way we view the professional development of competent future leaders. The road to the top in most organizations today is an uphill and bumpy ride – you simply can't float to the top. Mentoring is a key way to help us get to our destination. (Kunich and Lester, 1999: 117)*

Mentoring takes place in many organizations, but informally; it is a spontaneous relationship initiated unofficially by the mentor or protégé. In many African organizations mentoring is not formalized as a tool for development, but informal mentoring is common. Managers who take on mentoring responsibility do it because of their professional or social relationships with the employee. The objective is usually to provide psychosocial support, particularly to new employees who need friendship and guidance to enable them navigate their way through the political landscape of the organization. Because of its lack of formalization or institutionalization, mentoring easily attracts the pejorative term of 'godfatherism'. Neither the mentor nor the mentee would want to be seen in such light.

A major factor that may be militating against the establishment of a mentoring culture is that managers may not know how to mentor people because they themselves were never mentored or trained to do it. They cannot therefore share an experience that they have never had. Furthermore, some managers believe – wrongly – that mentoring could lead to emotional involvement in the private affairs of the protégé, especially if they are female employees. Finally, the pressures and demands of the job may be an inhibiting factor – managers may simply have no time for mentoring.

The primary role of a mentor is to assist the mentee or protégé to learn and build his or her technical and leadership capacity. The mentor also helps the protégé to clarify career goals and carry out a plan to reach the goals by sharing insights and knowledge they have gained through their experiences. The mentor could tell personal stories describe scenarios and offer examples to demonstrate the values and competencies required to be a good leader or to have a successful career. Not all the stories need necessarily be about success. Some will be about personal failures, what wrong decisions the mentor took, what opportunity was lost, what was not done right or well and the lessons learnt from them thereafter. Stories instruct, guide, reassure and show the human side of the mentor. The mentor's job is to give encouragement, support and wise counsel, and also to nurture self-esteem. The critical roles of a mentor include the following:

- acting as a role model to protégé in performance, integrity and professionalism;
- providing a holistic picture of the career opportunities available in the organization and how to navigate within the system;
- providing information about organizational culture and how to manage relationships with supervisors and colleagues;
- intervening in difficult relationships, particularly with supervisors which threaten to impact negatively on the career of the protégé;
- providing support and building confidence when the protégé is going through stress in a new position or a challenging project;
- counselling protégé on how to deal with challenging family situations that seem to interfere with performance or career advancement;
- helping the protégé to be visible by projecting his or her competencies and good qualities to top management in an unobtrusive manner.

A mentor could advise the mentee to undertake any of the following tasks as part of his or her development. The list is not exhaustive.

- Seek to participate in new projects or special assignments;

- Aspire to assume the leadership role when working in a team;
- Attend training courses, conferences and workshops to broaden knowledge and networks;
- Network within and outside the corporation;
- Write high-quality articles for a magazine or a professional journal;
- Seek to represent the organization at important external events.

Successful mentoring depends on both the mentor and the protégé, and their relationship is usually based on trust. The mentor should be an individual with a reputation for good leadership and should have the ability to inspire the confidence of the protégé to learn from his or her wealth of experience. Mentors should not be people with an unhappy career experience, but individuals who have positive experiences that can be shared; they should be knowledgeable, capable of coaching, counselling and networking, and be committed to development. Mentoring is driven by a strong and genuine concern for the growth and development of future leaders. Mentors are available for meetings as and when agreed; they provide information as promised to the protégé and protect his or her interests when the need arises. Both the mentor and protégé share the responsibility for the mentee's learning. The mentor has to create time for meetings, especially when the protégé has a concern that he or she wants to get off his or her chest.

Michaels, Handfield-Jones and Axelrod (2001: 118) give an interesting example of a mentor's commitment. The Senior Vice President of Arrow's Worldwide Operations who was a mentor to an employee, once travelled from London to Denmark to have dinner with someone she was mentoring. Incredible! That is how executives in organizations that value people conduct mentorship. Through actions like this, mentorship generates employee loyalty because employees are *ipso facto* convinced that management cares about their career and consequently commit to remaining with the organization – what an effective way to retain great people! For their part, protégés must be committed to learning, be receptive to new ideas, have a sense of personal responsibility and commitment, be willing to meet with the mentor on a regular basis and seek assistance when necessary, be open about their weaknesses, fears, concerns and career aspirations, and be committed to the common goal of both parties.

Certain guidelines are necessary from the outset to ensure successful mentoring. First, mentors must never be imposed on employees, and managers must not be forced to take up mentoring. Second, mentors should not be chosen from the direct chain of command: the supervisor of an employee cannot be his or her mentor. Preferably, mentors should be two or three levels higher than the protégé in the organizational hierarchy. Finally, mentors should not be allowed to have more than two protégés at a time so that he or she can find enough time for each of them. A manageable number ensures that the mentor does not suffer from burn-out.

The mentoring of a protégé is not a lifelong journey. Just as it has a beginning it also has a destination. Mentoring comprises three major phases: building trust, the learning process and the gradual dissolution of the relationship. The first three to six months of interaction is a period of getting to know each other and building trust. It is a phase when expectations and goals are discussed and agreed upon. In the second phase, confidence has been established. There are open and frank discussions. The mentor outlines the learning process, discusses his experiences, coaches, counsels and prods the protégé into taking risks, trying new ideas, solving problems and making discoveries through a series of activities such as those listed above. The protégé, for his or her part, becomes emboldened to challenge some of the mentor's ideas. In the third and final phase, the protégé has become a solid individual and feels capable of independently managing his or her career. There is a gradual reduction in the frequency of meetings between the mentor and the protégé until mentorship finally stops and they only meet as friends almost on an equal basis.

Mentoring has its own pitfalls. While managing a mentoring programme for management trainees, I encountered a number of situations in which either the mentors or the protégés were frustrated by the behaviours of the other party. In one situation the mentor was too busy to find time to meet with the protégé even when the latter needed immediate guidance on an urgent matter that related to his career advancement. In another case the mentee was a care-free individual who behaved so independently of the mentor that he took crucial decisions about his career without any reference to the mentor despite the fact that the latter was reputed for his wide experience and caring attitude to mentees. The mentee's decisions turned out to be wrong and, consequently, he lost a great opportunity to work on a high-profile and strategic project. The mentor pulled out of the relationship because he thought both of them were incompatible. The lesson is that a mismatch between a mentor and a protégé may result in the failure of mentoring. As in a marriage, they must be properly matched to be able to work together.

The mentor and the mentee should understand the objectives and process of mentoring. Often, both parties have different role expectations which impact on their relationship. In addition, confidentiality is crucial. The protégé might discuss with the mentor some unpleasant experiences he or she has had with his or her supervisor or team members. This information is provided in confidence. The protégé might just need some advice on how to deal with the difficult situation – it is not information for public consumption nor should it be discussed with those affected, no matter how close they are to the mentor. Like professional counsellors or physicians, mentors must consider themselves to be under oath not to discuss their protégés with other people. The basis for trust is destroyed the moment one party cannot abide by this ethical norm of confidentiality.

Mentorship could be a challenge in the African context where tribalism, ethnicism, favouritism and nepotism are sometimes unnecessarily attributed to decisions taken by top managers. It can easily be misinterpreted as 'godfatherism'. The tendency to misconstrue mentorship is due to the fact that it is not well understood and widely practised in many organizations. Top managers have a responsibility to create a culture of mentorship, especially as their organizations go global. Once it is institutionalized, there will no longer be any form of misinterpretation. Creating a culture requires a formal policy and consistent, constant communication, reinforced with behaviour modelling by top management.

Job Rotation

It was 1999. I was on vacation, and a former colleague decided to take me out for lunch at his company's restaurant. He had just emerged from an apparently stormy meeting with senior executives. Some of his colleagues had asked him, as the general manager in charge of human resources, to transfer certain of their subordinates to other functions or departments. He had told them that their requests were a tall order as he was not sure other departments would be willing to accept those employees. His colleagues were so angry with him that they almost chewed him up before the CEO intervened. My friend asked what I thought about his position, and I said that he was wrong as he had made absolutely no efforts at moving the employees in question. But, more importantly, the requests made by the senior executives were legitimate, except that they were made for the wrong reasons. Some executives wanted their subordinates to be transferred because of low performance, declining productivity or frequent absence from duty due to illness, while others asked for it because their subordinates were either difficult to manage or had low morale due to career stagnation.

None of the reasons for the requests was related to employee development and retention. This is a common malaise in many organizations. Lateral mobility or job rotation is often used for the wrong purpose and, with time, it acquires a stigma and becomes a plague that every employee wants to keep at bay. Ironically, though, it is one of the most potent tools for developing both technical and leadership capabilities. Morris (1956: 268) defines job rotation as a 'planned movement of employees from one position to another for the basic purpose of encouraging and stimulating the growth of the individual'. So ingrained is job rotation in most military institutions that it has become one of the unique features of the military profession. In fact, job rotation is the norm in the military. Job rotation is also a common practice in many organizations. For instance, banks and manufacturing companies recruit young university graduates as management trainees and generally rotate them through a number of functions or departments before finally deciding on the most appropriate job and organizational unit for them. Over the years, these individuals continue to rotate in different jobs and positions for development purposes.

Job rotation can be intra-functional or inter-functional. The former has the purpose of enhancing performance on the job within the scope of specialized function whereas the primary purpose of the latter is to prepare executives for advancement as well as for better performance in positions which require, or would benefit from, more generalized abilities and understanding. This is because inter-functional job rotation provides an opportunity for executives to gain experience in various spheres or functions of the business, such as marketing or strategic planning, and thus acquire a broad perspective and holistic understanding of the firm's operations. One of the advantages of job rotation, therefore, is that it removes the limitations that are generally inherent in narrow specialization, thereby preparing managers for better decision-making and, more importantly, for higher-level leadership positions.

Job rotation is of immense benefit to managers' career development and advancement in various ways. Managers who rotate in jobs accumulate experience *more quickly* than those who do not. In addition, managers who rotate in jobs accumulate experience in *more areas* than those who do not (Erikson and Ortega, 2002). There is a positive relationship between a manager's speed of advancement and the rate of job rotation. Not only does job rotation increase a manager's knowledge and understanding of general business challenges, it improves the ability to take effective decisions because the manager has a wider perspective of issues and a deeper comprehension of possible consequences of decisions on stakeholders. It also increases executives' personal confidence because they gain greater mastery of more jobs and a wider knowledge of the business.

Furthermore, job rotation is an effective way of reducing the effects of burn-out or career plateau because it provides the individual with fresh challenges, a new team and a new work environment. It also gives the employer the opportunity to learn about new dimensions of a manager's abilities. Without job rotation, the employer only keeps learning more and more about the same dimensions of employees' abilities and thus fails to tap their full potential. Overall, it has a long-term impact on employee retention, teamwork and organizational effectiveness. However, despite its potency as a career development tool, its effectiveness depends on how it is managed and linked to the succession plan. One of the reasons why job rotation is sometimes resisted by managers is because, in some organizations, it has no focus, its management is haphazard and it is perceived as a weapon used by supervisors to get rid of those they no longer want in certain positions, functions or locations. It thus acquires the notoriety of being a punitive, rather than a career development, tool. On the other hand, there are supervisors who would like to permanently retain certain high-performing employees even if such retention works against the individual's development and the overall organizational interest. It behoves management to communicate the purpose of job rotation clearly and consistently to all employees in order to forestall misperceptions.

Job rotation must be driven by employee development, which in turn must be linked to the organization's succession plan and the business model. For instance, if the General Manager of Human Resources were expected to retire in the next five years, it should be part of the succession plan to create a talent pool from which a possible successor would be expected to emerge. Those in the pool should go through a job rotation in all the major HR functions (recruitment, learning and career development, industrial relations, and compensation and benefits) with the objective that, in four or five years' time, there would emerge at least one or two managers in the HR talent pool who were fully equipped to take over the baton of leadership in the HR department as soon as the General Manager retired.

As noted above, sometimes job rotation is undertaken not necessarily to prepare the managers for higher level positions, but rather to inject new challenge into their jobs, especially where they have reached a career point beyond which they cannot be promoted (career plateau). The purpose of rotation in this context is to enhance motivation and productivity. Rotation could also be used to determine appropriate placement for high–potential, but low-performing, managers on the grounds that they are either in the wrong job or poorly led, and that rotation would help top management determine the most appropriate placement for the effective utilization of their talents.

If job rotation is not centrally planned and systematically linked to career development and succession plans, it could become counterproductive. Every rotation must have the objective of providing the manager with specific experience that will enhance his or her growth. The experience has to be related to future assignment. Both top management and the employee need to have a clear and common understanding of the exact skills that will be enhanced through the job rotation. The movement will therefore address skills and capabilities that are necessary for future performance and leadership. For instance, an HR manager who is on rotation to the industrial relations department as part of his or her development would be expected to acquire strong negotiating skills and a good knowledge of labour laws in the various countries in which the company has operations.

Every rotation sets in motion a chain of movements. There must be a plan for the replacement of the manager being rotated. This is precisely another reason why rotation has to be centrally planned and have a strategic focus. A rotation plan has to spell out who are to be rotated, when and for how long. The plan should also include the kind of initial support, such as training and coaching required to bridge the gap in knowledge, especially in a cross-functional job rotation. I recall that when I was on job rotation from the organizational development function to the industrial relations function in a steel plant, the first thing the company did was to send me on a two-week course on industrial relations management. It inspired me with greater confidence even though the terrain was already familiar to me. By the time I had attended another course, two months later, on 'collective bargaining', I felt even more confident that I was on top of the job. This kind of initial training is important, especially where some team members, including the supervisor, may be slow in accelerating the managers' learning curve. The period and cost of the learning curve can also be significantly decreased by providing relevant operating procedures and manuals.

Job rotation is only one component in talent development. It is not intended to be an end in itself. Hence, the duration of the rotation must be known by all the parties from the outset. Admittedly, the manager must acquire the relevant experience from the current position before the next rotation can take place or else the purpose of the rotation would have been defeated. The length of stay in each position will depend on a number of factors, such as the number of rotations necessary for the manager to be able to undertake the responsibilities of the next higher-level position, the manager's personal interests, his learning agility, and when management could consider him to be fully equipped and ready to assume higher responsibility.

International Assignment

In the past, international assignment was typically used to fill a skill gap because the required skill was not available locally in the host country. In some cases, it was used for the transfer of technical and managerial know-how, as well as for the implementation of organizational business strategy, policies and procedures in operations in other countries. Today, it is generally used to develop leadership competencies and give executives a global orientation characterized by cultural sensitivity, deeper knowledge of global competition and the ability to work independently and take critical decisions on the spot. In this regard, it is a developmental tool. Managers who work in different countries or regions tend to acquire a broader perspective of the organization's business opportunities and challenges, build a wider network of relationships with customers and service providers, and also acquire leadership skills.

Clearly, international assignment is expensive and carries the risk of losing managers during or immediately after the assignment comes to an end. Therefore, organizations should take necessary measures to ensure that the international posting does not become an exit route for valued talent. The following paragraphs provide tips on how to use international posting successfully for the purpose for which it is intended without losing executives.

First, it is important to prepare executives adequately for the assignment before departure. No matter how urgent it is to have managers at a particular location within a given timeframe, it is essential that they must be psychologically prepared for the assignment before their departure. This can be achieved in a multidimensional way. Employees need to have adequate notice to enable them take care of family challenges that will emanate from the transfer. For instance, they may want to sell their house or rent it out. They may want to put their children in a boarding school or make necessary arrangements for the care of an aged parent. The general view of managers who have had experience of international assignment is that organizations do not pay enough attention to the impact of international assignment on their families. The limited effectiveness of international assignment has been due largely to family resistance to mobility.

Second, it is extremely helpful to provide managers with transitional training in cultural awareness and understanding, global diversity, language skills and business practices in the host country. Some organizations hurriedly organize a one- or two-week language or culture-familiarization course prior to departure. Such crash programmes are never effective. Language training should be a major component in the corporate capability-building strategy for executives if an organization plans to send them on external assignment. They need to be trained to understand the economics, politics and cultural ethos of the new environment. The following are examples of cultural idiosyncrasies that they may have to deal with, depending on the country:

- In Japan, if you are making a presentation to a group of executives and some of them bend down their heads with eyes closed, the presenter should not be upset. They are not sleeping. Rather, they are listening with rapt attention to every idea you present.

- In many African countries, a subordinate may lower his head while receiving instructions from the boss and avoid looking at him or her directly in the eye. The employee is not necessarily timid or afraid. His or her behaviour is a cultural way of giving the boss the respect his or her position deserves. The same individual will demonstrate incredible assertiveness and self-confidence at a negotiating table with a client or service provider.

- In contradistinction to the above, a subordinate in the United States would probably look you straight in the eyes and even express disagreement with you, without intending to be rude. To the African executive this may be unacceptable; it is a clash of cultures.

- In Asian countries, team performance, consensus and 'saving face' (especially among the Chinese and Japanese) are important requirements for those who want to be leaders. African culture has the same ethos, but it has been corrupted by Western education and colonialism. In the United States and most of Europe, individualism and star performance are extolled.

- If you are invited to a diner in Korea, Japan or China, your host will be excited and impressed if you are able to eat with chopsticks rather than with a fork and knife.

Research has shown that pre-departure training, particularly language training, has a positive impact on the speed of adjustment of the employee on international assignment and also on that of the accompanying spouse, which in turn leads to improved performance (McNulty, 2005). Cross-cultural training is equally effective in facilitating cultural adjustment. Training should therefore be customized taking due cognizance of the purpose of the assignment, its location, and the needs of employees and their relocating families. Unlike executive training or mentoring, this is one developmental tool that could have profound impact on the family of the manager being sent on international assignment. Hence, employees and their spouses need to be sufficiently prepared not only for the cultural adaptation that lies ahead, but also for possible changes in marital dynamics. For instance, a spouse accompanying a husband/wife may not be able to find employment, and this new situation impacts not only on the family income but also, more importantly, on the self-esteem of the spouse as he or she may now have to depend on the partner for every purchase he or she has to make or financial assistance he or she wants to give somebody in need.

Top management must have a common understanding that international assignment is essential for leadership development. It cannot be a tool for dealing with unwanted managers. No organizational member is the exclusive property of any department or business unit. All employees, irrespective of their status, are a corporate asset. To that extent, they may be moved to work in any function, division or location of the organization, provided such mobility is mutually beneficial to both the employee and the organization. Employees will want to have a valid reason for their international assignment, its objective and duration, especially if it also involves geographical move to a country in difficult circumstances such as a political crisis, which may necessitate leaving the family behind. Consultation with the employees concerned not only enhances transparency, but also promotes employee ownership and commitment. The following story illustrates the need for adequate consultation in appointing managers for international assignments.

> Johnson is a manager in the marketing and sales division of a large manufacturing firm. Top management decided that, as part of his development to enable him take over from the General Manager, who was going to be the CEO of a newly created subsidiary, Johnson would have to go to a neighbouring country on an international assignment where he would head a production plant which embodies engineering design, production and quality control, as well as marketing and sales departments. He would have to be on the assignment for about two years to enable him have a broad understanding of the products and the challenges of marketing them.
>
> Johnson was never consulted before the decision was taken. Management's assumption was that he would be excited as his selection for the assignment was a manifestation of management's confidence in him and also an indication that he was being prepared for advancement to a higher-level position. On the contrary, he was thoroughly upset and threatened to resign when his supervisor, the General Manager, broke the news to him. The latter was shocked beyond words for some minutes. Johnson explained to his boss that he had just registered for a part-time MBA programme in the university in the city, and his wife had just taken up a new job so that she could be with their two children, having lived apart from them for over three years. He had a handicapped daughter who was being managed by one of the best specialists in the country, and she needed a lot of psychological support from both parents. Johnson sounded devastated. In one minute, he saw his future crashing down like a house built of cards. Yet, his plan for an MBA degree and his transfer by his employer had exactly the same objective – namely, career development and progression. Unfortunately, lack of timely communication and consultation had alienated Johnson and had portrayed management's plan for him as completely unfair and irresponsible.

The psychological readiness of an employee and the success of an external assignment depend not only on the preceding factors, but also on what the employee perceives as the prospects of the assignment on his or her future career. Dickman (2007), in collaboration with PricewaterhouseCoopers, did an interesting study on the value of international assignments. One of the things the study revealed was that, on average, 15 per cent of expatriate employees resign within the period of re-entry into the organization, and most of these people are high-performing individuals. High turnover rates are due to reluctance to return to previous jobs, ill-defined career paths and lack of opportunity to use newly acquired leadership competencies and experience. There have been instances when external assignments were so poorly managed that there were no more positions to which the expatriate staff could return at the end of their assignment. O'Grady (2001: 1) notes that about '68 per cent of companies do not guarantee expatriates a job upon their return'.

Besides the lack of clear definition of career progress, poor management is also a related cause of loss of expatriate employees. In many cases, executives are no longer in the organization's communication loop the moment they move into another country, despite pervasive information technology – e-mail, telephone, video-conferencing and so on. This is a critical and stressful aspect of international posting. Each employee must be assigned a mentor prior to departure. The mentor should be responsible for ensuring that: the executive has a reliable source of assistance; his or her career is protected by making sure that he or she is not disadvantaged by the external location; he or she is constantly in the organization's communication loop; and, finally, he or she does not stay longer than necessary in the external assignment. Some executives are inadvertently 'forgotten', thus casting the image of international assignment as a 'dumping ground'.

Action Learning

One of discoveries made by many organizations in the 1980s was that it is not generally easy for managers to apply the extensive knowledge they have acquired through management education to complex and rapidly changing circumstances in the business environment. Knowledge alone is no longer enough; managers must be able to innovate, adapt, resolve problems and take calculated risks, and behave as entrepreneurs. This change in paradigm is in recognition of the fact that the circumstances of organizations keep changing and managers inevitably have to operate in an uncertain and unpredictable situation. It was in an attempt to deal with this situation that Reginald Revans originated 'action learning'. Its philosophy is that managers must create a learning situation which enables them to explore, investigate and resolve, in a team, the problems which confront them at work. This is because training institutions and consultants may not be able to solve all organizational problems through executive training. Programmed knowledge, codified in books and manuals, is necessary but not sufficient for managers to manage their dynamic environments.

Action learning focuses on the dynamic and ever-changing and unpredictable situations which throw up new problems for managers every day. It involves dealing with risks. In Action learning, a group of five to eight individuals (referred to as an action learning set) is constituted to solve a specific work-related problem. Their main task is to seek a deeper understanding of the cause of the problem, investigate it, reflect on it and explore the possible and practical solutions. The action learning set usually chooses a work-based project that is strategically relevant to the organization, of interest to top management, and that would attract its support, ownership and mentorship. Action learning is supposed to involve some element of risk-taking. Selecting a project whose probability of failure is zero defeats its purpose, because learning occurs from mistakes and failures. Action learning also presupposes that top management has a high tolerance and acceptance of failure as part of the learning process. Indeed, it must be prepared to support the team with the resources they need to ensure success. Action learning seems to prevent the situation in which managers have no time to reflect on what they are doing because they are constantly busy or managing crises.

When action learning is properly implemented it achieves the following developmental objectives:

- It builds the leadership competencies of members of the action learning set.
- Members of the set develop the ability to work and learn in teams.
- Members develop systems thinking, innovativeness, creativity, risk-taking and problem-solving skills (Serrat, 2008).

Conclusion

The future of every corporation depends on its leadership development strategy because leaders are its veritable cornerstone. Gone are the days when people thought leaders were born. It is true that some people have what it takes to be better leaders than others, but no one can be a really great leader without development. Development helps to mould talented managers into the kind of leaders the organization needs and wants. Furthermore, succession plans are only worth the paper they are written on if they are driven by development programmes, which are the core of any succession plan. Development programmes have to be multidimensional and integrated to be effective. They have to take cognizance of the context of the corporation, its business strategy and rapid environmental changes. Executive leadership training should focus on issues and challenges, rather than on mundane topics.

10

Making Talent Development Effective

The Imperative of Talent Development

The effectiveness of organizations depends more on the quality of their human resources than on any other resource. Henry Ford once said that his machine could be taken away and his building and capital taken over, but if his men are left with him he should become Henry Ford. In other words, Ford Motors was built by no resource other than people. High-quality human resources are a product not only of careful, painstaking and intelligent recruitment and selection of talent, but also of continuous identification of development needs that are followed through with a systematic plan and the implementation of development programmes. Maxwell (2007: 5) makes the following vivid point which underscores the need for talent development: 'Talent stands out. It gets you noticed. In the beginning talent separates you from the rest of the pack. It gives you a head start on others. For that reason, natural talent is one of life's greatest gifts. But the advantage it gives lasts only for a short time.'

Development converts people's potential into actual capability to perform in a way that produces great results. Without development, employees, with all their talents, will diminish in value, skills and competencies and become less innovative, less engaged and less productive. They may ultimately become professional or managerial pygmies if they choose to remain in their organizations. As a consequence, the organizations will invariably reflect the stature of the managers and leaders they have, precisely because failing to grow and develop employees for leadership roles translates into failing to develop the capability of the organizations for higher performance and effectiveness.

The intellectual capacity of an organization is its greatest asset. People do not in themselves constitute an asset; they are mere statistics. It is their knowledge, skills, competencies and the relevance of such capabilities that represent an awesome asset or capital to an organization. In organizations where talent is highly valued and cherished there is a well-structured development process enshrined in a policy which is implemented in partnership with employees, because development is regarded as mutually beneficial to them and the organization.

A professional colleague was consulting for a multinational enterprise in 1996 when its CEO told him of his major concern with the low performance of some of his managers. On the recommendations of his division heads, he had promoted some six managers to senior managerial positions and deployed them to head the company's operations in different countries. They were to be global executives. They all had impressive performance records and great potential. Two years after the promotions, the CEO and his division heads were wondering if they had made a huge blunder in promoting the six managers; four were doing poorly while the performance of the other two was just fair. The dilemma was that the same managers who had demonstrated extraordinary performance before their promotion were now failing in their new responsibilities. They were micromanaging, had no strategic vision, were not providing effective leadership to their teams, and were failing to network and manage client relationships effectively. 'What went wrong?' was the question on the lips of the senior management team.

After discussion with the six managers and reviewing their files, the cause of the problem became crystal-clear. These executives were not effective in their new leadership roles because they were still behaving the way they did prior to their promotion to global leadership positions. They were fixated with using the same skills and competencies that earned them advancement. The irony was that those same skills and competencies that had made them successful managers in the national setting became inhibitors and the cause of their failures in their new responsibilities. These executives had each attended three one-week executive development programmes conducted by a renowned business school during their two-year incumbency in their present positions as part of the preparation for the new role. Yet they were not producing the results expected of them. The fundamental question therefore is: why do executive development efforts fail to yield the desired results?

Why Talent Development Programs are Generally Ineffective

According to Hollenbeck and McCall (2003), current development processes are not producing the executives required, and little has changed over the last 30 years. That precisely explains why competent executives are a scarce commodity and the competence of the few who are available is being called into question. Is it not also possible that the rapid turnover of CEOs could be the consequence of ineffective executive development? Could the ineffectiveness and inability of some organizations to compete in the global environment be attributed to their failure in developing their leadership corps? Many factors seem to be responsible for the ineffectiveness of talent development programmes.

FAILURE TO LINK DEVELOPMENT AND BUSINESS STRATEGY

One of the reasons why talent development programmes are not as effective as they should be is because they are not sufficiently linked to the business strategy and the specific needs of the participant's organization. The development needs of individual managers and the leadership needs of organizations vary from firm to firm because of differences in their bench strength, corporate strategy and corporate culture. Development programs therefore need to be situated within the organization's environmental and business context. It must be clear to the organization what core competencies are needed to achieve strategic goals. The process should consist of the following actions:

- Identify the current and future challenges of the company.
- Determine what core competencies will be required to achieve the desired results.
- Determine current capabilities in order to identify the gap between what is required and the existing capabilities.
- Identify those who have the capability or potential to deal with those challenges and provide them with the learning experiences they need to achieve the expected results. Development should be linked to challenges that are pertinent to the achievement of the business strategy.

The enterprise of executive development is therefore to bridge the gap between what is required in the future and what is currently available. For instance, if the strategy of a company in an English-speaking country like Nigeria or South Africa is to expand its business to Francophone countries, it should be part of the executive development programme to provide the executives with training in the French language, as well as in the economics, politics, cultural sensibilities and relevant knowledge of the legal framework of the countries concerned. The competencies required of a global executive in order to achieve results are not the same as those required by an executive who operates only within the national borders of his or her country. Given the business strategy of an organization, it is less productive to focus on generic leadership skills and competencies; rather, emphasis should be on those particular capabilities necessary for producing extraordinary leadership for the company.

While not ignoring today, executive development seeks to produce leaders for tomorrow because it is a strategic intervention aimed at effectively managing the future of the company. I have attended executive development courses, designed specifically for the managers of an organization, only to discover that in fact the learning events were generic and were in no way specifically related to the company's business strategy. Executive development programmes should be driven by the organization's business strategy.

LACK OF TOP MANAGEMENT OWNERSHIP

Talent development cannot succeed without the ownership of top management. Mere, passive support is inadequate to drive the enterprise. While the CEOs of some companies (Nestlé, Procter & Gamble and a host of others) consider development to be an organizational imperative and a critical aspect of their responsibility, there are many others who put it on the back-burner. The degree of importance attached to development is reflected in the size of the budget allocated for the activity or the speed with which the budget is reduced at the slightest financial distress. Sometimes, HR departments do not help the cause of development due to their inability to demonstrate how development programmes contribute to organizational performance and effectiveness. In the bid to justify their *raison d'être* and annual budget, many training departments lose sight of the essence of training, with the result that sheer volume of executive development training conducted, rather than the outcomes achieved, becomes the objective of development. Top management is enamoured with results, not the sheer volume of training events. The fact that talent development is an easy target for budget reduction is also a reflection of top management's perception that development is not substantially contributing to the business.

Top management's philosophy about talent development can greatly influence its effectiveness. Talent development cannot take place effectively without some underlying beliefs and values about how an organization intends to develop its leaders. The philosophy of some organizations is that development is the responsibility of the individual manager – they determine how they intend to navigate their individual careers and make efforts to acquire the necessary learning experience that could propel them to the next higher job. This is one extreme of the continuum. Other organizations have a paternalistic philosophy in which the organization unilaterally determines the kind of developmental experience each manager should be offered. This is the other extreme. The rationale is that the development of a manager is not necessarily for his or benefit but, rather, for the good of the organization. Yet other organizations have a philosophy that lies between the two – the organization and individual managers have a joint responsibility for development and it is for the good of both of them. The effectiveness of development is significantly reduced when top management's philosophy does not support it as a joint venture in which both the organization and managers are 'shareholders' and thus have a stake in it.

Although top managers generally accept the responsibility for determining the development needs of managers, they are passive or even reluctant to follow through the development plans to ensure that the desired results are achieved. The typical rationalization is that they are challenged for time. The reason sounds plausible, but what is missing in the reasoning is that managers cannot hire the best people from the market with a view to making their organizations effective and suddenly withdraw from developing the same people for the purpose for which they were originally hired. This is as absurd as of a mother telling a house help or a nurse that she is too busy or untrained to help her child grow and develop.

Developing people is a key responsibility of every top manager and leader. It cannot be abdicated to the HR department. The role of top managers involves the following:

- jointly identifying with individual managers their specific gaps in competencies and leadership capabilities;
- working with the HR director to determine the most effective development interventions and timeframe for implementation for each manager;
- following through to ensure that the development programmes actually take place as planned;
- when necessary, making presentations at learning events on topics of which the top manager has expertise and experience; and

- monitoring and evaluating the success of the development programmes – change in the behaviour and performance of the target people.

The most effective talent developers in any organization are the top managers. This is because they fully understand the vision of the company, its strategic direction, its business realities and the total job of management – its content, clients or customers, demands and pressures with concomitant stress, work environment, nature of work team, challenges, organizational politics and culture. These are the factors that make development meaningful and practical. It is therefore not surprising that, in organizations like Nestlé, the CEO himself participates in delivering training to his executives. He shares not only his vision, but also his wealth of experience and huge knowledge of the organization, which no business school professor can offer. Here lies the need for HR departments and top managers to review their paradigm, and approach development as a joint venture and not as HR's 'baby'.

As a management development manager in a steel plant, my most effective development courses were those designed and delivered by top managers. The case studies, examples, history and experiences they provided were rich, pertinent and easily assimilated by participants. Their analysis of the business environment and the relevance of the company's business model were certainly inspiring to participants at such seminars. This is not to suggest that consultants should not be used for executive training. Consultants can bring fresh perspectives and expertise that may not be available internally in organizations.

LACK OF A HOLISTIC APPROACH TO DEVELOPMENT

The reason for limited effectiveness in talent development varies from organization to organization, but experience has demonstrated that limited success is due, in many instances, to the fact that the development of human skills is usually divorced from organizational and institutional capacity development. The three dimensions are intertwined and interdependent, and therefore cannot be compartmentalized. No matter the volume and intensity of executive training in an organization, if the right psycho-social environment, policies, resources and incentives do not exist to reinforce motivation, engagement and commitment, the knowledge and skills acquired will never be used. The executives will remain stifled by the environment and organizational practices.

As part of its globalization strategy, a commercial bank opened operations in some African countries and deployed some of its best managers, well-trained and groomed, for these operations. They had immense responsibilities, but without commensurate authority. Consequently, they spent most of their time seeking approval for decisions that should have ideally been taken on the spot. With the epileptic status of African telephone networks, sometimes a simple transaction or deal that could be concluded normally in two hours remained unresolved for 24 hours because the executives were waiting for a response from headquarters. The thesis here is that organizations need to focus on the concept of capacity development because it is more holistic than training. In other words, companies have to develop their organizational and institutional capacity in tandem to sustain and reinforce the human capacity to use learning. It means removing organizational and institutional constraints that typically hinder the use of knowledge and skills at the end of training. Until this holistic approach is adopted, executive development programmes may continue to be less effective than expected.

PACE OF RESPONSE TO DEVELOPMENT NEEDS

Another factor that tends to impact on the effectiveness of executive programmes is the painfully slow pace at which organizations respond to the training and development needs of their executives. This could be due to bureaucratic inertia, lack of resources, gross incompetence and failure to see how the delay to provide timely development could hurt the business in the future. Modern organizations leverage technology to accelerate the pace of delivery of training and facilitate access to learning through distance, self-paced and web-based learning. Video-conferencing is a very convenient way of conducting training, especially where executives are in different locations. Executives operate in a very dynamic environment and therefore face new challenges on a daily basis. They cannot wait a year to learn what they need today in order to satisfy their valuable customers or assume higher responsibilities. The reality of today is that most executive training programmes can be delivered away from the classroom.

FAILURE TO FOCUS ON THE LEARNING ORGANIZATION

Today, progressive global organizations are shifting emphasis from merely training or developing capacity to becoming learning organizations. A learning organization is a place where employees excel at creating, acquiring and transferring knowledge; its building blocks are a supportive learning environment, concrete learning process and practices, and leadership behaviour that reinforces learning (Garvin, Edmondson and Gino, 2008). Training alone does not make an organization effective. As a matter of fact, highly trained employees can suffer from 'trained incapacity', a situation in which their current knowledge and skills make it difficult for them to operate effectively in a fast-changing environment because of their inability to adapt to change. A learning organization has a culture of continuous learning, and members use past experience to adapt to their changing environment. It means removing all barriers to the sharing of information and learning, providing opportunities for experimentation with new ideas, and opportunities to disagree with the supervisor or team without being penalized.

Learning organizations manage knowledge, which Kraiger (2002) refers to as establishing the right mechanisms and culture to encourage the sharing and application of knowledge. It involves gathering, structuring, storing and access to information. Knowledge management is important because, by virtue of their training and long years in an organization, employees become a great mine of knowledge, ideas and institutional memory. If they do not share this valuable resource, their departure could harm the performance of their division or the entire organization. When an organization loses a valued individual with all his or her institutional memory and expertise, it has failed to reap the dividend of its investment. Perhaps more damaging to its competitive ability is the fact that a competitor has benefited from its loss.

Experience and research have shown that most learning takes place informally in the workplace with professional colleagues or individuals committed to a common cause. Tannenbaum (2002: 19) noted that a study by the Center for Workforce Development reported that up to 70 per cent of workplace learning is informal. Other studies have also reported that informal on-the-job instruction is three to six times more prevalent than formal training. It is therefore important for organizations to devise means and ways of managing knowledge – ensuring unimpeded and continuous flow, sharing and exchange of novel ideas, learning, information and experiences.

Training in a learning organization is not just about bridging the gap in knowledge or skills. It is about how, through learning, an organization can continuously adapt, renew, reinvent and reinvigorate itself and remain permanently innovative in an environment that is constantly changing. Learning organizations recognize the compelling need to reward people not only for learning, but also for using the acquired learning to solve organizational problems. Reward is not based on ascriptive criteria such as seniority, status and quota, but on the skills and competencies acquired and their effective utilization.

Managing the Career of Low Performers

Every organization has low performers, as well as its high and solid performers. So far, this chapter has outlined the conditions for ensuring effective development for high performers and those with high potential, but whose performance may currently be low. Organizations should invest in employees according to their potential to yield high returns by producing extraordinary results or demonstrating extraordinary leadership abilities. Development should therefore focus on those who can benefit adequately from it. However, the organization cannot ignore those whose performance needs considerable improvement to enable them to perform satisfactorily. In this section we discuss how to be effective in managing the career of low performers.

At the time of recruitment, most employees generally showed great promise or else they would not have been employed in the first instance. They may have indeed performed commendably in the organization for several years before their performance declined to the point where it became a matter for concern. The poor performance of a new employee or the decline in the performance of a previously high performer should provoke some concern, curiosity and investigation. Unfortunately, managers are usually so busy that they hardly have time to investigate why some employees perform well and others poorly. Without a good knowledge of the specific factors that facilitate or inhibit high performance, an organization may not succeed in helping its employees improve performance or sustain high performance.

When confronted with low performers, managers react in a variety of ways. Some choose to ignore the problem and behave as if it does not exist, or assume, like Macbeth, that: 'Time and the hour run through the roughest day' – one way or another, the problem will be resolved. Others may decide to imagine that, having received consecutive poor performance ratings, the low-performing employees will resign and leave the company before they are shown the way to the gate. Other managers may ask the HR department to transfer the low performers to other departments or divisions. Yet others may confront the employees and threaten them with termination if their performance does not significantly improve. All these approaches are symptomatic of bad leadership, solution avoidance, lack of talent mindset and managerial insensitivity to an acute human need that is destroying a career and impacting adversely on the organization. They are completely inappropriate for talent management, particularly in global, multinational enterprises.

The truth is that when managers shy away, for whatever reasons, from dealing head-on with low performers there are grave consequences. Some people will naturally pay a price for such an abdication of responsibility – namely, the affected employee, other employees and, ironically, the managers who are derelict in their responsibilities. First, high performers are overloaded with additional responsibility that actually belongs to the low performers. Second, the low performers agonize over their situation because managers are not helping to pull them out from a situation that could end their career. Finally, the managers either don't get their jobs done at all or they get them done with more than the usual effort and with additional stress.

It is not uncommon for managers to believe that some employees are incapable of redemption from their current state, even though they have not been given them a chance to improve. With that kind of mindset, managers cannot see improvement even when it happens. They see only what they have programmed their eyes to see – low performance. Unknowingly, they communicate the same message to the concerned employee who comes to believe, out of frustration, that no matter what he or she achieves, it will always be rated as low performance. This becomes a kind of self-fulfilling prophecy.

Some low performers are worth saving not necessarily on humanitarian grounds, but because of the prospect of significant improvement in performance. Individual traumatic circumstances (divorce, loss or protracted illness of a loved one) could have a prolonged and devastating impact on performance. Line managers must identify the cause of poor performance. A manager who has consistently communicated with his subordinates should not find it difficult to detect the cause of poor performance. Once the cause has been diagnosed, the next step is to agree with the affected employee a structured action plan to address the problem. Quite often, this is not done. In 1994–96, I carried out a longitudinal review of over 200 performance evaluation reports in four different organizations. They revealed that, in many cases, the same weakness or area of improvement identified in the previous report had occurred in the subsequent reports for two or three consecutive years, thus suggesting that the management of the companies never took any deliberate action to help the employees address the aetiology of their underperformance. Yet, they were penalized every year for failure to overcome their weaknesses.

To avoid ambiguity and confusion it is important to state clearly in the action plan for improvement what is expected to be achieved and the desired timeframe for the improvement – usually six to 12 months. To ensure ownership by both the supervisor and the employee, they should jointly take an active part in designing, developing and implementing it as a partnership with a common objective. The role of both parties should also be clearly described and realistic targets agreed for the next six to 12 months to serve as milestones for monitoring progress and giving feedback on the employee's progress. Experience has, however, shown that six months is not long enough to yield meaningful results because, in most cases, managers are so busy that they provide support only on an irregular and sporadic basis, with limited benefit to the employee. Any action plan agreed upon must be implemented with sincerity and commitment, and in the spirit of the plan; it should not be a stratagem merely to meet legal obligations or provide the organization with an alibi for termination when it eventually happens. An action plan is intended to help the underperformer to close the gap in performance.

In helping low performers to improve, managers need to adopt a positive and genuinely helpful attitude because poor performers usually tend to be nervous and lacking in self-confidence because they perceive their careers to be on the line. Furthermore, being singled out as an underperformer in a team carries a social stigma in the eyes of colleagues. They therefore need to be repeatedly reassured that they could become great performers. Managers' body language usually speaks louder than their words in such circumstances. Managers must avoid unwittingly creating a self-fulfilling prophecy or 'Pygmalion effect'. This term is derived from Shaw's play *Pygmalion* (2003). In Greek mythology Pygmalion was a sculptor and prince of Cyprus who carved an ivory statue of an ideal woman. So beautiful was the statue that Pygmalion fell in love with it and begged goddess Aphrodite to bring her to life. The statue came to life and the couple married. The story was the basis of Shaw's play.

In the play, Professor Henry Higgins claimed that he could transform Eliza Doolittle, a flower girl, to pass as a duchess. But Eliza herself did not believe him. She tells Pickering, Higgins's friend that he (Pickering) could see that, apart from the things anyone could pick up (the dressing and the proper way of speaking, and so on), the difference between a lady and a flower girl was not how she behaved but how she was treated. She believed that she would always be a flower girl to Professor Higgins because he always treated her as a flower girl, but she knew she could be a lady to Pickering because he always treated her as a lady, and always would.

The implication of this story is obvious for managers, and indeed, for leaders. It is that the transformation from under-performance to star performance depends more on what managers expect, say and do than what employees actually do to improve their performance. If managers treat them as individuals who are capable of being star performers, they will be encouraged to fulfil the prophecy of their managers and become stars, to the amazement of their colleagues. By the same logic, their performance may not improve if they believe that no matter what efforts they make, they will always be rated as low performers. The improvement of underperformers depends more or less on their managers.

However, those who do not make efforts to improve their performance despite the necessary support, expectations and encouragement may have to be removed, but with respect and dignity. How? Organizations should have a policy that enables them to provide a reasonable financial separation package with a view to reducing the pain and humiliation of termination. Such a package will enable the employees to quickly pick up the pieces of their lives and chart a new career outside the company. More importantly, it promotes goodwill and does not leave an indelible scar of trauma in the psyche of the employees. If anything, honest employees will admit that the severance of the employment relationship is due to their own failing and that the organization has been fair and humane. Organizations should treat people with firmness, yet with a human face.

Indeed, organizations could make termination of low performers dignified by institutionalizing a group separation – essentially, a scheme for targeting low performers and all those who, for one reason or another, have become liabilities. This is a common practice in many private and multinational organizations. Such a group separation, with a generous severance package, removes the stigma and pain of exit before retirement age. The cost of the scheme may be enormous, but it has a dual advantage. First, it enables organizations to recruit more capable people and at lower salaries. Second, it is a signal to 'survivors' that the organization will keep people only on the basis of performance.

All the foregoing steps for saving a poor performer are like a therapy for a patient on a sick bed. But the illness could have been avoided by doing first things first – coaching and counselling (see Chapter 6). Growing people is a time-consuming but extremely rewarding activity, because it is like watering a plant or bringing up a child. Besides the inherent satisfaction in seeing the plant or child grow to maturity, the fruits of the labour can be enormous and take different forms. Because growing people is a great challenge, managers and executives must have an entrepreneurial view of their responsibility and be committed to their organization to be able to perform the duty effectively. The human resource department has a critical role in talent management, and this is the subject of the next chapter.

11

The Role of the Human Resource Function in Globalization

Globalization and the Emergence of MNEs in the Developing World

The most remarkable characteristic of globalization is the integration of national economies into a global economy through the instrumentality of information technology, especially electronic communication. Globalization involves trade, capital flows, mobility of human resources and diffusion of knowledge and technology across national borders. Czenter identifies two levels of globalization. The first is the political and economic level, which is the process of 'denationalization of markets, politics and legal systems' (Czenter, 2002: 7). At this level, globalization reduces barriers between countries, encourages integration of economic and political activities, and accelerates the interdependence of countries, with the result that events in one country tend to have an impact in other countries. For instance, a reduction in the production of petroleum due to the vandalization of pipelines or an attack on oil workers by the militant groups in the oil-rich delta region of Nigeria has an immediate impact on global oil prices. The implication of globalization is that no country can operate like an island.

The second level of globalization is the business level in which companies participate in the 'emerging global economy and establish themselves in foreign countries' (Czenter, 2002: 8). The growth and prosperity of organizations have come to depend, to a large extent, on their ability to compete effectively not only within national boundaries, but also across national borders. It has facilitated the creation of mega- and supra-organizations through mergers and acquisitions, and also the delocalization of enterprises. Multinational enterprises (MNEs) are taking advantage of low taxes and low compensation in certain countries by relocating their production units in such countries.

The developing world has also been affected by the impact of globalization one way or another. The annual rate of economic growth of African countries prior to the global financial crisis, which began in 2008, was about 5.75 per cent with the prospect of it rising even higher. This was made possible by reforms in the legal, political and governance systems of most African countries, which have created an enabling environment for foreign investment and regional mobility of resources. The growth rate has had a significant impact on the growth of banking and financial institutions, gas and oil, and telecommunications companies. The creation of regional economic communities, such as the Economic Community of West Africa (ECOWAS), has also fostered not only sub-regional trade, but also the emergence of multinational companies in Africa. Many of these companies are conducting business across national borders, competing in multiple countries and operating in diverse cultural, political and legal environments.

Many companies in South Africa, Egypt, Morocco, Nigeria and Tunisia are becoming giant multinational enterprises not only in Africa, but also globally. For instance, SABMiller, one of the world's largest brewers, has its origin in South Africa. It has over 69,000 employees spread over Africa, Asia, Europe, Latin America and the United States, as well as 139 breweries and 200 brands worldwide. Other large African multinational corporations include Anglo-American Platinum Corporation (South Africa), MTN (South Africa), Orascom (Egypt), Itissalat Al Maghrib (Morocco), Attijariwafa Bank (Morocco), First Bank of Nigeria, Zenith Bank (Nigeria), United Bank for Africa (Nigeria), Ecobank, and a host of others. MTN is a telecommunications company which operates in 21 African countries and also in the Middle East. It is the biggest mobile telephone operator in Africa. Ecobank is one of the leading pan-African banking institutions with operations in 22 African countries. The United Bank for Africa (UBA) is a mega-bank in Nigeria with a balance sheet of over $8 billion. It is one of the largest financial institutions in West Africa and has 6 million customers. It has operations in Ghana, Ivory Coast, Cameroon, Sierra Leone, Uganda, United States and the United Kingdom. According to Onwuamaeze (2008), the factors that have been responsible for the expansion and penetration of African firms into other countries include, amongst others, the use of information technology and changing political attitudes and mindsets on the continent. Many countries have come to realize that the private sector is the engine of growth and that foreign investment is catalytic in promoting economic growth and development.

Some of these organizations and others not listed here have done pretty well in the international arena. SABMiller, for instance, is indeed a great success story. But, as the global financial, economic and technological terrain keeps changing, there is no guarantee that many others, especially those that are just entering the international scene, will do equally well. The success of multinational enterprises in the developing world as global companies will depend on their ability to hire, develop and retain talent for their global businesses. The globalization of business has increased the need to identify and analyse ways in which multinational companies need to operate most effectively both now and in the future. It would be an error to assume that managers who have been successful in the domestic or national markets would be equally successful in international markets. This is because the mindset and competencies required to be effective in international operations are not necessarily the same as those required in the national environments. How can the human resource function integrate HR management practices with the firm's strategy and strategic needs? Schuler (1992) believes that the concern of strategic human resource management should be to ensure the full integration of HR management with the strategy and strategic needs of a company, and that HR practices should be adjusted, accepted and utilized by every employee as part of their daily work.

In essence, what this points to is that human resources are the key determinants of a company's competitive advantage. Of all the resources of a company – plant, technology, finance, natural resources, geographical location, protected market and so on – it is the human asset alone that can guarantee sustained competitive advantage. This is because it is the only resource that cannot be imitated or easily acquired by competitors (Pfeffer, 1998). However, a fundamental question is: has the HR management in African multinational enterprises undergone the kind of transformation necessary to enable it to give such companies a competitive advantage? Evidence everywhere seems to suggest the contrary. Bawa and Ali (1999) rightly noted that the changes taking place in the global business environment are often not accompanied by complementary changes in human resource management practices. It is a matter for regret that while functions such as operations, sales and marketing are generally quick to adapt to the global reality, the HR function typically lags behind in developing policies, systems and practices that support globalization. The situation raises the question about what the responsibilities of HR executives should be in globalization.

The Role of HR Management in Globalization

HR specialists need four basic competencies to be able to partner effectively in the strategic management process which is fundamental to fostering competitive advantage. The competencies are: business competence, professional and technical knowledge, integration competence and ability to manage change (Ulrich and Yeung, 1989). In general, most HR departments perform relatively well in the sphere of professional and technical knowledge, but not in the other three competencies. They have HR knowledge and skills in performing the traditional and usually transactional functions such as recruitment, compensation, benefits administration and welfare management. However, in Africa most HR specialists lack business-related competence. Not only do they lack a deep understanding of the core business of their firms, but they also do not know enough about the dynamic economic, financial and legal factors affecting the firm's business. They do not have business experience. Without business-related competence it is hard for the HR department to craft appropriate strategies to support the strategic direction or integrate HR practices with the firm's strategic needs. This is HR department's role as a strategic partner.

STRATEGIC PARTNER

The role of HR function as a strategic partner has become a buzzword in recent years, thus emphasizing the universally recognized need for HR departments to move away from personnel administration to the value-added function of helping organizations develop not only policies and practices, but also talent that will help the business. The reason why HR management has to be a strategic partner and be integrated into corporate strategy is that it is responsible for the firm's most important asset. To be a strategic partner, HR management has to be so aligned to the business strategy that changes in the strategy would require a change in the HR strategy, systems and practices. This is logically the reality if HR strategy is fully integrated into the design and implementation of the firm's corporate strategy. Partnership also requires internal coherence among the various elements of the HR system so that there is synergy and complementarity.

HR managers cannot be effective strategic partners in organizations in the developing world if they are not involved in defining the business strategy. Budhwar and Debrah (2001) note that there is no clear evidence in most African countries that HR managers are involved in strategic decision-making or policy formulation. They attribute this non-involvement to a tradition of personnel management in sub-Saharan Africa. HR executives cannot actively participate in defining the business strategy if the head of the HR function is not positioned at board or top management level where business strategies are crafted and strategic decisions made. It stands to reason that if MNCs in the developing world want to achieve a strategic alignment between globalization and talent management, the HR management team must be given the opportunity to provide their professional input into strategy formulation and also be invested with the authority to influence the decisions that their firms make. Sullivan (2010), a well-known HR guru, tried to trace the 2010 Toyota scandal, in which over 8 million cars were recalled, to the failure of the HR function. Although the problem with the Toyota vehicles was certainly technical, the HR expert was saying that you cannot compartmentalize technical and human resource management decisions.

MANAGING CONSISTENCY

As companies establish operations outside national borders, they soon realize that a one-size-fits-all approach cannot be applied to all countries in the management of talent. Česynienė (2008: 42) opined that global organizations have to think globally but act local, decentralize yet centralize, delegate but control, and differentiate yet integrate. De Cieri and Dowling (1998: 3) have noted that a fundamental issue is the 'tension between the needs for global coordination (integration) and local responsiveness (differentiation).' Thus the challenge which HR managers therefore face is how to manage with an international perspective while recognizing national idiosyncrasies. This is precisely the reason why HR departments must have the competence to balance the opposing dualities or apparent inconsistencies. HR approaches that have worked well in one country may not necessarily be successful in another country because labour laws, industrial relations, compensation and availability of talent may not be the same. HR practices, even in the same geographical and linguistic region like the Maghreb countries of North Africa or the French-speaking countries of West Africa, are not exactly the same. HR practices are influenced by their individual colonial histories, national cultures and levels of HR management development.

Sullivan (2004a) aptly states that HR managers have to get consistency in operations and information flow across the world while simultaneously allowing for some degree of local autonomy and control. He suggests that all HR solutions need to share a common consistent base while simultaneously providing for customization according to local needs. Consistency in HR practices across national boundaries is important because it promotes corporate culture and organizational effectiveness. Organizations can achieve a certain measure of consistency in HR practices through the following actions:

- development of an HR mission statement and strategy aligned to the strategic direction of the firm, thereby providing such a strong common base that even though there may be national variations, the objectives of HR function are consistently the same everywhere in the firm's operations, and are aligned to the HR strategic objectives;

- development of global policies and standardized HR systems in selection, development, performance appraisal and compensation.

SUPPORT TO GLOBAL EXECUTIVES

The general impression of line managers is that HR departments are insensitive, reactive and slow to respond to changing business and environmental needs. They are not close enough to hear and see the challenges faced by line managers. It may even be worse for global executives who operate at a long distance from the head office where most HR policies and decisions are made. In external operations where there is no HR specialist, virtually every decision on staffing has to be referred to headquarters. Global executives need support in the implementation of policies and systems relating to hiring (employment laws), training, performance appraisal, compensation (including taxation issues), and development and advancement of employees to higher-level positions. Because of the preoccupation with compliance procedures there is inflexibility and slow response to issues that deviate from the norm, thereby eroding the fabric of the partnership. The HR department therefore needs to be sensitive to the concerns of executives in external operations and to feel their pulse by providing opportunities for regular communication. They need to listen and respond to the executives' needs creatively and imaginatively, bearing in mind the peculiarities of each location.

MANAGING CULTURE CHANGE

Embedded in an organization's mission and vision statement are its values, beliefs and norms which constitute its culture. Organizations are dynamic and, in their attempt to meet the needs of clients and indeed stakeholders, they continually have to renew themselves by adopting new ideas, practices, processes and policies. They continually seek to change the way in which they do business. Such changes tend to impact on corporate culture. No matter how beneficial an idea or policy may seem, some employees will resist it. It is the responsibility of the HR department, as a cultural catalyst, to facilitate and accelerate the transformation from the status quo to the desired state in the organization. In this role the HR department is a change agent. This is one of the most important competencies of an HR executive working in a multinational company. The role involves identifying, defining and solving problems, building trust, building commitment to the change process, and ensuring that the change actually takes place as intended.

Quite often, the HR function is not proactive in translating a company's business strategy into HR priorities because many HR managers do not understand globalization and its implication for the HR function. This limited understanding of the firm's business and its international environment hampers HR managers' ability to provide strategic direction and respond proactively through appropriate policies and practices to external environmental pressures associated with globalization and competition. Therefore, they need to be trained to acquire broader exposure to, and deeper perspectives of, the role of HR management in globalization and the use of information technology to enhance HR efficiency. The continued relevance of the HR function will depend on the extent to which it performs a valued role in making the organization competitive and effective. Finally, top management also has the responsibility to provide the HR function its well-deserved place in the organizational hierarchy so that it can contribute more meaningfully to strategic goals.

12

Delta Steel Company – A Case Study of Talent Management

Delta Steel Company Limited, Ovwian-Aladja (near Warri) in Delta State is an integrated steel plant established by the Federal Government of Nigeria at a cost of about N1.26 billion (equivalent of US$1.89 billion in 1979 – exchange rate approximately N1 to US$0.6) to enhance the industrial capability of Nigeria. Another steel plant established by the federal government for the same purpose was the Ajaokuta Steel Company Ltd. The need for the steel plants emanated from the rapidly growing demand for crude steel in the country. It was projected that by 1980 the demand for steel would have risen to 9.168 million metric tons. In the event, the demand rose from 0.5 million metric tons in 1970 to 3.5 million metric tons in 1980.

Delta Steel Company (DSC) was incorporated on 14 November 1979, under the Companies Act of 1968 and commissioned on 29 January 1982. The company is located over an area of 175 hectares on the south embankment of the Warri River. It lies approximately 11 kilometres from Warri Refinery, halfway between the villages of Ovwian and Aladja. The selection of Ovwian-Aladja as the site for the steel plant took into consideration the abundance of natural gas in the oil-rich delta area. Natural gas forms the major energy requirement for the Midrex direct reduction process utilized by the plant. The site was also adequate for the potential expansion of liquid steel production to between 2.5 million metric tons and 3 million metric tons per annum in phase 2. In addition, the location provided easy access to the plant by sea, making it, in effect, a seaport plant like most modern steel plants all over the world.

The company was managed by a general manager who reported to a board of directors. The organization was divided into six large divisions, each headed by a deputy general manager. The divisions were administration, finance, commercial, production, technical services and estate management. Each division consisted of sectors headed by assistant general managers while the sectors in turn consisted of departments headed by managers.

When the steel plant was commissioned in 1982, its production process, known as Midrex direct reduction, was one of the newest and most sophisticated technologies in steel production. The technology was the handiwork of the Consortium of German–Austrian Companies (CSA) which built the plant. The term 'direct reduction' denotes the fact that ore reduction takes place directly without any melting whatsoever. Until the 1980s the blast furnace process was considered the only unrivalled economical process to extract iron from its ores.

Production begins in the pellet plant with iron-making. Iron ore, imported from Liberia and Brazil, is dried and ground in a ball mill. The fine ore is then mixed with hydrated lime and water thereby forming pellets. Hydrated lime is produced from limestone in the lime plant. The pellets are fired and hardened in the indurating machine at a temperature of 850°C–1,300°C. At the direct reduction plant, the iron oxide pellets are reduced with natural gas in a shaft furnace. The result is pure iron known as 'direct reduced iron' (DRI) which is stored in bins and protected permanently with an inert atmosphere of nitrogen.

The next stage is in the electric arc furnace. The temperature in this furnace is around 6,000°C. The melt charge is an average of 80 per cent DRI and 20 per cent scrap. Normally, the scrap is melted first, followed by the introduction of DRI fed in from the furnace roof through a vitro feeder. Impurities in the resultant liquid metal are removed as slag with the aid of burnt lime, and oxygen is used to aid refining. The steel is tapped into preheated ladles and transferred to the continuous casting shop where the molten steel is turned into preheated tan dishes which distribute the liquid steel into six moulds. Billets are then cast.

The last stage of the production process takes place in the rolling mills where the billets are reheated to a temperature of 1,200°C and passed through a roughing stand for the removal of scales and initial deformation. The billet size is reduced by approximately 50 per cent and deformed progressively into the appropriate shape for finishing operations. The final rolling operations take place here at the finishing stands. Additional processes in the rolling mills include the cooling of the products to ambient temperature, cutting to market product lengths, straightening if necessary, stacking and bundling.

The main products of Delta Steel Company were billets, plain rounds, ribbed bars, equal and unequal angles, tees, channels, flat bars and I-beams. The major consumers of billet products were the three inland rolling mills at Oshogbo, Kastina and Jos. The products of the steel plant were used mainly for construction and fabrication. Auxiliary or by-products from the steel plant included industrial gases (oxygen, argon and nitrogen), foundry products, burnt and hydrated lime, and direct reduced iron. The installed production capacity of the company was 1 million metric tons of liquid steel. Between 1982 and 1990 the highest production output was 243,893 metric tons, and that was achieved in 1985.

Attracting and Hiring the Best

The General Manager and Chief Executive Officer of the company was a young brilliant charismatic, Stanford-trained chemical engineer who provided strong leadership right from the establishment of the company. He was strongly committed to attracting, hiring, motivating and retaining talented professionals and managers. He personally head-hunted and attracted talent to the company. Delta Steel provides an interesting case study of the factors that can influence the attraction, motivation and retention of employees.

By 1983 the company had a workforce of about 4,000. Among them were some of the brightest professionals in the country. They were smart and with diverse experiences in various fields ranging from engineering, production, plant maintenance, marketing to finance and accounting, and human resources management. What is interesting, but puzzling, is that many of them left highly-paid jobs in oil and gas companies, banks and other manufacturing companies and took huge cuts in their pay to work for Delta Steel Company. This is in direct contrast to the usual practice of seeking pay increases when changing jobs.

The company's initial salary structure was adopted wholesale from the federal government civil service and remained so for ten years. Government salary structure can in no way be compared to the high and intimidating salaries in banks and oil companies. In fact, even as at January 1989 when a new salary structure was implemented, the salary range of top management (assistant general managers and deputy general managers) was N21,436–N27,000 per annum (approximately US$14,000–18,000 per year, using an exchange rate of US$1 to N1.5 at that time). Logically, the salaries of middle managers and professional staff were much lower than these figures. In my longitudinal study of the company extending over five years, I discovered that it was able to attract and hire people, in spite of the low salaries, for the following reasons.

THE COMPANY'S MISSION

The company's mission was to become the driver and bastion of industrialization in Nigeria, and this message was embodied and communicated in its advertisements, products, souvenirs, and so on with the popular mantra 'Reinforcing Nigeria with Steel'. It was powerful and captivating. Delta Steel Company was the first integrated steel plant in sub-Saharan Africa. Although established after the Ajaokuta Steel Plant, also in Nigeria, it went into production first. The first cohorts of employees were galvanized by the strong desire to make history – building the first steel plant and laying the foundation for an industrialized country. The commitment was palpable and inexplicably missionary. The effect was infectious and magnetic in attracting prospective employees to the organization.

CAREER PROSPECTS

The company presented prospective employees with opportunities for a great career in a green field, and in a new and fledgling steel industry. This was the magnet for those who left highly-paid jobs in oil companies and banks for the company. They were prepared to temporarily sacrifice higher pay in order to build a career that would ultimately compensate them in status, higher remuneration and visibility in the industry. The company also offered career opportunities to those who were apparently experiencing a career plateau and wanted new challenges. Such individuals were usually middle-aged and mature, and occupied managerial or leadership positions.

OPPORTUNITY FOR GROWTH AND DEVELOPMENT

Whatever the level and variety of skills and experience of new employees, the company insisted on every manager and professional being trained to acquire knowledge and skills not only in their respective professions, but also in the culture of steel companies. Right from outset, the Company's induction training was recognized as essential for effectiveness precisely because of the novelty of the steel production process. Steel production is also full of hazards which can be considerably reduced if employees have the right skills, knowledge and attitude to their jobs. Furthermore, intensive training was required in different operations to prepare Nigerians to ultimately take over the management of the company from the German–Austrian consortium.

The prospects of training and career development were particularly attractive to those who had never travelled overseas or worked for such a mammoth organization. Technical, supervisory and managerial training was provided for different levels and categories of employees in Austria and India, generally ranging between one and four months, with the exception of the project engineering design group whose training was for one year. The training department also went on an eight-month course at the training centre of the International Labour Office in Turin.

Most young college graduates joined the company in order to acquire skills. Besides the fact that they were attracted by the opportunity to make a career, some of them also had the aspiration that, with sufficient skills and experience, they could in future, as entrepreneurs, set up independent ancillary, operations downstream. Furthermore, the company established an educational assistance programme which provided opportunities to junior employees to acquire higher academic and professional qualifications while working for the organization. Evening courses were organized for a small fee.

TOTAL REWARDS

As earlier noted, the remuneration of the company was comparatively low. But it had an attractive basket of benefits that were unique to the company when compared to other organizations in Nigeria. In line with the tradition of many steel companies in other parts of the world, such as India, a captive steel township comprising over 6,340 housing units was built near the steel plant. Employees paid a small percentage of their salaries as rent and utilities. Employees owned nothing in their residences except personal effects such as television sets, musical equipment, clothes and so on. Each house was fully furnished with chairs, beds, refrigerators, air-conditioners, carpets, cookers and dining sets. They were maintained or replaced by the company if they became dysfunctional. As part of preparing the employees for retirement, the company had an employee housing loan scheme to enable employees to buy or build a house of their own. Employees were also entitled to a certain tonnage of rolled steel products at a reduced cost if they provided proof of actually building a house of their own.

Delta Steel operated a comprehensive healthcare system for its employees and their dependants (one wife and four children). The healthcare facilities included a 60-bed hospital located in the staff residential quarters and a clinic located in the plant to cater for emergencies and minor ailments of staff while at work. The healthcare system, including occupational healthcare, public health, health education, pest control and sanitation, was provided to employees free of charge. There was also a life insurance scheme.

Delta Steel Company owned and managed three high-quality and fully equipped primary and nursery schools with a population of about 3,000 pupils. In addition, there was a technical high school which provided post-primary, technical education to employees' children. The company provided recreational facilities – a club house, tennis courts, squash courts, swimming pools, a football pitch and so on – in the residential quarters. Furthermore, it operated a cooperative and credit scheme. Also provided was a family welfare unit which handled counselling, arbitration and support in matrimonial and inter-family disputes. The company supplied transport, at a subsidized rate, to and from work and granted vehicle loans to employees to enable them to acquire transport of their own. Management staff had official cars that were maintained by the company. Meals at the management and staff canteens were highly subsidized.

The low pay was not a great cause for concern to most employees initially, although the unions raised the issue of when there would be a change in the salary structure at almost every meeting with management. Employees were happy because the company basically provided what high salaries were needed for: namely, rent, children's education, health, transportation, utilities and recreational facilities.

BONDING

Living together in one location resulted in an unanticipated consequence for the company – bonding. The steel township was like one huge African clan, except that the people were of different descent, ethnic and linguistic backgrounds. Just living together was not what endowed it with the semblance of a clan. It was the social activities and a web of relationships that bound individuals and families together. For instance, the wedding of an employee was the affair of the employee's department and residential neighbours. Employees usually turned out in large numbers and supported the event financially. When an employee lost a spouse or parent, the company made transport available free to convey as many staff members as were willing and available to attend the funeral. In addition, employees provided material, spiritual and moral support to the bereaved.

Quite often, employees who did not even know each other were brought together surprisingly by their children who were in the same class or played together. The tennis and squash courts brought many amateur players together. There were sports competitions. Once a quarter, the social welfare unit organized a social or cultural event such as a musical concert or a drama that brought families together in a relaxed atmosphere. There was a spirit of familialism and the demonstration of the African concept of 'brother's keeper'. The significance of this bonding was that it was translated into strong teamwork in departments and production plants throughout the organization. There was easy communication within and across organizational units. 'Working in silos' was an almost alien concept to the company.

The Challenge of Employee Engagement and Retention

As earlier noted, the factors that usually inspire people to take up employment with an organization are not necessarily the same factors that are required to retain them and keep them highly engaged. By 1986 cracks were beginning to show – the euphoria of working for a steel plant had begun to wane because the anticipated great career and high salaries usually associated with steel companies were becoming a mirage. Some of the employees began to show signs of 'buyer's regret'. There was growing frustration, particularly among the young professional employees, because of unrealized dreams. Promotion was rapid in the first four or five years of the establishment of the company. After that, it petered away into a mere trickle.

UNFULFILLED DREAMS

I recall that in 1982–83 over 20 young engineers were recruited and trained as a team in India for about a year in steel design, production, maintenance, foundry work and so on. The cohort was to be an elite group in a newly created project engineering design department with responsibility for innovation and modification, if necessary, of the production technology and infrastructure. They were also to provide leadership for the installation of phase II of the plant. It was an exciting prospect, dream and responsibility. The cohort naturally appreciated the training they received because it had prepared them for the challenge ahead. Furthermore, it also met their initial motivation for joining the company. But by 1986 more than half of them had been poached by other firms. Why?

The reason was that Delta Steel Company could not provide them with a visible career path and prospects for advancement. Remuneration was still abysmally low. It did not compare with remunerations in the Nigerian National Petroleum Company in the same environment. Salaries in other companies like Shell Development Company, Chevron and Schlumberger in the oil sector were so many times higher that there was virtually no basis for comparison. Furthermore, most managerial positions had been filled by other equally young and talented men and women. Advancement prospects were diminishing and becoming bleak and more competitive. As if the situation was not bad enough, the plant had increasing difficulty securing adequate funds to purchase iron ore, spare parts and other raw materials for production. Lack of resources for operations further impacted on the motivation and commitment of the employees.

Delta Steel Company was originally established to have a second phase, which was to produce flat sheets. The ribbed bars, flat bars, channels, I-beams tees and angles that it produced were essentially good for construction and fabrication, but they did not constitute the basis for industrial take-off. Following the financial constraints deriving from the implementation of the Structural Adjustment Programme by the federal government, it gradually dawned on employees that phase II, which was critical for industrialization, might never happen. It really never did. It was a mirage. Consequently, some employees began to ask themselves, 'Is there a future for us here?'

Most of the young engineers were either not married or married with one or two young children who were not yet in school. They were therefore very mobile. The various benefits and the social bonding in the company were apparently of little relevance at that point in their lives. And, in any case, even the social bonding was gradually being whittled away by a conflict of attrition. Social services were also declining in quality, reflecting the general ill-health of the organization. And so the young professionals on whom the company had invested so much began to take their exit for other organizations.

TOXIC WORK ENVIRONMENT

In 1986 the company's work environment became toxic as a result of conflict within the top management. The general manager and his deputy were engaged in a melodramatic power tussle and, in the process, unwittingly divided the firm into two. Each of them had his supporters and apostles. The work environment became unhealthy, unproductive and fraught with suspicion and back-stabbing. The conflict led to the voluntary and involuntary departures of managers and professional employees. Unsurprisingly, liquid steel production declined significantly from 243,893 metric tons in 1985 to 134,638 in 1986. Low production continued for several years after. Healing the wounds inflicted on personal relationships and individual careers was difficult and took some time.

THE SURVIVORS

Why is it that despite all the imbroglio and turmoil some employees remained in the organization? Those who remained did so not necessarily because of any specific efforts or interventions to retain them on the part of the company. They simply had no better option. Some remained because they were no longer employable because of their age. Others had highly specialized skills in steel production that were not generally in demand in the labour market. Yet others were hoping that better days would dawn for the company. Whatever their reasons or rationalizations, they therefore needed the company just as much as the company needed them.

Conclusion

A number of deductions can be made from this case study. First, young talented employees are usually the first to flee from an organization when the psychological contract is broken and the value proposition ignored. They do not owe any organization loyalty. They are not seeking long-term tenure like their 'forefathers' or baby-boomers. They are propelled by personal ambitions and the Darwinian philosophy of self-preservation. They have age on their side, and their skills and talent are additional strengths and marketing tools. A lesson for organizations is to perpetually seek to meet the dynamic needs of talented employees. Losing them to competitors and replacing them is more expensive than keeping them. The Delta Steel Company actually went down until it was sold by the Government to a private steel-producing firm in 2005. Second, the needs of employees vary with age, marital status and personal circumstances. Hence, a one-size-fits-all approach to total rewards is inappropriate and ineffective. Flexibility should be the mantra. Third, the factors that make employees remain in an organization may not necessarily make them highly engaged, committed and productive. For instance, when salaries are low but benefits are generally satisfactory, older and married employees with children are not likely to leave the organization. Two main dangers are inherent in this kind of situation. First, it can engender unethical practices, such as employees conspiring with service providers and suppliers to cheat the organization. Second, employees may moonlight to augment their income. These options destroy engagement, commitment and loyalty to the organization.

The reason for employees' low engagement is that they cannot see a direct correlation between their efforts, contribution and performance, on the one hand, and the reward they receive, on the other. The mere fact that they are involved in external activities to earn more money significantly reduces their motivation, energy and the degree of effort they can commit to achieve high performance for the legitimate employer.

Finally, missions and visions tend to raise employee expectations, energize and inspire the workforce to extraordinary performance. But when they are not realized, the effects are like a broken dam on the workforce – disappointment, regret, fury, frustration and damage.

Bibliography

Abdullahi S-K. 2008. Universities need 60,000 lecturers for effectiveness – ASUU. *The Vanguard. 7 March*. Available at: http://www.allafrica.com/stories/200803070050.html. (Accessed: March 2010).

Aberdeen Group and Human Capital Institute. 2005. *Retaining Talent: Retention and Succession in the Corporate Workforce.* Available at: http://www.profilesinternational.com/articles/Aberdeen_RA_Retention_KJ.pdf. (Accessed: August 2010).

African Association for Public Administration and Management. 2008. Enhancing professionalization of human resource management in the public sector in Africa. PAS-HRMnet, 1–3. Available at: www.aapam-org/apsl.html. (Accessed: July 2009).

Amble, B. 2008. Still ignoring succession planning. 1–3. Available at: http://www.management-issues.com/2008/8/18/research/still-ignoring-succession-planning. (Accessed: 9 August 2010).

Anekwe, M.C. 2003. Brain drain: The Nigerian experience (1). 1–2. Available at: http://www.nigerdeltacongress.com/barticles/brain_drain_the_nigerian_experience.htm. (Accessed: November 2008).

Armstrong, M. 1991. *A Handbook of Personnel Management Practices.* London: Kogan Page Ltd.

Aryee, S. 2004. HRM in Ghana. In *Managing Human Resources in Africa*, edited by K. Kamoche, Y. Debrah, F. Horwitz and G.N. Muuka. London: Routledge, 121–134.

Axelrod, B., Handfield-Jones, H. and Welsh T.A. 2001. War for Talent, Part Two. *The McKinsey Quarterly*, (2), 9–11.

Baca, C. 2006. Clarifying competencies: Powerful tools for driving business success. *Workspan*, April, 52–56 .

Barab, S.A. and Plucker, J.A. 2002. Smart people or smart contexts? Cognition, ability, and talent development in an age of situated approaches to knowing and learning. *Educational Psychologist*, 37(3), 165–182.

Barker, J.A. 1992. *Paradigms – The Business of Discovering the Future.* New York: Harper Business.

Barner, R. W. 2000. *Executive Resource Management.* Palo Alto, CA: Davies-Black Publishing.

Barton, J. 2008. The HR business plan: A road map to talent management. *Workspan*, March, 50–54.

Bawa, M.A. and Ali, J. 1991. *The Challenges of Globalization and the Role of Human Resources*. Bangkok: ICC, 1–20.

Berger L. and Berger, D.R. 2004. *Talent Management Handbook*. New York: McGraw-Hill.

Berthiaum, J. and Culpepper, L. 2008. Hot skills – most popular compensation strategies for technical expertise. *Society for Human Resource Management Online*, 1–5. Available at: www.shrm.org/rewards/library-published/compensatin/nonIC/CMS-024139.asp. (Accessed: January 2008).

Beugré, C. 2004. HRM in Ivory Coast. In *Managing Human Resources in Africa*, edited by K. Kamoche, Y. Debrah, F. Horwitz and G.N. Muuka. London: Routledge, 135–149

Boshyk, Y. 2009. Developing global executives: Today and tomorrow. In *The 2009 Pfeiffer Annual: Leadership Development*, edited by D. Dotlich, P. Cairo, S. Rhinesmith and R. Meeks. San Francisco, CA: Pfeiffer, 1–32.

Brandon, C. 2005. Truth in recruitment branding. *HR Magazine*, 50(11), 89–90.

Branine, M. 2001. Human resource management in Algeria. In *Human Resource Management in Developing Countries*, edited by P.S. Budhwar and Y.A. Debrah. London: Routledge, 155–173.

Briggs, B.R. 2007. Problems of recruitment in civil service: Case of the Nigerian civil service. *African Journal of Business Management*, 1(6), 142–153.

Brown, J.A.C. 1954. *The Social Psychology of Industry*. New York: Penguin Books.

Brown, T. 2008. Putting pay for performance into practice. *Workspan*, February, 38–43.

Buckingham, M. and Coffman, C. 1999. *First, Break all the Rules*. London: The Gallup Organization.

Budhwar, P.S. and Debrah, Y.A. 2001. *Human Resource Management in Developing Countries*, London: Routledge.

Business Services Industry 2007. Top U.S. executives see rapidly shrinking talent pool. *Business Wire*, 1–3. Available at: http://findarticles.com/p/articles/mi_m0EIN/is_2007_Dec_13/ai_n27475084. (Accessed: August 2010).

Cadrain, D. 2008. Employers prepare to keep, not lose, baby boomers. *2008 HR Trend Book: Staffing Management, Special Supplement to HR Magazine*, 23–24.

Capelli, P. 2008. *Talent on Demand: Managing Talent in an Age of Uncertainty*. Boston, MA: Harvard Business Press.

Česynienė, R. 2008. Globalization and human resource management. *Ekonomika*, 82, 41–56.

Chingos, P.T. 2002. *Paying for Performance: A Guide to Compensation Management*. New York: John Wiley and Sons.

Clutterbuck, D. and Kernaghan, S. 1994. *The Power of Empowerment*. London: Kogan Page.

Collins J. 2001. *Good to Great: Why Some Companies Make the Leap ... and Others Don't.* New York: Harper Business.

Conley, P. Lasonde, R. and Larson, S. 2004. Using long-term incentives to retain top talent: Super rewards for superkeepers. In *The Talent Management Handbook,* edited by L.A. Berger and D.R. Berger, New York: Mc-Graw-Hill, 399–412.

Cooper, D., Robertson, I.T. and Tinline, G. 2003. *Recruitment and Selection: Framework for Success*. London: Thomson.

Corporate University Xchange. 2007. CorpU study cites inadequate leadership development as threat to business growth. Available at: http://www.hr-topics.com/wire-usa/leadership-development-inadequate.htm.

Coulson, C. 2003. Warming up benched players: Identifying future all-starts through succession planning. *Workspan,* March, 32–35.

Covey, S.R. 1998. *The 7 Habits of Highly Effective People.* New York: Free Press.

Covey, S.R. 2004. *The 8th Habit: From Effectiveness to Greatness.* New York: Free Press.

Covey, S.R. 2006. *The Speed of Trust: The One Thing That Changes Everything.* New York Simon & Schuster.

Crawford, D.L. 1984. Employee development. In *Human Resource Management,* edited by K.M. Srinivas. Toronto: McGraw-Hill Ryerson Ltd, 194–225.

CSA. 1979. Delta Steel Company Orientation Handbook.

Czenter, A.M. 2002. Labor market and globalization: Human resources management in global enterprises. Extract from a dissertation submitted to Centre International de Formation Européene, Institut Européen des Hautes Etudes Internationales, Nice, 65–95.

Dale, J. and Potts, H. 2007. Improving employee performance through coaching. *Workspan,* November, 22–27.

Dalziel, M.M. 2004. Determining every employee's potential for growth. In *Talent Management Handbook,* edited by L.A. Berger, and D.R. Berger. New York: Mc-Graw-Hill, 129–138.

Daniel's Blog. 2006. Management, innovation, innovation myths. 1–6. Available at: http://www.innovationzen.com/blog/2006/07/26/invention-vs--innovation. (Accessed: April 2007).

De Cieri, H.L. and Dowling, P.J. 1998. The tortuous evolution of strategic human resource management in multinational enterprises. *Working Paper in Human Resource Management and Industrial Relations,* No. 5, 1–21.

Delano, J. 2008. Executive development for strategic advantage. *Monitor Executive Development,* June, 1–8.

Dickmann, M. 2007. Measuring the value of international assignments. *Vedior HR Portal,* 1–3. Available at: www.vedior.com/vedior-hr-portal/english-articles-folder/measuring-the-value-o-international-assignments. (Accessed: October 2007).

Dieleman, M., Toonen, J., Toure and H., Martineau, T. 2005. How important is performance management in motivating in health workers in Mali? *Human Resources for Health.* Available at: http://www.human–resources-health.com/content/4/1/2. (Accessed: April 2010).

Director, S.M. and Schramm, J. 2006. Estimating future staffing levels: Implications for HR strategy. *Staffing Management, Staff Research,* October–December, 1–8.

Dooney, J. and Victor, J. 2006. Recruiting benchmarks: Defending and improving recruiting performance. *Staffing Management, Staffing Research,* July–September, 1–8.

Dychtwald, K., Erickson, T.J. and Morison, R. 2006. *Workforce Crisis: How to Beat the Coming Shortage of Skills and Talent.* Boston, MA: Harvard Business School Press.

Edoho, F. 2001. *Management Challenges for Africa in the Twenty-first Century: Theoretical and Applied Perspectives.* Westport, CT: Praeger Publishers.

Elegbe, B. 1985. The problems of transferring learning to job situations. *PERMAN,* 12(1), 19–21.

Emeagwali, P. 2003. How do we reverse the 'brain drain? A keynote speech delivered at the Pan African Conference on 'Brain Drain', 1–14. Available at: www.vimeo.com635651. (Accessed: November 2008).

Erikson, T. and Ortega, J. 2002. The adoption of job rotation: Testing the theories. Paper presented at Universidad Public de Navarra, 1–19.

Evans, P. and Pucik, V. 2002. *The Global Challenge: Frameworks for International Human Resource Management.* Boston, MA. McGraw-Hill.

Fako, T. Forchen, N. and Balogi, K.T.O. 2002. Productivity among nurses and midwives in Botswana. *African Sociological Review,* 6(1), 148–160.

Falcone, P. 2007. Big-picture performance appraisal. *HR Magazine,* 52(12), 97–100.

Farson, R. and Keyes, R. 2002. *Whoever Makes the Most Mistakes Wins: The Paradox of Innovation.* New York: Free Press.

FITC. 2000. *Issues in Human Resource Utilization: A Study of the Nigerian Banking Sector.* Apapa: Financial Institutions Training Centre.

Fleck, C. 2007. Cast a wide net. *Staffing Management,* April–June, 36–39.

Ford, N. 2009. Africa's top companies 2009: Low valuations hide true worth of Africa's best. *African Business,* (352), 14–33.

Foster, M. 2003. *Recruiting on the WEB: Smart Strategies for Finding the Perfect Candidat*e. New York: McGraw-Hill.

Fox, A. 2009. Effective hiring freezes require analysis, communication and continued recruiting. *HR Magazine,* 54(3), 28–33.

Frankel, L.P. and Otazo, K.L. 1992. Employee coaching: The way to gain commitment, not just compliance. *Employment Relations Today,* 19, 311–321.

Freeman, J. March 2007. Performance management: Working in theory but failing in practice? *LTDC News*, 1–6. Available at: www.loyalisttraining.com/index/php/news-detail/performance-management. (Accessed: May 2008).

Friedman, S.D. and Greenhaus, J.H. 2000. *Work and Family – Allies or Enemies?* Oxford: Oxford University Press.

Fulkerson, J.R. 2002. Growing global executives. In *The 21st Century Executive: Innovative Practices for Building Leadership at the Top*, edited by R. Silver. San Francisco, CA: Jossey-Bass, 300–334.

Games, D. 2008. South Africa: Standing out from the crowd. *The Africa Report* (10), 54–56.

Gara, T. 2007. The war for talent. 1–4. Available at: www.businesstodayegypt.com/article. (Accessed: November 2007).

Garvin, D.A., Edmondson, A.C. and Gino, F. 2008. Is yours a learning organization? *Harvard Business Review*, March, 109–116.

Giancola, F. 2007. Employee engagement: What you need to know. *Workspan*, October, 56–59.

Goleman, D. 1998. *Working with Emotional Intelligence.* New York: Bantam Books.

Grensing-Pophal, L. 2007. Coaching HR. *HR Magazine*, 52(2), 95–99.

Green, P.C. 1999. *Building Robust Competencies: Linking Human Resource Systems to Organizational Strategies.* San Francisco, CA: Jossey-Bass.

Gupta, V., McMillan, I.C. and Sure, G. 2004. Entrepreneurial leadership: Developing a cross-cultural construct. *Journal of Business Venturing*, 19(2), 241–260.

Gurchiek, K. 2008. Career development gets failing grade from many workers. *2008 HR Trend Book, Special Supplement to HR Magazine*, 49–50.

Hamilton, J. n.d. The entrepreneurial mindset – leadership implications. *Entrepreneurial Focus Champion*, Franklin University, 1–3. Available at: www.leadership.franklin.edu/LL037p.htm. (Accessed: May 2007).

Harrell-Cook, G. 2002. Human resources management and competitive advantage: A strategic perspective. In *Human Resources Management: Perspectives. Content, Functions and Outcomes*, edited by G.R. Feris, M.R. Buckley and D.B. Fedor. Upper Saddle River, NJ: Prentice-Hall.

Hassan, M.H.A. 2008. *Promoting Science, Technology and Innovation for Sustainable Development in Africa.* Addis Ababa: Economic Commission for Africa.

Hayes, J. 2008. Workplace and succession management in a changing world. *CPP Global Human Capital Report*, 1–23.

Hayes, M. 2007. Protect your company from the workforce shortage. *Workspan*, November, 64–67.

Hedge, J.W. and Pulakos, E.D. 2002. *Implementing Organizational Interventions: Steps, Processes and Best Practices*. San Francisco, CA: Jossey-Bass.

Heineman Jr, B.W. 2009. Integrity with global talent management. Available at: http://www.managehrnetwork.blogspot.com/2009/06integrity-with-global-talent-management.html. (Accessed: November 2009).

Hertzberg, F. 1966. *Work and Nature of Man.* Cleveland, OH: World.

Higgins, C.A. 2002. The emergence of person-organizational fit in organizational staffing process. In *Human Resources Management: Perspectives. Content, Functions and Outcomes*, edited by G.R. Feris, M.R. Buckley and D.B. Fedor. Upper Saddle River, NJ: Prentice-Hall.

Hofstede, G. 1980. *Culture's Consequences.* Beverly Hills, CA: Sage.

Hofstede, G. 1994. *Cultures and Organizations: Software of the Mind.* New York: McGraw-Hill.

Hollenbeck, G.P. and McCall, M.W. 2003. *Competence, Not Competencies: Making Global Executive Development Work.* Los Angeles, CA: Center for Effective Organizations, 1–29.

Horwitz, F., Nomo, S.M. and Rajah, M. 2004. HRM in South Africa. In *Managing Human Resources in Africa*, edited by K. Kamoche, Y. Debrah, F. Horwitz, and G.N. Muuka. London: Routledge, 1–17.

Howard, A., Erker, E. and Bruce, N. 2007. Slugging through the war for talent. *Development Dimensions International Inc.* Monster/DDI Inc. 1–7. Available at: http://www.ddiworld.com/pdf/selectionforecast2006-2007-es-ddi.pdf. (Accessed: August 2010).

Huang, H.J. 1999. Job rotation from the employees' point of view. *Research and Practice in Human Resource Management*, 7(1), 75–85.

Hundley, S.P., Jacobs, F. and Drain, M. 2007. *Workforce Engagement: Strategies to Attract, Motivate and Retain.* Worldatwork Press.

Idoko, C. 2010. Shagari laments deteriorating varsity education. *Naija-News, Nigerian newspapers extract*, 6 August.

International Council of Science (ICSU). 2007. *Health and Human Well-being in Sub-Saharan Africa.* ICSU Regional Office for Africa, 1–34. Available at: http://www.icsu-africa.org/sp_hh_rep_2007.pdf. (Accessed: April 2010).

Jackson, S.E. and Schuler, R.S. 1990. Human resource planning: Challenges for industrial/organizational psychologist. *American Psychologist*, 45(2), 223–239.

Janis, I. 1972. *Victims of Groupthink.* Boston, MA: Houghton-Mifflin.

Jay, A. 1968. *Management and Machiavelli: An Inquiry into the Politics of Corporate Life.* New York: Bantam Books.

Jibril, M. and Obaje, A. 2010. Internationalization activities in Nigerian Universities. *IIE Network.* Available at: http://www.iienetwork.org/page/133925/;jsessionid=cf69svnuprqr. (Accessed: August 2010).

Jones, K. and Schweyer, A. 2009. Recessionary management: The top DOs and DONTs for managing talent in the current downturn. *Human Capital Institute and Taleo Corporation*, 1–16. Available at: http://grid.taleo.com/sites/default/files/whitepaper-recessionary-management-hcl.pdf. (Accessed: August 2010).

Kamoche, K., Debrah, Y., Horwitz, F. and Muuka, G.N. 2004. *Managing Human Resources in Africa.* London: Routledge.

Kasekende, L., Ndikumana, L. and Rajhi, T. 2009. *Impact of the Global Financial and Economic Crisis on Africa.* Working Papers Series No. 96. Tunis: African Development Bank, 1–36.

Kiggundu, M.N. 1989. *Managing Organizations in Developing Countries – An Operational and Strategic Approach.* Hartford, CT: Kumarian Press Inc.

Kochanski, J. and Becom, A. 2008. Four key steps to performance management. *Workspan*, February, 32–36.

Kochanski, J. and Sorenson, A. 2005. Managing performance management. *Workspan*, September, 20–27.

Kotter, J.P. 1996. *Leading Change.* Boston, MA: Harvard Business School Press.

Kraiger, K. 2002. *Creating, Implementing, and Managing Effective Training and Development: State-of-the-Art Lessons for Practice*. San Francisco, CA: Jossey-Bass.

Krell, E. 2006. Branding together. *HR Magazine*, 51(10), 48–54.

Krisher, T. and Thomas, K. 2009. GM CEO Fritz Henderson to resign: AP source (breaking). 1–3. Available at: http://www.huffingtonpost.com/2009/12/01gm-ceo-henderson-to-resig_n_375890.html? (Accessed: August 2010).

Kunich, J.C. and Lester, R.I. 1999. Leadership and the art of mentoring: Tool kit for the time machine. *Journal of Leadership*, (1–2), 117–127.

Langley, M. 2010. BP's Hayward defends reign, spill response. *Wall Street Journal*, 30 July–1 August, 1 and 3.

Larson, P. and Richburg, M.T. 2004. Leadership coaching. In *Talent Management Handbook*, edited by L.A. Berger and D.R. Berger. New York: McGraw-Hill, 307–319.

Lawler, E.E. III. 1981. *Pay and Organizational Development.* Reading, MA: Addison-Wesley Publishing Company.

Lawrence, E. 1999. Strategic thinking: A discussion paper. Public Service Commission of Canada, 1–15. Available at: http://www.csun.edu/bus302/Course/Materials/Cases/strategic.thinking.pdf. (Accessed August 2010).

Lebovits, N.S. 2005. The next decade's talent war: Is your company prepared to win and keep the best and the brightest? *Ajilon Finance*. Available at: http://www.ajilonstaff.com/articles/Talent%20War-ext%205-26-05.pdf. (Accessed: August 2020).

Leka, S., Griffiths, A. and Cox. T. 2003. *Work Organization and Stress: Systematic Problem Approaches for Employers, Managers and Trade Union Representatives.* Geneva: World Health Organization.

Leonard, B. 2000. Online and overwhelmed. *HR Magazine*, 45(8), 36–42.

Lepsinge, R. and Lucia, A.D. 1999. *The Art and Science of Competency Models*. San Francisco, CA: Jossey-Bass.

Lockwood, N.R. 2005. Leveraging employee engagement for competitive advantage: HR's strategic role. *SHRM Research Quarterly*, 52(3), 1–10.

Lockwood, N.R. and Victor, J. 2007. Recruiting for workplace diversity: A business strategy. *Staffing Management, Staffing Research*, 1–9.

Loucks, P. 2006. Automation makes pay for performance work. *Workspan*, October, 52–56.

McClelland, D. 1975. *Power: The Inner Experience*. New York: Irvington.

McGregor, D. 1960. *The Human Side of Enterprise*. New York: McGraw-Hill

McKinsey and Company. 2007. War for talent – new ways of thinking. Available at: http:/www.mckinsey.com/clientservice/organizationleadership/warfortalent/newways.asp. (Accessed: November 2007).

McNulty, Y. 2005. Understanding expatriate ROI: Improving the bottom line. *SHRM Forum*, April, 1–7.

Manzi, F., Kida, T., Mbuyita, S., Palmer, N. and Gibson, L. 2004. Exploring the influence of workplace trust over health worker performance. *HEFP Working Paper, 07/04, LSHTM 2004*. Health Economics and Financing Program (HEFP), 1–68. Available at: http://www.hefp.Ishtm.ac.uk/publications/downloads/working_papers/07_04.pdf. (Accessed: April 2010).

Martin, A. 2008. Vocal contest gives McDonald's employees something to sing about. *New York Times*. 1–3. Available at: http://www.nytimes.com/2008/02/09/business/09idol.html. (Accessed: August 2010).

Maslow, A.H. 1954. *Motivation and Personality*. New York: Harper and Row.

Maxwell, J.C. 2007. *Talent Is Never Enough*. Nashville, TN: Thomas Nelson, Inc.

Mberu, B.U. and Ponguou, R. 2010. Nigeria: Multiple forms of mobility in Africa's demographic giant. Available at: http://www.migrationinformation.net/Profiles/display.cfm?ID=788. (Accessed: August 2010).

Meisinger, S.R. and Schiemann, W. 2009. *Reinventing Talent Management: How to Maximize Performance in the New Marketplace*. New York: John Wiley & Sons.

Michaels, E., Handfield-Jones, H., and Axelrod, B. 2001. *The War for Talent*. Boston, MA: Harvard Business School Press.

Mohrman Jr, A.M., Resnick-West, S.M. and Lawler III, E.E. 1989. *Designing Performance Appraisal Systems: Aligning Appraisals and Organizational Realities*. San Francisco, CA: Jossey-Bass.

Morris, J.R. 1956. Job rotation. *The Journal of Business*, 29(4), 268–273.

Mutume, G. 2003. Reversing Africa's brain drain. *Africa Recovery*, 17(2), 1–9.

Muuka, G.N. and Mwenda, K.K. 2004. HRM in Zambia. In *Managing Human Resources in Africa*, edited by K. Kamoche, Y. Debrah, F. Horwitz, and G.N. Muuka. London: Routledge, 35–51.

Neale, F. 1991. *The Handbook of Performance Management*. London: Chartered Institute of Personnel and Development.

Nduru, M. 2007. Brain drain is killing people. *Health-Africa*, 1–3. Available at: http://ipsnews.net/news.asp?idnews=37898. (Accessed August 2010).

Newsline. 2007. Inadequate leadership development a threat to business growth. *WorldatWork*. Available at: http://www.dialog.newsedge.com/newsedge.asp? (Accessed: November 2009).

Newsline. 2008a. Lack of skills major factor in UK recruitment, retention difficulties, 1. *WorldatWork*. Available at: http://www.worldatwork.org/waw/adimComment?id=26770. (Accessed: July 2008).

Newsline. 2008b. Two-thirds of companies are not prepared for sudden loss of leadership. *WorldatWork*. Available at: http://www.worldatwork.org/waw/adimComment?id=27904. (Accessed: September 2008).

Newsline. 2008c. 43% of working moms would take pay cut to spend time with kids. WorldatWork. Available at: http://www.workdatwork.org/waw/adimLink?id=26247. (Accessed: May 2008).

News Notes. 2007. Recruitment, Retention of skilled individuals: future leaders give CFOS serious cause for concern, *Workspan*, November.

Nnadozie, E. 2001. Managing African business culture. In *Management Challenges for Africa in the Twenty-first Century: Theoretical and Applied Perspectives*, edited by F. Edoho. Westport, CT: Praeger Publishers, 51–62.

NPR. 2007. Citibank loses billions, CEO Prince resigns. Available at: http://www.npr.org/templates/story/story.php?/storyId=15994978. (Accessed 13 August 2010).

Ofori-Sarpong, E. 2003. 70,000 scholars leave Afirica yearly – says don. *Ghanaian Chronicle*, All Africa.com, March 13, 1–3. Available at: http://allafrica.com/stories/200303130768.html. (Accessed: August 2010).

O'Grady, L. 2001. Using technology to de-stress on international assignment. *Canadian HR Reporter*, 1-2.

Ogrean, C. Herciu, M. and Belascu, L. 2009. Competency-based management and global competencies – challenges for firm strategic management. *International Review of Business Research Papers*, 5(4), 114–122.

Olita, R. 2007. Brain drain hits Uganda. *The New Vision*, 1–2. Available at: www.newvision.co.ug/D/8/12/577574. (Accessed: November 2008).

O'Neil, L. 2009. HR's time to lead. *HR Magazine*, 54(4), 8.

Oni, B. 1999. Capacity building effort and brain drain in Nigerian Universities. *Abstract*. Ibadan: NISER, 1–29.

Onwuamaeze, D. 2008. Looking beyond Nigeria. *Newswatch Magazine*. 1–4. Available at: http://www.newswatchngr.com/index/php?option=com_content&task=view&id=82Itemid=42. (Accessed: December 2008).

Orwell, G. 1946. *Animal Farm.* New York: Harcourt, Brace & Company.

Otite, O. 1978. *Themes in African Social and Political Thought.* Enugu: Fourth Dimension Publishers.

Paese, M. 2008. Global organizations are playing catch-up on growing executive talent, 1–4. Available at http://www.imakenews.com/ddi/e_article001095550.cfm?x=b11,0,w (Accessed: 13 November 2009).

Paese, M.J. 2009. Your next CEO: Why succession planning is more important than ever. *The Conference Board Review*, November/December, 18–23.

Paradise, A. 2009. Talent management defined. *Training and Development*, 63(5), 68–69.

Pfeffer, J. 1998. *The Human Equation: Building Profits by Putting People First.* Boston, MA: Harvard Business School Press.

Pucik, V. 1996. Human resources in the future: An obstacle or a champion of globalization? *Working Paper Series of Cornell University*. New York: Center for Advanced Human Resource Studies, Cornell University, 1–8.

Quinn, P. 2002. Recruitment branding. *Recruitment Extra*, October–November, 16–17. Available at: www.quinntenssential.com.au/article11.htm. (Accessed: September 2007).

Raelin, J. 2006. Does action learning promote collaborative leadership? *Academy of Management Learning and Education*, 5(2), 152–168.

Ready, A.D. and Conger, A.J. 2007. Make your company a talent factory. *Harvard Business Review*, 85(6), 68–72.

Reich, R. 2010. More profits, fewer jobs. *International Herald Tribune*, 30 July 30, 6.

Rioux, S.M. Bernthal, P.R. and Wellins, R.S. 2000. The globalization of human resources practices. *HR Benchmark Group*, 3(1), 1–17. Available at: http://www.ddiworld.co.uk/pdf/theglobalizationofhrpractices_fullreport_ddi.pdf. (Accessed: August 2010).

Roberts, G. 1999. *Recruitment and Selection: A Competency Approach*. London: Institute of Personnel and Development.

Robinson, D., Perryman, S., and Hayday, S. 2004. *The Drivers of Employee Engagement*. Report 408. Brighton: Institute for Employment Studies.

Rothwell, W.J. 2005. *Effective Succession Planning*, New York: AMACOM.

Runnion, T.T. 2005. Expatriate programs: From preparation to success. *Workspan*, July, 20–22.

Rustomji, M.K. and Sapre, S.A. 1981. *Incredible Japanese.* Delhi: Macmillan India Ltd.

Sammer, J. 2008. Calibrating consistency. *HR Magazine*, 53(1), 73–75.

Scholl, R.W. 1981. Differentiating organizational commitment from expectancy as a motivating force. *Academy of Management Review*, 6(4), 589–599.

Schuler, R.S. 1992. Strategic human resource management: linking people with the needs of the business. *Organizational Dynamics*, 21(1), 18–32.

Schuler, R.S. and Jackson, S.E. 2005. A quarter-century review of human resource management in the US: The growth in importance of the international perspective. *Management Revue*, 16(1), 1–25.

Schuler, R.S. and Jackson, S.E. 2009. The global talent management challenge: Drivers and HR actions for attaining and sustaining global competitive advantage, 1–35. Available at: www.dgfp/de/perdoc/document.php?id=8143. (Accessed: October 2009).

Senge, P. 1990. *The Fifth Discipline: The Art and Practice of the Learning Organization*. New York: Doubleday/Currency.

Seijts, G.H. and Crim, D. 2006. What engages employees the most or the ten C's of employee engagement? *Ivey Business Journal*, March–April, 1–3.

Serrat, O. 2008. Action learning. *Knowledge Solutions*, 19, 1–3.

Shaw, G.B. 2009. *Pygmalion*. Rockville, MD: Wildside Press.

Smith, D.K. 1996. *Taking Charge of Change: 10 Principles for Managing People and Performance*. Reading, MA: Perseus Books.

Smith, A. and Rogers, R.W. 2003. *A Blueprint for Leadership Success*. White Paper. Available at http://www.ddiworld.com/pdf/leadershipBlueprintWP.pdf. (Accessed August 2010).

Soyinka, W. 1972. *The Man Died*. Harmondsworth: Penguin Books.

Spreitzer, G. and Doneson, D. 2005. Musings on the past and future of employee empowerment. In *Handbook of Organizational Development* edited by T. Cummings. Thousand Oaks, CA: Sage, 1–12.

Stahl, G.K., Miller, E.L. and Tung, R.L. 2002. Toward the boundaryless career: A closer look at the expatriate career concept and the implications of an international assignment. *Journal of World Business*, 37, 145–157.

Stern, S. 2008. Human resources departments are unloved but unnecessary. *Financial Times*, 18 April.

Stilwell *et al.* 2004. Managing brain drain and brain waste of health workers in Nigeria. *Bulletin of the World Health Organization*, 1–3. Available at: www.who.int/bulletin/bulletin-board/82stilwell/en. (Accessed: November 2008).

Sullivan, J. 2004a. *Rethinking Strategic HR*. Chicago, IL: CCH Incorporated.

Sullivan, J. 2004b. The worldwide war for talent II is coming: are you prepared? 1–6. Available at: www.ere.net/articles/db/4004B40657A1402190F2B7B152856152.asp. (Accessed: November 2007).

Sullivan, J. 2010. A think piece: How HR caused Toyota to crash, 15 February. Available at: http://www.ere.net/2010/02/15/a-think-piece-how-hr-caused-toyota-to-crash/print/. (Accessed: August 2010).

Tannenbaum, S. 2002. A strategic view of organizational training and learning. In *Creating, Implementing, and Managing Effective Training and Development: State-of-the-Art Lessons for Practice*, edited by K. Kraiger. San Francisco, CA: Jossey-Bass, 10–52.

Telberg, R. 2007. War for talent goes global. *On Career*, April, 1–3. Available at: www.cpa2biz.com/conent/media/producer_content/newsletters/articles. (Accessed: November 2007).

Tessmann-Keys, D. and Wellins, R.S. 2007. *The CEO's Guide to Preparing Future Global Leaders*. Pittsburgh, PA: Development Dimensions International Inc.

Towers Perrin. 2003. Working today: Understanding what drives employee engagement. *The 2003 Towers Perrin Talent Report*. Available at: http://www.towersperrin.comm/tp/getwebcachedoc?webc=HRS/CAN/200408/Talent_canada_eng. (Accessed: August 2010).

Towers Perrin. 2006. Talent takes on new meaning for companies struggling to retain critical skills. Available at: http://www.highbeam.com/doc/1G1-154058302.html. (Accessed: April 2010).

Trahant, B. 2007. Debunking five myths concerning employee engagement. *The Public Manager*, 53–59. Available at: http://goliath.ecnext.com/coms2/gi_0199-6433218/Debunking-five-myths-concerning-employee.html. (Accessed August 2010).

Tropman, J.E. 2001. *The Compensation Solution*. San Francisco, CA: Jossey-Bass.

Tuedon, N.T. 2006. *Human Resource Management: An on the Job Perspective*. Lagos: Pages and Pictures Ltd.

Tulgam, B. 2007. Superstars need managers. *HR Magazine*, 52(6), 135–139.

Tyler, K. 2007. Cross-cultural connections. *HR Magazine*, 52(10), 77–83.

Ugwuegbu, D.C.E. 2001. *The Psychology of Management in African Organizations*. London: Quorum Books.

Ulrich, D. 1996. *Human Resource Champions: The Next Agenda for Adding Value and Delivering Results*. Boston, MA. Harvard Business Press.

Ulrich, D. and Brockbank, W. 2005. *The HR Value Proposition*. Boston, M.A. Harvard Business Press.

Ulrich, D. and Yeung, A. 1989. A shared mindset. *Personnel Administrator*, 34(3), 117–134.

Vandu, C. 2010. Reforming academia in Nigeria. the new black magazine. Available at: http://mhtml:file://F:\Nigeria In Search of PhDs.mht. (Accessed August 2010).

Vogel, A.J. 2005. Guidelines for the preparation of expatriates on international assignments in South African multinational enterprises. Dissertation submitted in fulfilment of the requirements for the degree Doctor Commerce II (Business Management) at the University of Pretoria.

Vroom, V. 1964. *Work and Motivation*. New York: John Wiley and Sons.

Want, J. 2006. *Corporate Culture: Key Strategies for High-Performing Business Cultures*. New York: St Martin's Press.

Watkins, M. 2003. *The First 90 Days*. Boston, MA: Harvard Business School Press.

Welch, J. 2005. *Winning.* New York: Harper Business.

Wells, S.J. 2005. Driving in. *HR Magazine*, 50(3), 54–59.

Whyte, W.H. 1956. *The Organization Man.* New York: Doubleday.

Wiener, Y. 1982. Commitment in organizations: A normative view. *Academy of Management Review*, 7(3), 418–428.

Wikipedia. 2010a. List of countries and territories by fertility rate. Available at: http://en.wikipedia.org/wiki/List_of_countries_and_territories_by_fertility-rate. (Accessed: August 2010).

Wikipedia. 2010b. List of universities in South Africa. Available at: http://en.wikipedia.org/wiki/List_of_universities_in_South_Africa. (Accessed: August 2010).

Wikipedia. 2010c. List of universities in Uganda. Available at: http://en.wikipedia.org/wiki/List_of_universities_in_Uganda. (Accessed August 2010).

Williams, S. 1991. Strategy and objectives. In *The Handbook of Performance Management* edited by F. Neale. London: Institute of Personnel Management, 7–24.

Woodruffe, C. 1999. *Winning the Talent War.* New York: John Wiley and Sons Ltd.

World Bank. 1995. *Retaining Teaching Capacity in African Universities: Problems and Prospects, Findings.* Africa Region No. 39, Washington DC: IBRD.

Yesufu, T.M. 1996. *The Nigerian Economy: Growth Without Development.* Benin Social Science Series for Africa. Benin: University of Benin.

Young, S. 2003. Micro inequities: The power of small. *The Workforce Diversity Reader*, Winter, 40–43.

Zachary, L.J. 2009. Filling in the blanks. *Training and Development*, 63(5), 63–66.

Index

Locators shown in *italics* refer to figures and tables.

For Product Safety Concerns and Information please contact our EU representative GPSR@taylorandfrancis.com Taylor & Francis Verlag GmbH, Kaufingerstraße 24, 80331 München, Germany